W9-AOJ-283

06/24
STAND PRICE
$ 5.00

CAMILLE DIRAIMONDO
415 Old Country Road
Deer Park, NY 11729

BEST
OF THE
GRAPEVINE

The AA Grapevine, Inc.
New York

Alcoholics Anonymous is a fellowship of men
and women who share their experience,
strength and hope with each other that they
may solve their common problem and
help others to recover from alcoholism.

The only requirement for membership is a
desire to stop drinking. There are no dues or
fees for AA membership; we are self-
supporting through our own contributions.
AA is not allied with any sect, denomination,
politics, organization or institution;
does not wish to engage in any controversy,
neither endorses nor opposes any causes.
Our primary purpose is to stay sober and
help other alcoholics to achieve sobriety.

The AA Grapevine, Inc.
Box 1980
Grand Central Station
New York, NY 10163

Copyright © 1985 by The AA Grapevine, Inc.
All rights reserved
First printing 1985
ISBN 0-933685-00-9
Printed in the United States of America

CONTENTS

PART THREE
Men and Women Who Share

(The AA group — group life; sponsorship; Traditions and guiding principles; the unique nature of leadership in AA; a new group forms)

PART FOUR
Experience, Strength, and Hope

(The AA program — the Twelve Steps; wisdom from the Big Book; other tools)

PART FIVE
Not Allied with Any Sect or Denomination
*(Spiritual experience — the spiritual roots of our Fellowship;
variety of beliefs among members; universal principles)*

PART SIX
Neither Endorses nor Opposes Any Causes
*(Trends and issues in AA — an overview of problems and
controversies within the Fellowship, from founding days to
the present)*

PART SEVEN
Alcoholics Anonymous Is a Fellowship

(The Fellowship as a whole — past, present, and future; significant historical writings; personal glimpses of the cofounders; more about the Twelve Traditions)

FOREWORD

READERS OF THE AA GRAPEVINE magazine have called it their "meeting in print" since the first issue came off press in June 1944. In this *Best of the Grapevine*, scores of those readers, along with the writers, artists, and editors who joined them in putting the book together, welcome you to a marathon meeting — 288 pages of articles selected by Grapevine enthusiasts as those that best nurtured their sobriety and developed their understanding of AA principles.

So sit back, relax, keep an open mind, and "listen" to AA friends from all over the world. Prepare to meet co-founders Bill W. and Dr. Bob; come to know the men and women who through trial and error forged AA's Steps and Traditions; welcome some non-AA friends into your hearts and minds; and widen your circle of friends among the AAs new and old who keep our Fellowship, and therefore ourselves, alive and growing.

You are invited to enter the world of the Grapevine, a sober world filled with the love and laughter, the hard work and spiritual growth, that stand at the heart of the life-saving Fellowship of Alcoholics Anonymous.

Turn the pages, and let the meeting begin.

"Alcoholics Anonymous is a fellowship of men and women who share their experience, strength, and hope with each other..."

ONE

THAT WE MAY SOLVE OUR COMMON PROBLEM

You Don't Know What Lonesome Is!

December 1947

YOU DON'T KNOW WHAT LONESOME IS until you have taken your first slip after being exposed to the Alcoholics Anonymous program. You thought you were lonely *before* you ever attended an AA meeting. Sure, the alcoholic is the loneliest person in the world — isolated, ignored, scorned. You can admit no one to your little twilight world.

Then you are exposed to AA. Dozens of friendly hands are extended to you, dozens of warm voices say, "Hello, pal. Have a cup of coffee." You start to tell them your story and they say, "Sure, we know. We've been there, too. We know what you're talking about."

So you bask in the cheerful warmth of their friendship, you listen to their talk, you study the program and try to clear the fog out of your brain. Pretty soon things begin to look rosy. Why, say, this is peaches and cream; this is the life you've been looking for. Somebody gave you a dollar and a clean shirt. Maybe they even got you a job. The program is easy.

All you have to do is follow it, and that's a simple matter when you're traveling with people who are struggling toward the same goal you are. Life is a bed of roses, and someone has kindly removed all the thorns. That's what *you* think.

Then comes the first bump. The boss says something that hurts your feelings. Or you see a girl you want, but she doesn't want you. Or maybe it rains, or the sun shines too much. Whatever the reason, the old despair comes into your heart, the old glaze dulls your eyes, and you head for the nearest tavern.

So you start pouring it down. You could quit after the first one. Then you remember that it doesn't matter now; you've already taken the first one. There's a meeting tonight, but you can't go. You may be a heel, but you're not that much of a heel. You've shut yourself away from those people, and you sit there crying in your beer, remembering how good they were to you, how they tried to help you.

So the sun goes down, and twilight comes on, and the tavern fills up, and you're beginning to understand what lonesome is. That bleary blonde over there is watching you, and the look in her eye makes your stomach churn a little. The tavern is full of loud, hoarse voices, and there is no sense in what they are saying. And the juke box is playing "When You Were Sweet Sixteen" and you try to think back to a girl you knew who was sweet sixteen, but you can't remember her name, and she's probably dead anyway, and life is a pretty sad mess, so you cry a little more and call for another beer.

The meeting will be starting just about now, but you can't go. Everybody is standing, someone is reading the Twelve Steps. "We admitted we were powerless over alcohol — that our lives had become unmanageable.'' The words of those Steps are written on your heart, and the first thing you know you are repeating them out loud, and the guy next to you gives you a fishy look and goes over and whispers to the bartender.

Remember how you looked when you were drunk — like an old sick cat that has been left out in the rain too long? Remember how you felt — like the frazzled end of a misspent life? Remember what went through your mind — the bells and birds and bees, and the little slithering things that nobody could see but you? But you didn't remember soon enough. You struck a blow at your last hope, you tried to tramp it to death in a senseless frenzy for one more drink. And those friends you had made — you struck a blow at their defense as well as your own.

And the great beacon light burns on, trying to light your way through the fog. And you know that it will always be there, burning bright when your eyes become clear enough to see it. But you're sitting there, and at last you *really* know what lonesome is.

I. S., Portland, Ore.

Slips and Human Nature

by **William Duncan Silkworth**, MD

January 1947

T HE MYSTERY OF SLIPS is not so deep as it may appear. While it does seem odd that an alcoholic, who has restored himself to a dignified place among his fellowmen and continued dry for years, should suddenly throw all his happiness overboard and find himself again in mortal peril of drowning in liquor, often the reason is simple.

People are inclined to say, ''There is something peculiar about alcoholics. They seem to be well, yet at any moment they may turn back to their old ways. You can never be sure.''

This is largely twaddle. The alcoholic is a sick person. Under the techniques of Alcoholics Anonymous, he gets well — that is to say, his disease is arrested. There is nothing unpredictable about him any more than there is anything weird about a person who has arrested diabetes.

Let's get it clear, once and for all, that alcoholics are human beings. Then we can safeguard ourselves intelligently against most slips.

In both professional and lay circles, there is a tendency to label everything that an alcoholic may do as "alcoholic behavior." The truth is, it is simply human nature.

It is very wrong to consider many of the personality traits observed in liquor addicts as peculiar to the alcoholic. Emotional and mental quirks are classified as symptoms of alcoholism merely because alcoholics have them, yet those same quirks can be found among nonalcoholics, too. *Actually, they are symptoms of mankind!*

Of course, the alcoholic himself tends to think of himself as different, somebody special, with unique tendencies and reactions. Many psychiatrists, doctors, and therapists carry the same idea to extremes in their analyses and treatment of alcoholics. Sometimes, they make a complicated mystery of a condition which is found in all human beings, whether they drink whiskey or buttermilk.

To be sure, alcoholism, like every other disease, does manifest itself in some unique ways. It does have a number of baffling peculiarities which differ from those of all other diseases.

At the same time, many of the symptoms and much of the behavior of alcoholism are closely paralleled and even duplicated in other diseases.

The slip is a relapse! It is a relapse that occurs after the alcoholic has stopped drinking and started on the AA program of recovery. Slips usually occur in the early stages of the alcoholic's AA indoctrination, before he has had time to learn enough of the AA technique and AA philosophy to give him a solid footing. But slips may also occur after an alcoholic has been a member of AA for many months or even several years, and it is in this kind, above all, that one finds a marked similarity between the alcoholic's behavior and that of "normal" victims of other diseases.

It happens this way: When a tubercular patient recovers sufficiently to be released from the sanitarium, the doctor gives him careful instructions for the way he is to live when he gets home. He must drink plenty of milk. He must refrain from smoking. He must obey other stringent rules.

For the first several months, perhaps for several years, the patient follows directions. But as his strength increases and he feels fully recovered, he becomes slack. There may come the night when he decides he can stay up until ten o'clock. When he does this, nothing untoward happens. Soon, he is disregarding the directions given him when he left the sanitarium. Eventually, he has a relapse!

The same tragedy can be found in cardiac cases. After the heart attack, the patient is put on a strict rest schedule. Frightened, he naturally follows directions obediently for a long time. He, too, goes to bed early, avoids exercise such as walking upstairs, quits smoking, and leads a Spartan life. Eventually, though, there comes a day, after he has been feeling good for months or several years, when he feels he has regained his strength, and has also recovered from his fright. If the elevator is out of repair one day, he walks up the three flights of stairs. Or he decides to go to a party — or do just a little smoking — or take a cocktail or two. If no serious aftereffects follow the first departure from the rigorous schedule prescribed, he may try it again, until *he* suffers a relapse.

In both cardiac and tubercular cases, the acts which led to the relapses were preceded by wrong thinking. The patient in each case rationalized himself out of a sense of his own perilous reality. He deliberately turned away from his knowledge of the fact that he had been the victim of a serious disease. He grew overconfident. He decided he didn't have to follow directions.

Now that is precisely what happens with the alcoholic — the arrested alcoholic, or the alcoholic in AA who has a slip. Obviously, he decides to take a drink again some time before he actually takes it. He starts thinking wrong before he actually embarks on the course that leads to a slip.

There is no reason to charge the slip to alcoholic behavior or a second heart attack to cardiac behavior. The alcoholic slip is not a symptom of a psychotic condition. There's nothing screwy about it at all. *The patient simply didn't follow directions.*

For the alcoholic, AA offers the directions. A vital factor, or ingredient of the preventive, especially for the alcoholic, is sustained emotion. The alcoholic who learns some of the techniques or the mechanics of AA but misses the philosophy or the spirit may get tired of following directions — not because he is alcoholic, but because he is human. Rules and regulations irk almost anyone, because they are restraining, prohibitive, negative. The philosophy of AA, however, is positive and provides ample sustained emotion — a sustained desire to follow directions voluntarily.

In any event, the psychology of the alcoholic is not as different as some people try to make it. The disease has certain physical differences, yes, and the alcoholic has problems peculiar to him, perhaps, in that he has been put on the defensive and consequently has developed frustrations. But in many instances, there is no more reason to be talking about "the alcoholic mind" than there is to try to describe something called "the cardiac mind" or "the TB mind."

I think we'll help the alcoholic more if we can first recognize that he is primarily a human being — afflicted with human nature.

Anybody Seen My Dragon?

February 1967

YOU'RE STILL DRINKING, FRIEND? Then you're just the man I want to see. Want to ask you a question. Over here, where we won't be disturbed.

Question's this: Wonder if you've seen my dragon? Name of Beastly. Nice little guy. For a dragon. Green, with pink spots. Believe me, you couldn't miss ole Beastly!

I was sobbing my eyes out one night because the park bench I was on was going through red lights and I was scared stiff. Suddenly this dragon whammed into the bench and stopped it cold. If I'd thought I was scared before, Friend, now I was petrified. A dragon! Imagine!

"What'th the matter with you, Mithter?" he asked, and that started me laughing like a school kid. Somehow you can't be really scared of a dragon that lisps.

"Thtop laughing!" he fumed, and believe me, Friend, I thtopped. I mean stopped. On second thought, you *can* be scared of a lisping dragon, especially when he closes the damper and flames shoot out of his mouth.

"Thanks for stopping the bench," I said.

"Nothing. Nothing at all." At least he was modest.

Turned out the li'l fella didn't have a name, so I called him

Beastly, which described him pretty well. Besides, he liked the name. Beastly also liked the smell of sherry. He always came around when I drank it, and sometimes stayed for days after.

Usually, however, he would disappear when I was broke and had to work for a day or two (as a rule I took a position as Asst. Director of a Dishwashing Dept., Wet Arms Division), but Beastly always showed up again when I got a crock of sherry.

When Beastly stopped that park bench he was about three feet long, but it was amazing how he grew. About a foot a month. At first, he was fun to play with. Throw sticks, that sort of thing. He'd bring 'em back unless he got confused and burned 'em up. But in six months it got to the point where he could stop a Sherman tank with his breath, the ground shook under him when he ran, and if he ran too close to me, the wind would knock me down.

Once a cop found me in that position and asked, "What's the matter with you, fella?" I said, "It was Beastly," and he agreed, but wouldn't accept it as an answer. Then he smelled the sherry and hauled me off to the cooler, which was dragon proof.

I never saw Beastly again. You see, an AA visited me in jail last month and I got on the program, and since they don't allow spotted dragons to join...

Well, I smelled the sherry on you, Friend, and just thought you might have seen my old pet Beastly. Greatest little dragon I ever met.

Anonymous

The Fear of Feeling Rejected

October 1973

I N MY FIRST AA INVENTORY, taken almost six years ago, I listed as my primary shortcoming an inability to cope with feelings of rejection and defeat. In pre-AA years, whenever I had been willing to make a sincere effort to achieve anything, I often experienced gratifying success. But ordinary setbacks, which my normal friends seemed to shrug off, would throw me into a seething anger and resentment. I would withdraw from the contest and, wallowing in depression, would lock my door against the entire world, comforting myself with the bliss of alcoholic oblivion.

Then came AA. For the first time in years, I became willing to be possessed by an honest desire to achieve something — in this case, sobriety. The willingness came easily, because my life depended on it. As my obsession was being lifted, I got down to the causes and conditions mentioned in Chapter Five of *Alcoholics Anonymous*. This first inventory revealed that my old fear was still thriving, that I was still a moral coward, albeit a sober one.

For example, fear of being turned down because of my unstable employment record kept me from trying to land the kind of job for which I was qualified. When I finally did work up the nerve to apply (to just one employer) and was refused the position, my resentment-depression hung on for weeks. Caught in this dilemma, I reverted to form, refused to try again, and as a result, worked below my capacity for many months.

This fear of feeling rejected shortchanged me in the people department, too. I was afraid to choose. Surrounded by these well-meaning but self-assertive friends, I found little opportunity to cultivate any social courage. The men and women I wanted and needed most seemed to move in a sphere of their own, just beyond my grasp.

This insidious feeling even crept into my periods of prayer and meditation. What if God said no? I hesitated to ask, even though I knew such a request should have a qualification: that it be granted only if it was his will and if others would be helped. Thus, God rarely refused me — because I rarely asked him. Hung up in the limbo between fear and anger, what was I to do?

I would like to say that I turned promptly to AA for the answer, that I immediately applied spiritual principles to solve my problem. But I am an alcoholic, with the alcoholic's hard head, and it was necessary for me to waste much effort exercising my right to be wrong, before I finally yelled for help at my home group's meeting.

The first thing I discovered was that I was not alone. Almost without exception, my AA friends admitted that they had struggled with these same feelings. Some claimed that their fear of rejection stemmed from a lack of self-worth; some of the men laid the difficulty to feelings of inadequate masculinity stimulated by years of drinking. It was also asserted that we couldn't stand the responsibility of being loved and so sought rejection in subtle ways. About the only thing that everybody agreed on completely was that this problem, like our drinking problem, had a spiritual solution.

That night, restless with a new energy, I paced the silent city streets, thanking God over and over again for having given me the strength to reveal my shortcoming and to receive a wealth of shared experience. My friends had bridged the chasm of human limitations and had put something in my soul that hadn't been there before. Who could reject me if God accepted me? Who could defeat me unless I defeated myself?

I began to reach out. Through the amazing capacity of AA members to love, I received acceptance and the strength to go forward in spite of my qualms. I continued to pray for removal of my defects. Although the big step of willingness had been taken, my personality didn't reverse itself overnight. I can still feel a little bad at the moment I'm refused a position for which I'm qualified; I may suffer a slow burn for a few minutes after my date has pulled away just as I am courageously about to kiss her goodnight; even God turns me down more often now. But (and here is the miracle) I continue to try; I persist in the face of defeat. I can risk being rejected now, because I no longer have to feel resentful and depressed when it happens.

Soon, I expect to celebrate my sixth AA birthday. Some of the people I will be with on that day will be those I found the courage to reach toward. I will be doing work that is interesting and fulfilling and came only after many setbacks. Most important, if my Higher Power points out that my desires do not happen to coincide with his will, I can accept gratefully and continue the great search a day at a time.

V. C., Venice, Calif.

Ever Been on a Dry Drunk?

April 1962

AFTER TEN YEARS OF EXPOSURE to the AA program, I still experience that periodic phenomenon referred to as the "dry drunk." To my own amazement and everlasting gratitude, the last seven of those years has been a period of uninterrupted sobriety. This fortunate condition has certainly been brought about by a Power infinitely greater than my puny capabilities. I believe that the times of the greatest danger of self-destruction during these years were those when I, consciously or otherwise, attempted ego-tistically to take over the reins of my life and tried to exercise total control over my own affairs.

This usually resulted in a dry drunk. What is a dry drunk? The following description is based on a personal viewpoint, but is also supported by those ideas which I have heard expressed at many meetings.

An alcoholic appears capable of emotional extremes ranging from feelings of unbounded elation to depths of dark despair. As an imperfect but perhaps helpful analogy, we might compare the personality of an alcoholic with a weather map: *A dry drunk is an emotional storm.* The emotions of an alcoholic can fluctuate much in the manner of weather fronts.

When all seems to be comparatively well for the recovered alco-holic, his general feeling of well-being is like a "high-pressure" weather area. This is a large mass of cool, dry air, usually accom-panied by clear, blue skies and lots of pleasant sunshine. As long as we try to carry the message to others, attend meetings regularly, and seek God's guidance every day, we are frequently gifted with a sunny, love-filled spirit — our own inner high-pressure area.

You know, of course, that the weather changes: day by day, little by little, the cool, stimulating air may be replaced by uncom-fortable, oppressive, moisture-laden air. There develops a turbu-lence and confusion in the atmosphere, similar to the turbulence and confusion in the mental atmosphere of an alcoholic on a dry emotional jag.

October 1974

"Whenever I have a problem, I ask myself,
"How would a grown-up handle it?"'

This is why we are cautioned against fatigue. Take a particularly difficult day with a sufficient number of negative events, mix in normal amounts of twentieth-century stress, give this dose to a fatigued alcoholic and you have a nice dry drunk in the making. Of course we can help it along by skipping lunch, rushing at a double-time pace all day long, and engaging in the doubtful luxury of such emotions as anger and worry.

I learned that, in my own case, I was more likely to become irritable and confused toward the end of the work week, when accumulated tensions and lack of rest were at their worst. Things looked darker on Friday than they did on Monday morning. In time, I was able to realize that the things which seemed so important on Friday were really minor, and that such an outlook was due mostly to my failings and not to circumstances.

We all realize that there are ways of modifying or preventing dry drunks. A dry drunk is basically an illustration that we have much progress to make in our application of the AA program.

The antidote is contained in the Twelve Steps. We should seek ways to help other members — even a simple telephone call to inquire about a fellow member can shake us loose from our exaggerated self-concern. No one can express love and self-pity at the same moment; showing concern for others helps us to see how foolish we have been, how we have literally trapped ourselves in the familiar mental "squirrel cage."

When nothing else avails, we can say, "Today I am sick." Of course, this does not mean *physically* sick, but refers more to a spiritual disorder — a separateness from God as we understand him. During an emotional bender, the admission that we are powerless over our own rampant thoughts, and that our lives are even more unmanageable than usual, is an act which equates with Step One.

I believe a dry drunk is a period of temporary insanity for the sober alcoholic. Step Two says: "Came to believe that a Power greater than ourselves could restore us to sanity." A dry drunk is a self-imposed separation from others and from God. We try to run on our own current, like a battery without a generator, which soon runs down and becomes quite dead.

Step Ten — the Step of continuing personal inventory — should certainly be emphasized following a dry drunk. We should attempt, in a spirit of humility and deep reflection, to see clearly where we were wrong. It helps to discuss these failures with other members, in order to crystalize our mistakes and prevent their recurrence. A series of unexpected conditions may have helped to bring about our emotional upheaval; this does not justify it, but only indicates that we are in definite need of further spiritual development.

Perhaps, in the last analysis, a dry drunk is mostly a childish tantrum, an interval of immaturity, a regression to those frantic drinking days of self-will run riot. Nevertheless, it can still be a perilous period for the alcoholic struggling for recovery. I know that there have been dark days when a will infinitely greater than my own has been responsible for my sobriety.

M. E., Dayton, Ohio

Those Depressions — Make Them Work for Good!

August 1948

MOST OF US HAVE THEM, I guess — those depressions that attack us without warning and apparently without adequate cause. I am sure they are not limited to alcoholics; but for us, they are dangerous, much more dangerous than they are to the average nonalcoholic, for they induce a craving, not necessarily for liquor, but for the effect of liquor.

I remember reading an article some time ago about mood cycles. I think it said that the mood swing for an average normal person took place in a matter of fourteen to eighteen days, as a rule. It advised us to keep track of our feelings — that is, if we wake up feeling unaccountably happy and go through the day in that frame of mind, mark it down on our calendar, and see how long it is until we have another such day. Do the same with the sad days.

This might be an interesting experiment and prove helpful enough if it were not for the fact that our mood swings are wider than those of the average person. Our sad times are sadder; our happy periods, perhaps because we have gotten used to doing without them, cause an elation that is unrealistic and almost as dangerous to us as the depressions. We make plans that are out of all proportion to our abilities, at least without years of sustained effort.

We are not too long on sustained effort, and when a few stabs in the direction of our goal, whatever it may be, don't produce immediate results, we are prone to give the whole thing up.

To make these violent changes in mood safe for ourselves, I think we will have to do something about them, turn them to account in some way. I wouldn't know what to do about the elations except to pull ourselves down out of the clouds by main force and go out and do something active instead of daydreaming — do something that is within the realm of possibility and keep on doing it until we have accomplished something concrete. At such times, our self-confidence is high, and we are likely to do a good job.

Our depressions vary in length and intensity — at least, mine do. Sometimes, they are deep indeed and last as long as a month. Sometimes, they are less severe, and I get over them in a few days. Dark or light, they are distressing, unproductive times, when life seems like a very dull business. Even AA loses its reality. I go to meetings and come away bored and dissatisfied. If it is a discussion meeting and I contribute any optimistic thought, I listen to myself cynically and think, "Why don't we stop kidding ourselves? We'll never really amount to anything. We missed our chance long ago. We are way behind in the race."

These, to my mind, are the times to go to work, fight it out with yourself, answer yourself back. Say to yourself: "All right. Perhaps I never will do anything spectacular. Maybe I'm not any ball of fire, never was, never will be. Suppose I have to plod along in the middle of the road just like the vast majority of human beings — scoring a small success here, a small setback there, never getting very far ahead, trying not to get too far behind."

If we face these thoughts honestly and without shame, we have done something. We have turned our depression into an adjustment that is a necessary one for most of us. It is quite probable that our lives will be spectacular only in that they are so much better than they were during our drinking years. We will be important only to ourselves and the few who are close to us. If we stay sober, and we know that we must, we can say these things to ourselves and go on from there.

To us as active alcoholics, the word "mediocrity" meant all the dull, boring aspects of life that we were trying to escape. If we couldn't be tops, we didn't want to play at all. Well, most of us — not all of us by any means, but most of us — are pretty run-of-the-mill individuals. We can do a job as well as the next fellow, but perhaps not any better. We can make as much money if we work as hard as he does, and if we can stop this frantic drive to prove that we are remarkable people, it is quite likely that we will settle down and really enjoy whatever life has to offer us. And it offers a great deal now that we are sober and can appreciate it.

There is one job that we *can* do superlatively well, and there isn't anything that can keep us from doing it if we are serious in wanting to. That is the job we do on ourselves, inside ourselves. It means clearing out a whole mess of false values, unrealistic ambitions, and worn-out resentments, and putting in their place the qualities we want to have — kindness, tolerance, friendliness, for instance. We can begin to see what the real values of life are, and they are very different from the hazy, distorted dreams we had of becoming famous overnight.

If we can really talk to ourselves in this manner during our depression, we have made use of it. Instead of letting it submerge us and perhaps drive us into a slip, we have used it as a stepping-stone toward a better understanding of what our sober lives can hold for us.

In our happier moods, we will still daydream, and I wouldn't want to stop. But they will be constructive dreams, rather than mere flights of fancy, and if we keep them within the bounds of possibility, we will have a good chance of making them come true.

M. N., New York, N.Y.

Just Keep On Going

April 1976

I'VE HAD A LOT OF DEPRESSIONS during my sobriety. Many have lasted for six months, some for a year, or two or three years. I have stuck to the AA program, also to friends in AA, and this has saved my life. I've tried everything from psychiatry to special diets and megavitamin therapy. Nothing has worked except putting one foot in front of the other and keeping going.

I believe in a Higher Power, and I believe that my Higher Power, if I really turn over my depression, will free me. I am working on this now, because I am beginning to come out of a depression. I am becoming able to change those things I can while accepting the things I can't change, at least for the time being.

I was overwhelmed by money problems, by the death during the last few years of six dear friends, and by a life situation that looked totally unmanageable. But I didn't reach for the bottle; I didn't hit a psychiatric ward; I didn't jump off anything higher than a horse or a New England stone wall; nor did I swallow anything more detrimental to my health than caffeine, tannin, or chocolate sauce.

I know from past experience that sitting around and brooding is the worst thing to do. Trying to figure it all out in my head brings on waves of fear, anxiety, and self-reproach. So I say, "What can I do today for myself and others?" I always write out a list of things, check them off as they get done, and carry those I don't get done over to the next day. When bleak thoughts come up, I remember that I have already turned them over. They mostly have to do with the past and the future. What I can do *now* is what counts.

I also try to laugh at my own state of woe. I find something funny to say about my attitude. And laughter is great, even if it's forced at first, by and by, you can really laugh.

I am grateful for a lot of things: the long stretches of good life that I have had; the pleasures of the outdoors with young members of my family. We love each other; we are good friends. Because I have leveled with them about my past drinking, they've been able to unburden themselves about their own problems. This has closed the generation gap, and we are able to talk about everything and anything.

As a writer, I haven't worked as consistently as I might have. But some of my things have been published, and I'm not ashamed of them. I certainly don't write well when I'm depressed, but I do it anyway. Without AA, I wouldn't be writing, because I'd have been dead years ago.

Thank God for all the wonderful people, professional and otherwise, who have helped me or tried to. Even when the help has not succeeded, it has kept me going, kept me trying. And I have been able to use some of the help and advice.

I try to help people, in and out of AA. I speak when I can. I meet with a group of other AAs who are prone to depression, and we help one another. We tell one another to accept the state we are in and to relax and keep going. We encourage one another to regain self-esteem by pointing out the progress we've made. Depression and anxiety can breed all kinds of unpleasant symptoms, such as loss of memory and attention, giddiness, heart palpitations. We discuss this, because we have resolved not to fight unpleasant feelings, but to accept them and go about our business. We sometimes telephone one another when we are feeling at our worst.

Once a week I go to a painting class for handicapped people and the nonhandicapped who bring them, and I help set up the paints. I have just joined it and haven't done much yet except help my friend, who founded the group. She has no use of her arms or hands, but she drives her own car with her feet and drives *me* to class.

Spending a whole day alone or eating dinner alone is hard when I'm depressed. This is when "poor little me" really sets in. However, I read the papers, try to watch news programs, and really enjoy reading books. I get to movies and plays and concerts. Walking in the woods or on the beach is a joy, and I do it every chance I get. I always have my car radio on for news and music. I have friends in and cook dinner for them or ask somebody in for coffee. And bless my friends, I'm asked out a lot.

I am immeasurably grateful for the sense of values I have learned from AA and psychiatry — but especially AA. I know that I am not a total loss, even when I think I am. I know that freedom and usefulness, love, outgoingness, and sharing are the important things in life. But even more important, I have to care for me and achieve a sense of self-worth. So I continue to listen. I am still open to suggestions. I continue on my way. And I am on my way up.

F. M., New Canaan, Conn.

Self-Pity Can Kill

February 1973

OVER AND OVER, through the gaiety of the preholiday season in December 1965, I chanted this litany of despair: "I gave all I had to give, and it wasn't enough." And on Christmas night, I made a drunken and almost successful suicide attempt. Consciousness returned in the special-care ward of the local hospital, where doctors waited to determine whether brain damage had occurred during the moments when my heart had stopped beating, thirty-six hours earlier.

It would be nice to be able to say that I promptly joined AA, stopped drinking, reconstructed my collapsing marriage, and never again suffered an attack of the Ploms — the poor-little-old me's. But a divorce was to come and two more drunken years were to elapse before I took my last drink.

This dirty linen might have been washed in the privacy of the Fifth Step if I was not convinced that its obvious message should be passed along: Self-pity can kill.

True, alcohol was the catalyst. It required a combination of alcohol, self-pity, and a bitter quarrel to provide the impetus for my nearly fatal gesture. And it required ignorance of the underlying causes. It became necessary for me to go back to my childhood, to the time when the seeds were planted that had their noxious blooming so many years later.

My mother, doubtless for well-meant reasons, did not believe in coddling me. She used to tell me proudly, "You have to *earn* my love."

Too young then, and too unquestioning, I failed to realize the truths that one is not always unlovable and that others are often unloving. That ignorance almost cost me my life.

I went down the potholed, mud-bogged path of the years, struggling against my legitimate anger, excusing the faults of others, though never my own, measuring myself by the yardstick of perfection and despising the gap between, dismissing my virtues as inadequate or condemning my recognition of them as egotism, and nursing each failure with an aching pain.

And when it got too bad, when my demands on myself had squeezed the juice from life, I drank. I might have gone on forever, fighting the battle of my disintegrated ego — drinking for release, sobering up amid the wreckage the release created, making impossible demands on myself, then drinking again — had I not finally become convinced that I had achieved my goal. In the midst of a family disaster, I had behaved almost perfectly.

My unbelieving joy was monumental. All the efforts of the years had paid off. I examined my actions for flaws — went over every word I had said, every gesture I had made, every letter I had written, every attitude I had held. I bathed them in the clinical, unsparing light of objectivity and justice, and found them valid. Joy-suffused, I turned toward love.

And met hate. I had been wise, and my wisdom was resented. I had been compassionate, and they wanted intolerance. I had been understanding, and they called for condemnation.

Blinded with tears, I headed for the bottle. And drank. And said over and over (though no one listened, they had their own problems), "I gave all I had to give, and it wasn't enough." And almost died.

Looking back, more than six years later, I still feel that I had behaved exceptionally well. I did deserve, if not love — which depends on the capacity of the giver, rather than the acts of the

VICTOR E.

recipient — at least approval. And I didn't get it.

Poor little old me. I had the Ploms and almost died from them. Sober, I would probably have recovered with a few new scars on an already badly dented ego, and my life since would have been a different one. Yet I had survived many a maudlin drinking bout without resorting to suicide attempts. It was alcohol *plus* the Ploms that almost did me in.

Though I no longer use alcohol, I must still guard against self-pity, a defect as "cunning, baffling, powerful" as alcohol. I have wrestled with self-pity many times since joining AA, four years ago. It was a tough fight, but I won — until very recently, when the old "I gave all I had to give, and it wasn't enough" syndrome rose phoenixlike from the ashes of Christmas 1965. Although my symptoms were identical, I didn't recognize them. When I first became aware of deep depression, I put it down to the aftermath of moving and getting settled in a new city and in an old house. "I'm just tired from papering and painting," I told myself firmly. Or "I'm a little depressed because the excitement of shopping is over and the money's all spent."

I decided to celebrate Be-Kind-to-Me Week, which is generally helpful in treating mild depression or fatigue. I took long naps, and awoke more tired and disconsolate than when I had gone to sleep. I gorged on sweets, then hated myself for my spreading waistline. Nothing seemed to help.

In fact, things grew worse. I fought tears, and when I had successfully swallowed them, anger and hostility toward everyone and everything welled up in their place. When I forced these back — or, unfortunately, spilled them out to anyone who would listen — despairing loneliness enveloped me.

April 1976

It was only through the grace of God that I was free of the compulsion to drink during the four or five days that I felt these symptoms with such intensity. The old feeling of "To hell with it! I'll get drunk" recurred only once, when I had dropped my husband at his office and faced a return to the empty house, which I had come to loathe. AA had given me a weapon to combat that feeling. I hadn't been around long enough in my new AA group to have acquired any phone numbers for telephone therapy, so I did the only thing I could think of to postpone a return to the house — and to the bottle kept for nonalcoholic guests. I took care of some neglected errands. Not many, not important, but when I returned to the house, forty-five minutes later, I had gained some perspective, been in contact with other people — and completely forgotten any thoughts about bottles for guests. Sometimes, playing for time is all it takes.

I did something else. Though I didn't believe a word of it with my heart, I *knew* intellectually that "this, too, shall pass." I reminded myself constantly that I had been badly depressed in the past and that, *if I didn't drink*, I had always bounced back up — and would this time, too. All I had to do was wait.

Then I started listing in my mind the exact possible causes of this depression. Gradually, the old, tired pattern emerged: I had given all I had to give, and it wasn't enough. I had moved even farther south, although I am one of those nuts who *like* cold weather. I had practiced economy in the purchase of the house and its contents, in spite of my predilection toward extravagance. I had cheerfully done backbreaking labor, although I incline toward the horizontal plane if left to my own devices. The list was a long one, but what it boiled down to was that I had been pretty saintly. So where was my laurel wreath?

Poor little old me — same song as before. And I hadn't had the remotest notion that *self-pity* was again the root of my problem!

Without knowing what I was fighting, however, I had used another weapon that AA had given me. Never thinking of it as practicing the Tenth Step, I had continued to take personal inventory, and when I was wrong had promptly admitted it. And that Tenth Step, practiced with unsparing honesty, had ended my dry drunk, cured my self-pity, and saved my sobriety.

There are additional weapons that can be used in fighting the Ploms, once the disease is recognized for what it is. First, for me, is to recognize that most of the time when I give all I have to give and

even a bit more, I am doing it by my own choice. No one was pointing a gun at me and making me paint walls — I chose to do it for the reward of enjoying the fresh paint. If I overdid it to the point of aching muscles and exhaustion, whose fault was that? What reason did I have to expect paeans of praise?

Second, if I occasionally do not receive what I have earned and have a reasonable right to expect — who ever promised me justice? Often, I do not get my just deserts when I behave badly!

It is my belief that all of us have more control over our feelings than we generally suspect. Once an unhealthy attitude is seen clearly, it can be scrapped. If someone has given me cause for self-pity, I can opt to resent and even try to punish him, ignoring the fact that I might better leave that up to God. But do I *want* to hurt him? Do I really want, however justifiably, to be bitter, hostile, and judgmental? Do I want to live inside that sort of person? Wouldn't I rather forgive, make allowances, understand? Is self-pity, feeling abused, so precious that I will not trade it for self-liking?

I can also fight self-pity by considering the lot of others. Whom do I know who always gets what he wants, whose life is so fine that I would eagerly exchange mine for it? And whom do I know who has much less than I?

Last, suppose life deals me one crushing blow after another, none of them deserved. What can I do about it? Well, I can weep and whine. If that doesn't improve things, I can get drunk. And if *that* doesn't work, I can kill myself. Or I can accept the situation and live. Those are my only options.

Living appears to be the best; if things should happen to improve, I will be around to benefit. As drinking alcoholics, we all ran from life and toward death. When we join AA, we reverse the process — we give ourselves to life *as it is,* rather than as we would like it to be. We stop fighting the inevitable and start growing up.

I will never totally overcome self-pity. It will lie in ambush along the road ahead. It will wear many skillful disguises so that I will not always recognize it immediately. But, with the help of God and AA, it will never cause another night like the one of Christmas 1965.

J. W., Key West, Fla.

The Green Demon

May 1962

I CAN MARK ONE THING WELL in looking back at my whirling nightmare of drinking — it was the only time I was ever completely jealous of total strangers! It amazes me now to remember that I had ugly and envious thoughts about innocent people I passed on the street — people who never knew me and had never done me the slightest harm. I resented their good fortune, their fine clothes, their poise, their normalcy. I wanted to see them taken down a peg or two, or even down many pegs to where I was!

I am no longer jealous of strangers. Yet this is not to say that I have been purged of the terrible emotion. It is only to say that my capacity for jealousy has become more subtle, often cloaking itself in seemingly righteous feelings. It is now directed toward people whom I know personally. What used to be blind jealousy, seething almost on the surface at all times, has now become "conditional" jealousy, kept under lock and key unless certain nerve ends in my life are rubbed the wrong way. Then, in almost an instant, the cold fury rises, as it always did.

Fortunately, it does not usually rise all the way. For I have done battle with this demon jealousy, and I charge that he is a great destroyer of happiness and stability. It is impossible to be both jealous and happy; the two conditions are what engineers call "mutually exclusive." I want to be happy, I want to be sober, and I want to progress. Therefore, I must exclude the very beginnings of jealousy at all costs, for the pain of rooting it out is nothing compared to the pain of being its victim.

Most of the jealousy I suffer from today is in a disguised form; I have simply allowed it to appear in a new mask. It makes itself known abruptly, however, when I feel something good is

Well, the old hands in our area were dry five to six years when I went shyly through a meeting hall door for the first time. As I became aware of them as people, there developed in me a sense of awe for the old-timer of the day.

From my own insecure stance, I thought: "How wonderful to have a platform of sober years to work from. Surely, these men and women who have been dry for so long have a security from the horrors of alcoholic drinking."

I longed for that security.

Then a decade whirled and I became conscious that in some eyes I, too, had become an old-timer. A friend who was to be chairman of a special "big meeting" asked me to dig up a speaker for him.

"I want all the speakers to be in the six- to eighteen-month group," he said. "They are the ones who pack a real punch."

I pondered this.

I pondered it even harder after attending that meeting. The speakers had great power. All talked out of the remembrance of recent agony and great gratitude for their release.

Freedom! Freedom from alcoholism was the theme. How purposeful they made AA life seem!

For the last couple of years I have been uneasily aware of once-active members who have disappeared from meetings, and disturbed by reports of slips suffered by people with years of sobriety. Where was their platform of security? Where was my own?

Recently, a bouncy twelfth-stepper, just over a year dry, brought a slippee to my door. Both were in varying degrees of desperation. The AA man wanted my help in solving a difficult hospitalization problem. The sick man, it appeared, had made himself unwelcome at almost every institution in the area.

The sick one was babbling and arrogant. I became resentful and irritated. A couple of phone calls solved the problem and I made a half-hearted offer to accompany them to the sanitarium. The offer was politely turned down.

When they left, I was overwhelmed with shame. True, I had given of my past Twelfth Step experience, but nothing else; no compassion, none of the essential friendship of AA. A chore had been accomplished and my friend knew that for me it had been nothing more.

Is this a common problem of the older AA member — remoteness in time and feeling from the sick alcoholic stumbling in his search for recovery?

One does not, I think, become suddenly remote. It creeps up, as smugness and security displace concern for our own sobriety and that of others.

How secure is my eleven-year sobriety today? As secure, I am forced to admit, as that of any other self-deceived older member who, to the dismay of his friends, has returned to drink. As secure, insight tells me, as that of the newest member, because my sobriety and his are attached to the same branch of earnest desire for freedom and to the same root of spiritual principles.

I am facing the truth that there are no platforms of security in AA. Because if one tarries on a platform, he leaves the living stream of AA life. He becomes alone.

And I am remembering that when an alcoholic tries to stay sober alone, he returns to drink. At least I always did.

J. M., Vancouver, B.C.

Tradition One

Our common welfare should come first;
personal recovery depends on AA unity

November 1969

MY AA HISTORY CONSISTS of two extended slips during an otherwise sober quarter-century. I have not taken or wanted a drink since May 1952, but I have learned much about alcohol and AA, and a little about myself. I no longer have quick, simple answers for staying sober, although at times I sound as if I do. For example, I have said I had sobriety of the head, not sobriety of the heart, in my first year, and I've been so proud of this eloquence that I was deaf to the vanity revealed: the implication that my own superior ability at rational thinking kept me from drinking.

More honest thinking suggests that what kept me sober those first days was not any of my doing at all. Obviously, it was not rules or laws, either, since we have none. In fact, our Twelve Traditions had not even been written yet, the first year I spent dry, sit-

*Articles on the other Traditions appear later: Tradition Two, page 95; Three, page 39; Four, page 104; Five, page 67; Six, page 250; Seven, page 114; Eight, page 259; Nine, page 264; Ten, page 222; Eleven, page 70; Twelve, page 191.

ting around in New York City's old 41st Street clubhouse, glum and stiff in one of the musty pews of that barnlike old church building where meetings were held.

I made a few mechanical gestures that year, doing my turn at desk or telephone duty, reading the AA publications (very few then), and speaking at meetings. I even typed copy for the early, tabloid-size Grapevine. But none of this was based on any real desire to change myself.

When I came to AA, I had not wanted sobriety so much as I wanted to stay out of the trouble that came with my drinking. I had been terrorized by blackouts and a searing fear that I was really losing my mind. I had been sick with shame at the way I had treated my family and friends, even if I did think they often deserved it for some of the things they did to poor me. I had been unemployable, hopelessly in debt, and sure that jail or an insane asylum was deserved and inevitable, unless a suicide attempt worked out some time.

The vanity which so often had propped me up had given way to self-loathing. I was a dirty, gaunt, unshaven, quaking wreck. I was no good. The world would be better off without me.

The state of AA dryness I found in that old clubhouse in 1945 was highly desirable, every precious 24 hours of it. It did not promise any rosy future, but it was beginning to exorcise the past.

I kept going through the AA motions, relieved enormously by the knowledge that I had a disease, that it was not my fault, and that others like me, or worse, were recovering. (Didn't I see hope sitting row on row at every meeting?) I was memorizing AA state-

February 1975

"I got no drinkin' problem. My problem is when I ain't drinkin'."

ments and not drinking, more because AA seemed to expect it (and my family approved) than because I really wanted the AA way of life.

It is, of course, a miracle that I stayed sober at all. Those wonderful AA people, when I first came for help, certainly had far more to do with keeping me sober than my own reluctant efforts. I believe now that those sober members acted out twelve specific ideas of AA behavior, and I want to celebrate in Grapevine ink those twelve ways, because they saved my life and still do, over and over.

Chronologically, one of the first things AA members ever did, which eventually made my own recovery possible, was simply *sticking together*.

The first AAs fast got the notion that we need each other if we are to survive. As has been said well and often, we may not all like each other, but we have to love each other. Communicate or die! When put into action, the power of that one idea alone can keep a guy sober, to his own surprise, a very long time. It did that for me, I know.

Then someone got the idea that AAs ought to put down in writing just how it was they were staying sober. Many agreed; others were fearful. The real crunch was agreeing on what to put into the book. What a miracle that those early members, despite misgivings, disagreements, distrust, and fierce devotion to high principles that were poles apart, could agree, not only on the Twelve Steps, but on enough material to fill a whole book! If the early AAs had not stuck together at that point, if they had broken up in hopeless disagreements, there would be no book, no Twelve Steps, no AA, and no me.

Ancient history? Not for me. I turned myself in to AA on a bitterly cold January day during World War II. AA members had already decided to have a publicly listed telephone number. The simple act of getting in touch with AA that first time washed out in an instant the dark loneliness that had encompassed my life. When I fearfully crept into that old building that first day, I was greeted with a gentle invitation: "Come on in. Let's talk it over." And everyone assured me I was not alone and *need never be alone again*.

All the suggestions I heard then were based on our sticking together. "Come to meetings" meant that I would be with other AAs, fulfilling the purpose for which meetings had been started in

the first place. "Don't get lonely; telephone before you take a
drink; talk to another member and get your troubles off your
chest." All these powerful tools of sobriety assured me that *together* we could get well and stay well.

Less than a year later, there were so many meetings in the New
York Area that those of us who answered the telephone had difficulty remembering which groups met which nights and where. So
we typed up a list we could refer to. Where would I be now without
my meeting list and the central office that publishes it? These two
things are absolutely necessary if we AAs in New York or in any
large city want to stick together. To remove the last traces of loneliness, there is the *World Directory*, assuring me that we are now a
worldwide Fellowship with the shared strength of hundreds of
thousands. And now the General Service Conference, many GSO
bulletins, and the treasured Grapevine, of course, make it easier
for all of us to keep in touch.

About five years after my last drink, I found myself pretty
sick one day with an illness not related to alcohol. At home alone,
scared, I needed help. The natural thing was to call an AA friend,
right? Who else would come to help? To whom else could I un-
ashamedly admit I was afraid? Who else knew the inside of fear?

But the only nearby AA member I could reach on the telephone at that time of day was a fellow I did not like. Never had,
and the feeling was mutual; he had no use for me, either. Yet he
came at once and helped me through the day with incredible, tactful kindness.

That is not an unusual AA story, I know. Almost always,
when the chips are down, we forget our differences and observe
our First Tradition. We may not quote its words very often, but
apparently each AA realizes, deep down, that if it were not for the
"we" of AA, there would be no "I."

The Tradition has also made a difference in the quality of my
AA life beyond sobriety. One sleepless night some years ago, I was
again feeling lonely and isolated, although I had been as regular as
ever in going to meetings and participating in other AA actions. I
felt surrounded by AA, but insulated against it. Somehow, I was
wrapped in a cool cocoon that kept the warm AA spirit from getting to me.

Again, it took the experience of begging another AA member
for help to melt away the chilly walls. This time I reached a dear
AA friend, and the help I got was anything but tactful. I was told

bluntly where the trouble was. It was self-importance again! It seemed that I had subtly and unconsciously come to think of myself as somewhat of an example, if not a font, of AA wisdom. My AA talks pointed out, not only how stupid I had been, but also — and mostly — how much smarter I was now. In discussion meetings I never asked questions; I just answered them. I overflowed with AA know-how, and insidiously it put me out of touch. Secretly, I did not mind at all when someone once referred to me as an oracle.

True, I was sharing my experience, and what I revealed was honest. But it was not the whole truth. I kept hidden from others the yet-unsolved problems, the shameful secrets of today, admitting them fully to no one.

I was furious at the old AA friend who punctured the vanity balloon, but she was right. I had been so busy giving fellowship that I had forgotten to accept any. And she finally goaded me into doing something about it. I began to spill it all out, at last sharing the other parts of my total experience, including the bad and the embarrassing. Believe me, it was a liberating experience, and the help was enormously strengthening.

I still marvel that our Loners and Internationalists, who hardly ever get to meetings, stay beautifully sober. But I also remember that originally the Grapevine began as a message from the AAs back home to the AAs overseas in World War II. And I recall a letter from a private, who wrote from Normandy, "Even thousands of miles away, I know I am not alone, since all of you are always with me in spirit."

Maybe those isolated members — perhaps because they have to dig so deep into our literature — sense better than some meeting-goers like me the meanings and values of fellowship. They are constantly reminded that the Twelve Steps say *we* admitted, *we* came to believe, *we* made a decision, and *we* tried to carry the message.

This beautiful *we*, this sticking together in our brotherhood of love — which can heal my individual sick soul, as well as cementing together our Fellowship — is set forth for all of us in the words "Our common welfare should come first; personal recovery depends upon AA unity."

B. L., Manhattan, N.Y.

Tradition Three

*The only requirement for AA membership
is a desire to stop drinking*

January 1970

W HO CAN MEASURE what is in the heart of another? No one presumed to measure the sincerity or quality of my motivation to get well when I first approached AA. Our Third Tradition is based on group experience, and its wisdom has truly been proved to me in personal experience. It is a powerful tool for safeguarding my own recovery.

When I first offered myself to AA, some twenty-five years ago, I met almost no requirements for joining any decent gathering. The preceding months had been nothing but drunkenness, accompanied by a sickness at heart which few but alcoholics can fathom. I could have completed no questionnaire or application blank. I had no address, no telephone, no references. My last few employers would have warned anyone not to let me inside the door. My estranged family would have agreed. I had no religion, no job, no clothes except those I was wearing. I could not have paid for entertainment in a penny arcade. From my past behavior, I could not prove that I deserved any kindness or help. I was dirty, and I stank. I had only a highly undesirable sickness to offer AA, and that was all AA asked of me.

I was so chilled inside, so bleak and numb that, although I had no overcoat, I did not notice the bitter wintry weather on the January day when I first walked, zombielike, up the steps into the old AA clubhouse on New York's West 41st Street. What shakes I could not control, I pretended were deliberate, if weird, gestures. My mouth was cottony; I had not had a drink for about thirty-six hours. I knew from gloomy past experiences that I must just hold on for one more minute, make my legs take one more step, try to think of some great happy moment in the past (or invent one), steel my will just one more time, and sooner or later I could get a drink, after I had investigated this Alcoholics Anonymous business. Or, mercifully, I would suddenly die. I had no strength to ask for help. I was taking this dangerous risk — getting near strangers who, I was told, did not ask for names and had been pretty bad drinkers themselves — just to see whether I could observe while being unobserved.

Although I did not know what to expect, I was prepared — with lies, naturally. I had to be. If anyone asked me how much I drank, I always lied; the quantity was irrelevant to how drunk I got or what happened to me. If I was asked what I would do to get a drink, I would have to lie, because if I admitted the truth, I would surely be punished. If I was asked how I behaved when drunk, I would lie, partly to cover up the blackouts, partly to hide the bits of shameful truth that I did recall.

Since this was in 1945, before our Third Tradition was written, the AA woman who spoke to me first had no formal printed guidance for deciding whom to admit to AA for help. But she had compassion. She did not begin with a blunt "Are you an alcoholic?" If she had, I would have said, "Certainly not," with my usual nasty aloofness. Nor did she ask, "Do you want to stop drinking?" In my state, the question would have seemed absurd, if not insane. The one thing in the world I needed and wanted that minute was a stiff drink. But I was afraid to take one. That fact glued my feet just inside the door of the old building, where I pretended to be reading a handy bulletin board.

But she spied me lurking about, and, in a kind but not over-gooey voice, she said, "Are you having trouble with your drinking?" I was thunderstruck. It was the one query I had not prepared a lie for. Before I knew what was happening, I told the truth. I nodded yes.

"Well, I'm a drunk myself," she said. "Come on in and we'll talk it over."

She spoke easily, with no emotionalism. I had thought I was beyond surprise, but I could only stare in disbelief. She seemed so serene, so content, so clean, so respectable. How could she say she was a drunk?

We sat down, and my education began. *She asked no questions*, so I did not have to be cautiously alert; I could just listen with full, intense attention. I heard about her disease, alcoholism, and her recovery in AA. It was more comforting, more nourishing, and more enduring than any drink had ever been. Probably my face remained frozen, but my heart thawed, and I had to keep blinking rapidly and blowing my nose. Finally, warm inside, I began to feel the cold I had come in out of.

Dreading the answer, I was afraid to ask what was in my heart: "Will you, *please*, let *me* join?" I knew I did not deserve it, so, with a disdain often practiced, I tried to sound casual while managing to murmur, as if only impersonally interested, "How does one join?"

She said that my simply coming there meant I wanted help, and if I just wanted to be a member of AA, then I already was.

I hope I never forget the floods of relief those words brought. I particularly need to remember them when I am disturbed or inconvenienced by "improper personages" who sometimes intrude on nice, clean, sober, orderly AA meetings these days. A group near my home has "banned" two alcoholics from its premises. Impossible types, I heard. Most uncooperative, very undesirable.

I was not in on these exclusions, but during my early AA days I sometimes led the pack in verbally stoning an alcoholic out of the one place where he could have found help at that time. We had many rules of membership then. They were a nuisance, because we had to keep changing them almost weekly to keep the "wrong" people out and let the "right" people in. Sometimes one week's sergeant-at-arms was himself excluded the next week because he was drunk. Me.

Perhaps today's would-be rule-makers for AA membership, or guardians of the premises, are those whose drinking lives had such virtue as to earn for them the "privilege" of AA assistance. But no member I know claims such deserts, and I know I do not. As you see, I am now as intolerant of rule-makers as they are of the sick alcoholics they find undesirable.

Honestly now, if in order to get into AA we had had to meet any standards more rigid than the one given in the Third Tradition, who of us would be alive? Think of all the wonderful people, including the nonconformists, eccentrics, and kooks who make such valuable additions to our number, who would have been kept out of AA if we had any requirement for membership other than a desire to get well.

Although I know it is impossible to judge what is in anyone else's heart, and arrogant even to try, I still find myself trying at times. I have heard myself on the telephone at Intergroup screening would-be members, as if judging whether or not they were worthy of our help, whether or not they merited our love.

I have even asked a drunk such an awful question as "Do you *really* want to stop drinking forever?" Or "Have you had any AA contact before?" — as if prior membership were a requirement, or perhaps grounds for disqualification. Or "What kind of pills do you take?" I have been impatient with a slipper, too, forgetting that this binge could be his last, as one of my own finally was (so far).

In fact, just today I found myself deciding that I do not care for so-and-so's brusque and hypocritical brand of AA; nor do I like what that fanatic such-and-such says so rudely about spiritual matters; and I can't stand the phony-sounding piety of still another fellow AA.

I fear that in my heart I am ruling out of *my* AA anybody who does not meet my own high and mighty requirements for membership. It is as if, each time I disdain an alcoholic for whatever reason, I add another brick to a wall supposedly safeguarding my recovery, or at least keeping it cozy and comfortable for me. And

November 1959

"Just one more — then I've got to dash."

if I keep on adding rejection bricks or exclusion bricks to my wall of safety, you know where I'll wind up: isolated behind the wall I have built, right back where I was before AA, *alone*.

One of my own first AA contacts did suggest that, later on, I could earn my AA membership if I wanted to. And I wanted to desperately, because I was already feeling smothered by the enormous debt of gratitude that I felt I owed to AA. I do not think I could have survived the burden of owing so much if AA had let me go on thinking it was all being done only for unworthy me. But I was assured that AA people kept *themselves* sober by trying to help me. It was also a great relief to be told that I could, in a sense, pay off my debt simply by talking to someone else, some day, as I had been talked to. It was *not* suggested that I help only the clean, the proper, and the unpilled, the nonbrusque and unhypocritical, the nonfanatics, the pious, or the impious.

Apparently, for me, the price of our AA fellowship (First Tradition) and of our fearless trust of each other (Second Tradition), if I want them, is learning unstinting acceptance of others — a love which can be claimed by anyone who wants it. He may not say he wants it, or act as if he does, but if the desire is in his heart, even unknown to himself, that is enough.

B. L., Manhattan, N.Y.

Caught in Hateland

December 1966

D URING MY DRINKING YEARS I was a general all-around expert on all subjects. Now I feel that my experience qualifies me as an expert on only two, resentments and rationalizations.

Although there is a relationship between them, since resentments are developed against the people and situations which we think are the cause of our trouble, it will be simpler to discuss them one at a time. This is about resentments.

After working on a personal inventory for about eight months, it became clear that one of the worst of my character defects was a tendency to harbor resentments. Tendency did I say? My mind was one big total resentment against the world and everything in it. It didn't know how to think any other way. My thoughts were *automatically* resentful — and that is a clue as to why I believed I had no resentments at all.

I really believed that all the things I *thought, were true.* I thought my boss was a dope, that my wife was constantly putting upon me, people on the sidewalks and in the subways got in my way. I was critical of my friends, business associates, the government and the world in general. I constantly had hurt feelings because people didn't treat me with the kindness and thoughtfulness I deserved. Just the opposite.

But there was little I could do to change all these things and people. I couldn't help it if my boss was a dope or that people behaved so miserably. True, I suffered for it, but it was not my fault, and there was almost nothing I could do about it except fight back and make the best of it.

On looking back, I can see that during my whole life before AA, I believed that I judged other people objectively. What I *believed*, was to my mind, *fact*. It never occurred to me that the "facts" might be wrong.

So after joining AA, when my new friends and club members talked to me about resentments, I said, "Who me? I don't have any" — and I was completely honest about it.

After a few months in AA I began making attempts at the Fourth Step — efforts which repeatedly turned out to be neither searching nor fearless. Many years of rationalizing kept forcing me to turn the painful spotlight away from me onto others. But persistence paid off. After about eight months of effort on the Fourth and Tenth Steps, the only sudden thing that ever happened to me in AA happened!

In one flash of insight I saw that if I were to wait for all the other people to shape up, I was going to get drunk and stay drunk a long, long time. In that instant I saw that all the things I had considered facts, were not facts at all, but my own thoughts. And that this was very fortunate, because I could do something about changing my thoughts but nothing about changing the people around me.

So the fault was mine after all. I felt humiliated; but there was a sense of relief, too. While I felt totally inadequate to deal with the faults of the world and its people, I did not feel quite so inadequate to deal with my own mind. So I think that the most important factor in eliminating resentments is to know you have them. You can't fix something if you don't know what's wrong.

So then, what to do? Well, I decided that every time a resentment came into my mind, I'd toss it out. Is that so? After a few days I found it wasn't that easy. Resentments were so automatic that I didn't recognize them unless I consciously thought about them. Here the Tenth Step was invaluable because, although it doesn't say so in so many words, I interpreted it to mean that I should do it every day. Each night before going to sleep, I reviewed the day, and every day I found that I had been building up resentful thoughts. And I also found that if I recognized them before they grew into big ten-megaton size, it was not difficult to toss them out. Merely recognizing them seemed to do the trick. But if I

didn't recognize them, and they got to be real big massive resentments, I found that I could *not* just cast them out. In spite of my efforts to get rid of them, they rankled around in my mind for days, until time finally wore them out, and my mind went on to other things. Oddly enough, the hardest ones to deal with were the ones in which I happened to be right about the underlying facts.

As time passed, I recognized resentments more readily, and I began to learn little devices that helped me in getting rid of them.

For instance, I learned to reason about them this way: A resentment is made up of two parts: (1) the facts, and (2) the emotional content. As to the facts, I may be right or I may be wrong, but that's not important right now. As soon as I can, I will review them and try to find out the actual truth of the matter. Right now my stomach is turning over, and that's wrong. It's *my* stomach, and I'm the one who's suffering, and it's totally unnecessary. Worse, it incapacitates me to a degree that is relative to the strength of the anger. If it is very strong I can't think straight. In fact, it blocks me completely from thinking about anything else. For a while, my mind is consumed with it.

What I am really doing is giving up my own liberty and freedom. I am putting myself at the mercy of anyone who comes along, who either consciously or unconsciously chooses to make me unhappy and to interfere with my effectiveness.

As a practical matter, if I react angrily I lose every chance of convincing anyone that my view is correct. In business, I am able to convince others of my point of view (assuming I happen to be correct) only if I respect the opposing opinion, and present mine in an agreeable and friendly manner. Only that way can I be convinced, never by someone angrily trying to cram something down my throat.

Such reasoning helps, but it is not all-powerful against emotions. For reason alone can't do it all. So I learned another tactic at meetings — to do something nice for someone, anyone. Give someone a deserved compliment. Say "How are you today" to the phone operator. Just show a little human interest in anyone around you. Invite someone to lunch. Order some tickets to take your wife to a show. It is amazing how little of this sort of thing it takes to make the resentment vanish.

If the occasion calls for it, some self-ridicule helps. We learn to laugh at ourselves in AA, and it's a good thing, too. One time a member had some small folders printed and on the cover was the title RULE NO. 87. When opened, it read, "Don't take yourself so damn seriously." When I found myself getting into a disagreement with someone, felt the ire rising, and heard myself thinking "how can anyone be such a big jackass," this inspired me to say to myself, "Look out now, you might learn something." This would make me change my attitude and listen respectfully to the jackass's opinions.

And then there is another very powerful little thing you can do if you have made just a little progress in the life of the spirit, and that is to say to yourself, about whomever you feel the resentment, "God bless you." And really mean it. If you don't feel quite that spiritual, you can at least say, "I wish you well."

As you practice you learn many tactics in fighting resentments. And you can be absolutely certain that your handling of them will keep improving just as long as you keep practicing.

                                                    R. S., La Verne, Calif.

TWO

STAY SOBER AND HELP OTHER ALCOHOLICS

Not Today, Thanks

October 1983

U SUALLY, WHEN THE LEADER of our closed discussion meeting asks whether anyone has an alcohol-related problem the group might help with, nobody speaks up. On this particular night, our newest member, Marcie — two months sober — did.

"I have, Jerry. You may think it's silly."

"We won't think it's silly, Marcie. If it's important to you, it's important to us. Tell us about it. Helping one another is what we're here for."

"Next Saturday night, I'm going to a big cocktail party. My husband's boss is giving it, and we have to be there. It's the first one since I came to AA, and I'm scared — not so much because I'm afraid I'll drink — but what can you say to people about not drinking? How do you explain it?"

Murmurs of sympathetic understanding sounded all around the table, and a few reminiscent chuckles. People started recalling their first involvements in drinking occasions after reaching AA. No one tried to dismiss her anxiety as trivial. How to fit our newly sober selves into a drinking society without embarrassment is a legitimate cause for concern to most recent arrivals in AA.

"I take it you want to be inconspicuous about not drinking?" Forrest asked. Marcie nodded. "Then don't make the mistake I did. I was on a real pink cloud, three weeks sober, and when my host offered me a drink, I announced in a loud, clear voice that I had joined AA and was never going to drink again. That got their attention! Not surprisingly, with that attitude, I was drunk again the next week. That taught me two things: to do it one day at a time, and to stay low-key at social affairs.''

Cleve spoke up. "You'll discover, Marcie, as we all did, that people don't notice what we drink. They aren't interested in *our* drinking — they're totally concerned with their own. If you quietly ask for a soft drink, chances are no one but you and the bartender will know your drink is nonalcoholic.''

"Your question about how you explain your not drinking reminds me of me,'' Irene said. "When I was new in AA, I thought I had to explain — almost apologize for — refusing alcohol. We have no obligation to explain ourselves. People who drink don't think they need to explain it. At the same time, it doesn't hurt to be prepared with an answer on the slim chance someone notices, and says something. A person who knows you used to drink might. Or a host trying to look after his guests could be a bit insistent. Have a smooth answer ready, like 'Little digestive upset. Thought I'd go easy tonight,' or 'It isn't on my diet.' Anything you feel easy with.''

Mike suddenly laughed. "I haven't thought of this for years. I was at a party when I was very new to AA, and was trying to be both sober and sophisticated. So I bellied up to the bar and ordered Perrier and water. I can still see the bartender's expression at this nut asking for water and water. Now, I am supremely indifferent to what anyone thinks about my choice of drinks, but I was supersensitive then and let it spoil my evening.''

"Take one precaution, Marcie,'' Kenneth advised. "If someone else is getting your drink for you, sniff before you taste. Glasses are easy to mix up, and you could get the wrong one by accident.''

"We've been talking about affairs where mixed drinks are served and nonalcoholic beverages are readily available,'' Lewis observed. "Once in a while, you may hit an occasion where only alcoholic drinks are offered. Alison, tell Marcie your story of how you handled that.''

"I was really on the spot,'' Alison said. "I was on a study tour of the Far East with a group of women in my line of work. In Taiwan, we were entertained at a luncheon in Taipei's best hotel, with an hour of wine drinking before the meal.

"Our hosts were Oriental, and I didn't want to do anything

that might offend them, or make me appear critical of their hospitality. So I couldn't ask for anything that was not offered; I couldn't simply refuse the wine; and I couldn't drink it."

"What on earth did you do?" Marcie asked.

"Something so simple and workable it must have been an inspiration from my Higher Power. For the first thirty minutes, when I was offered a drink, I said, 'Not just yet, thank you.' And the last thirty minutes, I said, 'Not any more, thank you.' Not a soul there so much as suspected that I hadn't touched a drop."

"You see, Marcie," Jerry assured her, "an AA member who really wants to stay sober can always find a way, and without attracting attention."

"It's not only possible," Alison added. "It's fun!"

E. E., Tulsa, Okla.

On Cultivating Tolerance

by Dr. Bob

July 1944

D URING NINE YEARS IN AA, I have observed that those who follow the Alcoholics Anonymous program with the greatest earnestness and zeal not only maintain sobriety but often acquire finer characteristics and attitudes as well. One of these is tolerance. Tolerance expresses itself in a variety of ways: in kindness and consideration toward the man or woman who is just beginning the march along the spiritual path; in the understanding of those who perhaps have been less fortunate in educational advantages; and in sympathy toward those whose religious ideas may seem to be at great variance with our own.

I am reminded in this connection of the picture of a hub with its radiating spokes. We all start at the outer circumference and approach our destination by one of many routes. To say that one spoke is much better than all the other spokes is true only in the sense of its being best suited to you as an individual. Human nature is such that without some degree of tolerance, each one of us might be inclined to believe that we have found the best or perhaps the shortest spoke. Without some tolerance, we might tend to become a bit smug or superior — which, of course, is not helpful to the person we are trying to help and may be quite painful or obnoxious to others. No one of us wishes to do anything that might act as a deterrent to the advancement of another — and a patronizing attitude can readily slow up this process.

Tolerance furnishes, as a by-product, a greater freedom from the tendency to cling to preconceived ideas and stubbornly adhered-to opinions. In other words, it often promotes an open-mindedness that is vastly important — is, in fact, a prerequisite to the successful termination of any line of search, whether it be scientific or spiritual.

These, then, are a few of the reasons why an attempt to acquire tolerance should be made by each one of us.

Why Don't We Talk About Sex?

November 1969

AN INTERESTING ASPECT of our Fellowship is that one of our most serious problems, collectively speaking, is mentioned very little or not at all, either at meetings or in our literature. That problem is sex, in all its various forms and sublimations. It is involved in, if not the prime cause of, as many as seventy-five percent of slips, according to one rehabilitation center worker I know.

More curious still have been the reactions of various AAs to my rather tentative explorations into the possibility of discussing the subject. While a few have responded in a mature manner, many have reacted either negatively or with smirks and grins reminiscent of a teenage locker room. A few have even branded me as a "sick fiend."

Nevertheless, my basic aim is still to yank the problem of sex out from under the rug and expose it to some light.

Now, you readers who are hoping for some spicy material might as well quit reading. I am not going to record case histories. If you want that sort of thing, you know where the stores are, al-

though if you read the rest of this piece, you may stay out of them.

To begin with, it is not my purpose to espouse any particular code of conduct, morality, or ethics. The only thing I'm going to talk about is sex in relation to staying off the sauce, which is AA's primary purpose.

Whether we like it or not, the sex drive is a powerful force in every human's life, shaping each of us in many ways and providing the next main motivation after survival. In its direct form, it is responsible for continuing the race, and in its sublimated forms it is the power behind all creative arts. In all these things, it is a good force, and a necessary one.

It is not necessarily good when it is turned in directions that either are impossible to accomplish or will, if accomplished, be at direct variance with the person's *own* moral code. Such sex is called obsessive sex. It is one kind that is unhealthy enough to get people drunk.

But even healthy sex can be a problem powerful enough to make people slip. For many people (including many AA members) have come to believe that all sex is bad, wrong, dirty, etc. This attitude may be manifested by abhorrence of physical contact or, more subtly, a lessening of regard for one's partner. When this partner is one's spouse, the problem can become acute.

Yet even if a person is free of feelings of sinfulness and guilt, he or she may still be so plagued with a sense of inadequacy or inferiority that drinking becomes a prerequisite for sex.

Compounding these hang-ups is the complication that many of them function chiefly on a subconscious level, making them particularly hard to solve. But solve them we must if we are to stay sober.

It would be wonderful if we were all suddenly *able* to talk about these problems with one another. If we were, the problems of sex that bug many of us so deeply would immediately be brought out in the open where they, like all our other problems, would not long survive. But that isn't likely to happen. The mere fact that we *cannot* talk about it is one of the main reasons sex is such a problem.

Generally speaking, we are concerned with two categories. First, there is Type A: people whose drives and desires are, by any logical criteria, perfectly normal. Their problem is that somewhere in their early years they were given to believe that sex — any kind of sexual activity — is bad. The moral code that Type A people try to live up to is totally impossible for normal human beings.

Type B people are different: Their moral codes are normal or nearly normal, but their behavior before, during, or after drinking is anything but normal. Such behavior can vary widely, but it has the common denominator that the person condemns his or her own behavior.

It is important to note that according to my investigations and discussions, the power of the sex drive to get people drunk lies in the *divergence* between behavior and personal morality, not in specific actions or standards.

In my travels, I have met people who followed some really outlandish practices without shaking their serenity or their sobriety. Those activities are not my bag; if I engaged in them, I would be bothered. And that is the key. According to Dr. Ruth Fox, a prominent New York psychiatrist who treats mainly alcoholics, "Sex is a problem only because it is treated as a problem. If people would just go do whatever they are going to do anyway and stop worrying about it, they'd be a lot better off."

I must hasten to point out that Dr. Fox is in no way advocating behavior at variance with a person's own morality. What she is advocating is putting things in the proper perspective. While sex may be an important drive, the act itself can hardly be called time-consuming, so why spend all the rest of the time worrying and stewing over what you did and didn't do? But that, in a way, is only begging the question. Sex *is* a problem, and just saying that it shouldn't be is no answer at all.

The answer, or at least the answer for me, was in dragging the whole mess out into the light where I could look at it, and in giving it the same treatment that had taken care of my other, less demanding problems: spelling out to myself just what the score was, and then talking to someone else about it. To my intense surprise, my confidant did not look horrified and condemn me. On the contrary, he was most sympathetic and even felt free enough to talk about his own problems, which were bugging him as badly as mine were me.

That was the beginning of my coming to terms with this basic drive. I will not pretend that I am now a 100 percent winner. I'm not, but most of the time I am indeed comfortable. And on those days when desires I'm not fond of rear their ugly little heads, I can usually remember that it is only today. By tomorrow, they will be only a memory.

As time goes on, the bad days grow farther apart and become less intense when they do come, and as they fade, a bright clean flame of love has begun to burn at home, a flame that was at first just a flicker, but is now a steady, bright light. It is a flame I never expected, but am grateful to see again.

P. S., Greenwich, Conn.

Responsibility Is the Name of the Game

November 1966

WHEN I CREPT INTO MY FIRST AA meeting, sober, and sank into the corner of a room, it didn't occur to me that I was finally discharging a responsibility to myself.

Actually I didn't have anywhere else to go. Yes, I had a wife, a home, and a bank account, but still I had no other place to go. My home had become alien to me; I'd run my wife out of the house on my last day of drinking; the money couldn't buy what I was looking for. All my life I'd looked for something outside of me, not for the answers to being comfortable within. Some "thing" would make me happy, some person would change my life, and I would find my place. "Seek and ye shall find" meant to me trying to fulfill the distorted values I had come to hold.

It never occurred to me that I was using alcohol as a medicine in an attempt at a self-cure, to make me comfortable while I was rehearsing my way to the bottom. That knowledge only came to me after I'd "cured" myself into AA. God works in strange ways, and he had allowed me to beat myself almost to mental and physical death in an attempt to get me to face up to the responsibility of becoming a human being. Alcohol was the runaway freight train I used in my no-brakes, downhill ride. Even though I was in the caboose, I rode in the cupola above the rest of the train and had a good view, but I was busy looking down at the book I was writing, Dante's *Inferno*.

There are still times when I just plain and simple don't like responsibility. Responsibility irks me. As a young boy, I wouldn't enter sports because it carried with it the responsibility of winning. School carried with it the responsibility of studying and making good grades. As a young man, work carried with it the responsibility of making good. Marriage carried with it the responsibility of making a home, being true to one woman, raising kids. I backed off from them all. The feeling of inadequacy was awful. Since coming to AA, I've found that my feeling of inadequacy was a rationalization to enable me to escape responsibility. I used the guilts of the past to feel that no matter what I did I would never be forgiven by God, if there was a God. Until I came to AA, I didn't realize what a magnificent rage and hate I had for people, life, living — *me*.

I told myself I wasn't responsible for wars, murder, rape, arson, mayhem. Didn't people know that was all wrong? Why did they do it? I didn't realize that it was my responsibility not to add to those horrors, but add to them I did, especially when I slipped

December 1981

LIVE AND
LET LIVE

"Twelfth Step work requires tolerance, persistence, understanding, and resisting the urge to take the phone off the hook."

into my vodka bottle. People became indistinct shadows to me; they were bent upon my destruction; everybody threatened me. I was escaping the responsibility of living, true, but I was also adding to being responsible for the curtain going up on opening night with me flat on my back, asking for help from the only prompter who can rescue me.

The job looked much too big when I came to AA. It bugged me that I was responsible for attending meetings. I was hurt and enraged when my sponsor didn't call or stop by and take me to a meeting — thereby making me responsible for going to meetings by myself. I disliked meetings because those present didn't talk about things I wanted to hear, or they said things I didn't understand. When some members seemed serene and competent, my defenses went up — who did they think they were? When I asked a question at a discussion meeting and it was answered, I became enraged because I thought everyone was after me, looking at me, putting me down.

If we hit bottom with a public bang, the time will come in our AA tenure when we will have to venture out of the house and face that public. Face the very same people who were eyewitnesses to our final day of disgrace, whatever it may have been. This is definitely a responsibility. By the time I exposed myself to the view of my knowing neighbors and business associates and acquaintances, I'd fortified myself with months of AA. Some of the first things I learned were: that if I thought God could forgive me, who was I not to forgive myself?; that now I had a new life, was a member of a Fellowship that cared; that there were understanding people standing behind me; that I should not fear; that I had a responsibility to stand up and be counted, sober. As our Big Book says, I could go anywhere, do anything within my capabilities, as long as my motive was right, as long as I felt I was putting myself under the big director, my Higher Power.

Even today it bugs me to feel that I am responsible for my actions. Worse yet, I am responsible for the thoughts that lead to the actions. At times the whole shebang becomes so overwhelming I am forced to go back and start all over again — "First Things First"; "one day at a time." I must put one foot carefully after the other; be careful that I don't always look down, but also look up to see where I am going and note that the sun is shining, that I am sober, physically well, my mind cleared of booze and pills. I must be grateful in the knowledge that there is a Power greater than myself. Perhaps I am not responsible at all times for the adversity in my life, but I certainly am responsible for trying to cope with that adversity sober.

To my chagrin, I've learned the hard way that I am responsible for slipping into mental and emotional depressions. I can usually take action that will forestall a depression when I conjure up one and begin to slide into it. My depressions are mostly brought on by frustration, fear of the future, self-pity, rage at my lot in life, but above all *fear*.

AA has taught me that I will not be asked to bear more than I can, regardless of what I think, but that I am responsible for reporting for duty and making the effort to overcome the adversity, and in so doing to overcome myself, which is my first responsibility.

D. W., Van Nuys, Calif.

Coping with Unemployment

April 1978

ONE AFTERNOON IN JUNE, the boss called me into his office. The result of our dialogue was, "You'll be much happier with the next company." I was fired.

This employer, nine years ago, had given me every opportunity to straighten out my drinking problem. He was overjoyed at the change in me through AA and had promoted me several times during my sobriety. But there had been an organizational change, and my job no longer existed.

How could this happen to a good guy like me? Some tears followed for my sorely bruised ego. A conversation with my sponsor assured me that my worth as a human being has nothing to do with a job. Was he right? I believed it in my heart, but my stomach wasn't sure.

The self-knowledge and spiritual awakenings gained through work with the Twelve Steps enabled me to go on without a break in stride. The boss was considerate. The organizational change did not take place for three to four months, and I was invited to stay on till then. I decided to show them. I dived into the job search and almost landed a terrific position back in the hometown. The disappointment was bitter at coming in second. My sponsor told me that God does not sober you up to throw you on the woodpile.

Sent out 300 resumes. Lots of activity, some interviews, no job offers. The sponsor said that you don't get any cross to bear without the strength to carry it. I knew from experience this was correct. Why did I need to be reassured all the time? Thank God for sponsors and the Fellowship.

I was stripped of responsibility at work. Everyone was whispering about me behind my back. One day at a time. The sponsor promised that wherever I wound up, it would be where I was supposed to be, and better. I doubled up on prayer and meditation to an hour a day.

Time was up! Then, a last-minute extension to the first of the year working on special projects at half salary. Could I take it? Yes, one day at a time. Add another half hour to meditation, and be grateful. The sponsor said the reprieve was probably connected to the increased prayer and work on the program. I thought so, too.

Sent out 400 resumes. Some activity, some interviews, elections, holidays, and no job offers. I was starting to worry about money, but I knew I had what I *needed*. When would this end? The Serenity Prayer was a great help.

Unemployed and a statistic! I wasn't alone. Lots of AAs had gone through this sober. They came forward to offer support. I stood in the unemployment line for three hours. I increased my work with others and stayed close to newcomers. A new moral inventory revealed a lot of resentments and problems over work. Was being fired an answer to my prayers? Be careful what you pray for — you might get it.

Sent out 400 more resumes. Back to the hometown to renew old friendships and business acquaintances. All the people I thought I would never need. You do meet the same people going down as coming up. Please, God, don't let me forget this lesson. People were kind. They seemed to understand they could be on the other side of the desk some day. Why didn't I ever think of that?

A break — an outstanding job! They said bring the wife down. Then a last-minute phone call: Sorry, we decided to promote from within. The sponsor said that if I was meant to have that job, I would have gotten it. Thy will be done!

Ten months later. No job, but making it a day at a time. The

Big Book is right; sobriety can be maintained with or without a job. A job is a circumstance. A job is not a survival matter like sobriety. Everyone gets a job sooner or later. My faith was being tested. Had God misplaced my file? Was I a failure? No, God has a perfect plan for me. This process has given me a closeness to people and God that would not have been possible otherwise. My life is continuing to change steadily for the better.

Several weeks later, I landed a good job. My wife and I have relocated and are comfortable in our new area. The program is the same, and we look forward to going on from here. Without a doubt, this has been the most significant sober living experience of my life.

If I work my program, I will be okay. All my experience says, exactly as the Big Book states, I get everything I need in Alcoholics Anonymous. And when I get what I need, I invariably find that it was just what I wanted all the time.

B. K., Freeport, Ill.

The Impossible Dream

November 1971

D URING MY DAYS as a practicing alcoholic, I had a maudlin habit. At some point during the evening, I would weave woozily from the kitchen, fresh drink in hand, and stack a pile of mawkish ballads on the record player. Then I would settle down to wail my off-key accompaniment. Two or three drinks later, I would be supine, a steady stream of tears coursing across my cheekbones and rolling wetly into my ears as I agonized and empathized with the heartbroken vocalist.

I am grateful for one thing: When the song "The Impossible Dream" came along, I was newly sober. Even sober, I wept over that one! And today, when I play that record, I still feel the old familiar longing for the lovely, perfect things — heroism, chivalry, nobility.

I suspect it is a siren song for many alcoholics, because most of us cherish an impossible dream. Perennially immature as long as we drink, we share with true children an unshakable faith that, if

The Impossible Dream

Sobriety demands that we accept life as it is, with all its good and all its evil

During my days as a practicing alcoholic, I had a maudlin habit which I would guess is uniquely feminine. At some point during the evening, I would weave woozily from the kitchen, fresh drink in hand, and stack a pile of mawkish ballads on the record-player. Then I would settle down to wail my offkey accompaniment. Two or three drinks later, I would be supine, a steady stream of tears coursing across my cheekbones and rolling wetly into my ears as I agonized and empathized with the heartbroken vocalist.

I am grateful for one thing: When the song "The Impossible Dream" came along, I was newly sober. Even sober, I wept over that one! And today, when I play that record, I still feel the old familiar longing for the lovely, perfect things — heroism, chivalry, nobility.

I suspect it is a siren song for many alcoholics, because most of us cherish an impossible dream. Perennially immature as long as we drink, we share with true children an unshakable faith that, if only we find the magic word, we will get the moon for Christmas. Like children, we are prone to tears and tantrums when we don't. Our tears and tantrums require special medication — and all the prescriptions contain a high percentage of alcohol.

In the motion picture *Days of Wine and Roses,* the alcoholic wife

3

only we find the magic word, we *will* get the moon for Chrismas. Like children, we are prone to tears and tantrums when we don't. Our tears and tantrums require special medication — and all the prescriptions contain a high percentage of alcohol.

In the motion picture *Days of Wine and Roses,* the alcoholic wife is unable to stop drinking because, she explains, the world is so ugly when you see it sober. I had no trouble identifying with that excuse.

During the years of my sobriety, I have been one of the lucky ones who seldom think of a drink; but if I like, I can remember what drinking did for me in the early days, the good days. I can remember the release, shyness dissolving, love welling up toward everyone, even myself. I stopped judging and criticizing; the self-defensive chip fell from my shoulder and left me weightless and free; the moon was mine at last, shining silver in my arms and worth whatever it cost!

The only trouble is that inflation sets in early in the impossible-dream market. Too soon, for alcoholics, the price skyrockets; the modest hangover escalates to a day home from work, to several days home, to lost job, lost family, accidents, hospitals, jails.

"Why don't you just stop drinking?" our nonalcoholic friends ask when they see our situation. We shrug, and we smile with the charm most alcoholics can muster when necessary, and we change the subject quickly. But in the dank miasma of the predawn sweats, when we lie sleepless and sick in the rumpled sheets, we ask ourselves the same question, and we cannot reply.

In my opinion, there is an answer — an answer we don't want to face because sobriety also has a high price tag: We must give up the impossible dream.

For each of us, the impossible dream differs. For one, it may be great wealth; for another, a dramatic rise to fame. For me, it was a world in which love, joy, beauty, and truth (to name a few things) were the rule, not the exception. But for all of us who cherish the impossible dream, it has one common denominator: It is, as the name indicates, a totally unrealistic demand for perfection in one form or another, and it requires of its disciples a fanatical devotion that permits no compromise. We will not settle for less, and we are proud of our refusal.

We look with amused or bitter condescension at the lowly earth people who actually *enjoy* the mediocrity of their surroundings, their friends, their jobs, their children. Not for us, we say (going to mix another drink); at least *we* have the perception to spot the manifold flaws in *our* environment and the sensitivity to be miserable over them. Never let it be said that *we* are so lacking in discrimination that we would permit ourselves to *enjoy* imperfection. So we stagger through the dreary drunken days in pursuit of the impossible dream, worshiping with narcissistic preoccupation our steadfast rejection of the world around us.

Listen to the words of that song the next time you hear it. If they still move you — as they sometimes do me — watch out! Unless you happen to be a nonalcoholic masochist, you are heading for trouble.

After a reasonable number of 24 hours, I have begun to realize certain truths. It is not admirable to rush in where angels fear to tread; it is stupid and self-destructive. It is not heartwarming idealism to hate life for its imperfections; it is rank ingratitude. It is not intellectual superiority to single out the shortcomings of the world; it is self-inflicted, selective blindness. Throughout my drinking years (and for the first arrogant months of my sobriety), I had a field day judging, condemning, and hating. I had to get drunk to escape being poisoned by my own venom.

Eventually I had to free myself from the impossible dream of a perfect world in order to love and accept the real world. Judged by human standards, life is *not* perfect; to demand perfection of it is asking the impossible. Life is an incredible totality that ranges from good to evil, from beauty to horror, from bliss to agony. One extreme cannot exist without the other. There would be no music if high C were the only note, no art if spectrum red were the only color, no joy in pleasure if pleasure were the only feeling — and, paradoxically, there would be no perfection without imperfection.

What does this mean to me? Well, first it means that *I don't have to be perfect*. All I have to do is grow at a pace natural to me — and that is all I have a right to expect of others. If I can remember these truths, then love — real love, as opposed to drunken sentimentality — is finally within reach. It is not stupid to accept myself and others complete with our imperfections. It would be stupid not to.

It means that I am free to like and enjoy *what I have*. I don't need to exhibit my high values by hating my rowboat for not being a yacht, my house for not being a palace, my child for not being a prodigy. In all aspects of my actual life, there is room to grow. More important, my appreciation of what they *are now* has room to grow. Perfection would limit me; imperfection offers me the freedom of a million potentials. All the excitement and interest and wonder of adventure are mine to explore, ever-new, ever-changing, ever-becoming.

Thank God, as a result of AA and sobriety, I am liberated from *dreaming* the impossible dream and free, finally, to start *living* the possible dream.

J. W., Islamorada, Fla.

Children

March 1980

LAST NIGHT, OUR MEETING TOOK a turn into a familiar subject: our kids, the monsters. I had gone to that meeting hoping to raise the topic of our children, but in quite another context. I was thinking about my daughter, prompted by a magazine article I had read concerning alcoholics' children who grow up looking good and acting perfect and then, later in their lives, begin to fall apart. What seems at first to be their healthy self-reliance proves to be unhealthy loneliness brought on by a parent or parents who could never be trusted. I was hoping we could discuss this — see, perhaps, whether there were danger signs in our own children, ask ourselves what we might do to heal such an injury. The meeting never did get around to this; but for me, the topic was far from closed.

When I came home, my wife told me, with some emotion, of a conversation with our six-year-old daughter earlier in the evening. She had asked our little girl to be especially kind and patient with Ben, her fellow first-grader, who lives on our block. Ben's mother, she explained, has a crippling disease that keeps on getting worse, and she cannot do most of the things that other mothers do. Ben has talked about his mother's sickness, and he knows that she'll never get better. He probably thinks of it a lot and gets sad and frightened, and that is why he seems to be hurt so easily and cries a lot.

Our daughter seemed to understand immediately, and this was her response: "Oh yes, I know. Remember when Daddy was sick and you both would argue so loud at night? I would go into the bathroom by myself and just cry and cry — and I was so scared!" And then, after a thoughtful pause: "It sure is lucky that you both had things you could get better from!"

I had no idea that such a thing had ever happened even once, let alone repeatedly. But that is not so surprising, for in my drinking, I had become totally insensitive to everyone and everything about me, and the blackouts wiped away what few thoughts I had. But we were surprised that my wife had not seen the child run from the room to hide. And why had she waited all this time to say anything about it? It hurts me to accept the obvious explanation: Her memory was triggered because her feelings on those awful nights were as terrible as those she thought Ben must have at seeing himself being left more and more alone, looking with dread toward the

VICTOR E.

time when that abandonment would be total.

These thoughts came tumbling out, along with a flood of painful memories. Painful they will always be, but thank God, they are kept from being bitter memories by one thing — the new life that the AA program has given to all three of us. My disease has been arrested. As my daughter said, it is something I could "get better from."

I don't pretend to a perfect understanding of her young mind on this or any other topic, but last night did give me a fresh insight. On our vacation last year, I spent one of our precious evenings in Paris getting to a meeting at the American Church on the Quai d'Orsay. My daughter was a bit annoyed by this, and asked me why I had to go to all those meetings anyway. I told her it was something I had to do to keep from ever getting so sick again from alcohol. I finished with the rhetorical question "You don't want that to happen, do you?"

"Oh no!" she said. "It's no good for anyone to be alone!"

I wasn't sure whether she was thinking of me or of herself as being alone, or even whether those rather cryptic words simply reflected her limited command of language, rather than the more profound significance I was attaching to them. Now, I see that she really had felt the terror of loneliness, of estrangement, of isolation beginning to envelop her. She has just told us that the memories of those past days are still with her. I hope with all my heart that no more than the memory is there, that the feelings themselves are gone.

I do not take her for granted. All I have to do, if I think "our kids, the monsters," is remember how my drunken ravings sent her fleeing in terror, I want to do all that I can for her and, espe-

May 1963

cially, with her. I expect no praise for this; it is neither a penance
nor a burden. It's one of my greatest joys, one of the rewards
beyond price of my new life.

K. C., Racine, Wis.

Don't Hide in AA

January 1967

AROUND OUR AA PROGRAM we generally hear, "Keep active in
AA and it will help you to remain sober." What about our
activity on the outside, in our daily lives? I have seen AA members
whose entire personal activity seems to be centered on AA to the
exclusion of everything else. I may be wrong, but I do feel that this
is a form of hiding, something like what we did when we hid behind the bottle, and just another escape from reality. It is actually
using AA as a crutch.

Of course for those who have little or nothing else to focus
their lives on, AA *must* be the pivot of their existence in order to
keep them sober. But for the average AA member, who has a job,
a family, good health, and is, of course, sober, it seems to me that
activity in all areas is essential for his well-being. People in AA
aren't the only ones who can benefit from our sobriety, and the
world, as I see it, now that I have been sober nearly three years, is a
wonderful place filled with wonderful things to do. I, for one,
can't find the time to accomplish all the things I want to do each
day.

A word of warning here, too. Don't overstep yourself. Activity, like all of man's pursuits, should be done with moderation.
Overreaching ourselves may lead to overtiredness, to fatigue, to
rotten thinking, to drinking; it's as easy as that.

Inactivity, to me, is a form of death, and I see AA as a program of action. I came into AA in order to live, and everything
that lives grows. None of the Steps, except the First and the Second, can be taken without action. We have to work hard in order
to change ourselves, and we have to learn to grow outside AA as
well as inside it. We *can* close ourselves up behind four walls and

emerge only for AA activities and remain sober, but I don't think we can achieve happiness that way.

I may offend some good AA members by my next statement, but I do feel that some of us in AA think we have achieved Nirvana by getting sober, and that this is an end in itself. We may go on for several years giving lip service to the program and not reap its full benefits because we are still afraid to rejoin the human race and go out and face reality — that is, lead a normal, productive life.

We are told very often, especially by old-timers in the program, "Utilize, don't analyze." This, to me, means living my life the way God meant me to live it and not the way I *was* living it while I was drinking. I had lost my husband and was in danger of losing my three lovely young children and my sanity and finally my life, through the use and abuse of alcohol. With the help of my sponsor, good AA friends, and the Twelve Steps of our program, I have been able to stay sober, one day at a time, for nearly three years, and today am fortunate in having not only my children, but my husband (who is now also in AA) again with me.

I realize I am one of the more fortunate ones, and can show concrete evidence of the benefits of sobriety in terms of my own life. I believe that without AA I would certainly be dead. Instead I have a home and family, my health and sanity and, greatest of all, sobriety. I know that I am fortunate in being able to enjoy life because I have a lot of physical energy. In terms of my own sobriety, I find that to sit around doing nothing for too long is bad for me. I need a certain amount of time for quiet and meditation, but in general I have to be up and doing; this is my nature. The restlessness that, while I was drinking, was nothing more than a destructive drive can now, through sobriety, be channeled in constructive areas, and the same energy be applied for good, not evil.

Action to the newcomer may mean just taking a walk when he gets the jitters. Even reading can be a form of activity — at least we are thinking of something besides ourselves while we are doing it. Keeping busy, no matter how, is a good way to avoid self-pity. We can find new interests, new scope for our returning enthusiasm for life (which may seem a long time in coming, but does return).

"Hard work never killed anyone" is an old maxim, and a true one, but apathy can stunt and warp the mind. And what did we get sober for if not to live and enjoy life? AA gives us the tools to do this. In our Twelve Steps we have a blueprint for living. I read things into them which I could not do in my first year of sobriety. I am learning to work them to the best of my ability, and I see constant changes in myself and my attitudes, and in this way I know I am growing.

But, most of all, I think we should try to get with it, get back into the swing of life. We all belong to society and we each have our role. If we don't like the role we have, we must try, if we can, to change it. Our Serenity Prayer, in which we ask for the courage to change the things we can, is therefore, in part, a prayer of action. Nothing will change for us if we don't give a helping hand. Neither God nor AA can help us if we are not open to help.

There are many physical and mental outlets for our pent-up energies. Don't let them atrophy, or I believe the precious gift of sobriety will turn back on itself and decay. In my own case I know that doing my housework was a form of therapy in the first days of sobriety. I still use it to work off pent-up emotions and sometimes can actually get rid of a resentment or anger that way. My husband calls me a compulsive housewife. In my drinking days I used to argue and resent this, but now I just smile because I know (and I know *he* knows too) that for *me* this form of activity is essential to

my well-being. We all have our own gimmicks to hang onto, and this is one of mine.

So to all AAs, newcomers and oldsters alike, I say again, *keep busy*. Rejoin the world, and find it again the exciting place it can be when we are not viewing it through the distortion of an upended bottle. And don't use AA as a crutch. Come out from behind that shell and give a little to the outside world and you will get back a lot in return. Use the wonderful AA program in all areas of your life.

Take heart; live your lives to the utmost now that you are sober. Isn't this our way of giving thanks to God and AA for the wonderful gift of sobriety? Use your sobriety, don't abuse it with inaction both in and out of AA. To me, an active sobriety is a happy sobriety, within the reach of us all.

B. G., Forest Hills, N.Y.

Tradition Five

Each group has but one primary purpose —
to carry its message to the alcoholic who still suffers

June 1970

ON MY FOURTH SOBER AA DAY, I was sitting alone in one of our musty old meeting rooms, very sad and very broke. All the AAs had seemed very kind in their desire to help, but none of them had mentioned money. And, like thousands of other new members, I believed my biggest problems were financial. Yet not one person had offered a loan.

Then, suddenly, one of those big, handsome, gray-templed, well-dressed old-timers strode in with a friendly smile widening his face. He stuck out his hand and squeezed mine. "If I can help you any way at all, just say so, and I'll do it!" he declared heartily.

Trying to sound as if I were merely asking for a match, I said, "I hope so. You see, I need to borrow two thousand dollars."

His silence was total.

But finally he spoke. "You're in the wrong place," he said firmly. "We don't lend money here, my friend. That's not what this place is for."

I froze, but he went on and on. "We won't help you with a money problem. We won't help you with a family problem or a job or clothes or a medical problem or food or a place to spend the night. All we will do in AA is help you stay sober," he explained. "Then you can take care of these other problems yourself. You *can* take care of yourself, can't you, if you're sober?"

I hated that word "sober?" But what could I say? "Certainly," I snapped, humiliated that, in my ignorance of AA folkways, I had been caught in a *faux pas*, as if someone had found me eating peas with my fingers.

What the man had said made perfectly good sense. I *had* been sober a few days and *could* take care of things. So I put my gradually clearing mind to it, remembered a cousin I had not tapped for months, sent a wire, and got some dough.

To my astonishment and sorrow, I almost instantly found myself drunk.

Within a few hours, my new AA benefactor had given me in very blunt words a sharp summary of Traditions Five, Six, and Seven. And, by getting drunk, I had illustrated perfectly the special sense behind Five. What I needed most was not money, obviously. After getting it, I still had the *drinking* problem that had made me think of approaching AA in the first place.

This happened in January 1945, and the first hint of the Twelve Traditions was not to appear anywhere in AA until the July 1945 issue of the Grapevine, when Bill W. wrote, "I would like to discuss in coming issues such topics as anonymity, leadership, public relations, the use of money in AA, and the like."

Therefore, what I encountered in AA during my first few months, before the Traditions were formalized, were customs of AA behavior followed by members who had learned that some AA ways would work and others would not.

That is the authority of the Traditions in my personal life. I honor them, not solely because of their authorship or their having the mystical number twelve or their being adopted by the Fellowship at the First International Convention in Cleveland in 1950. I cherish them because they work. They enable me and my fellow AAs to stay sober, together, and to carry our message to other alcoholics.

But I did not like the Traditions at first, especially when they conflicted with what I wanted. I was a suspicious character, often turning phony operator to get what I wanted. During those first weeks, I kept wondering what "those AAs" were really up to or out for, and what I could get out of them.

The real miracle is that most of them acted with extraordinary kindness. No matter what I tried to maneuver out of them, they tried just to give me the message.

In subsequent years, I tried to misuse AA in two ways; that is, I tried to get more out of it than the sobriety message. Once I wangled a part-time job from a fellow member, then took advantage of him. Coming in late, I would excuse myself by thinking, "After all, we're both alcoholics; he ought to excuse my little weaknesses." He exploited me, too, expecting long hours of unpaid work simply because I was a fellow AA. We began to concentrate on what we were owed, not on what we as AAs owed each other. Neither of us got drunk, but our friendship did not survive.

Another time I tried to use AA for romance, and really did find balm for a lonely heart with an AA partner. We found romance, all right, but we lost our sobriety.

Years have gone by since I had my infancy in AA as an excuse for my "gimme" tendencies. Today I try to look at the Fifth Tradition as a giver, not as a taker. But the picture is not pretty enough to brag about. It isn't always easy, even now, to keep my personal wants out of the way when I try to carry the message. I want applause as an AA speaker, compliments as a Grapevine writer. I want to be a "success" as a sponsor — that is, I want to be the one who sobered somebody up!

I have found I prefer to carry the message to pleasant, attractive, grateful alcoholics who do what I say and give me full credit for their sobriety. Sometimes I wish I did not even have to *carry* the message at all; I wish I could just wait where I am for people to come and pick it up.

On the other hand, I rejoice that I can now participate in so many good ways of fulfilling our primary purpose. I can help put on public meetings and other public information activities to carry the message to the alcoholics who are still out there drinking — sick, scared, completely unaware that we want them, and completely wrong in their notion of what our sober life is like. I can be on our hospital- and jail-visiting committees. I can serve on my group's hospitality committee, to welcome the ill-at-ease newcomer. I can attend or lead beginners meetings. I can help support our local intergroup office and the AA General Service Office, which reach drunks in places I cannot get to. I can have coffee with the new AA after the meeting, instead of running off to chin and gossip with my old friends.

Yes, my group (made up of individual AAs, including me) has improved a lot in its respect for our Fifth Tradition — in its ways of carrying the message. My own AA history has lengthened considerably since I first caught glimpses of the sobriety-preserving wisdom in the AA way of doing things, summed up in our Traditions. But I have recently discovered something else quite wonderful about the Fifth: It does *not* say that AAs should help only newcomers.

I do not agree that the newcomer is *the* most important member at any meeting. In my opinion, equally important are those old-timers who showed me the way, and any middle-timer who may today be suffering. If newcomers are indeed the lifeblood of AA, old- and middle-timers are its skin and backbone. What a bewildered mess we would be in without them!

So in your next meeting, when that Tradition about carrying the message "to the alcoholic who still suffers" is mentioned, please give a thought, not only to newcomers, but also to the alcoholics older in AA who are sitting there. One of them might be me. I still suffer, sometimes. I still need to hear the message, always.

B. L., Manhattan, N.Y.

Tradition Eleven

Our public relations policy is based on attraction rather than promotion; we need always maintain personal anonymity at the level of press, radio, and films

July 1971

THE NAMES OF JOE DIMAGGIO, Henry Ford, Fiorello La Guardia, Mrs. Thomas A. Edison, Admiral Richard E. Byrd, Senator Harry S. Truman, the Duke of Windsor, Earl Baldwin, and Generalissimo Chiang Kai-shek may not seem to fit together. But they were all listed in New York newspapers as joint "sponsors" of the Oxford Group, an evangelical religious movement very popular in the 1930s. (Actually, it had no ties with the renowned English university; but people thought it did, so the name was used because such an image had obvious prestige value.)

When Bill W., who codified AA customs into our Twelve Traditions, first sat down to write them out (for the Grapevine) in 1946, he had very much in mind this Oxford Group practice of exploiting celebrity names to promote its cause. And that, he told me once, was one reason he proposed "attraction" rather than such "promotion" as the basis of AA's relations with the public.

In fact, AA had already pretty much adopted the nonpromotion policy as the young Fellowship's way of doing things. Ex-drunks knew from their own experience that the hard sell generally does not persuade a rumpot (or anyone else) to give up his pot. Tradition Eleven just put this idea into capsule form.

But none of this was known to me, or of any use or interest whatsoever, one hot summer day in 1942. I stood in a seedy old joint on lower Main Street in Fort Worth, Texas, trying to get a glass of cold beer down before my shakes made me spill the damn thing.

Three thousand years and two bottles later, I had begun to get it all together, and I realized, to my mild surprise, that it must be afternoon. The evening-paper boys were delivering their wares.

I bought a paper and turned to my favorite gossip columnist. He had a funny piece that day about a bunch of folks in town who called themselves Alcoholics Anonymous. They sounded like awful fools, or some kind of fanatic reformers, just like the fellows who ran that rundown, shabby old mission next door to the tavern I was in. They had gone all sanctimonious, I figured, and had given up drinking and almost everything else I liked to do, which the mission preachers called "sinful ways."

Despite my scorn for both the mission and this AA business, I did tear out the AA story and slip it into my wallet. I explained to the bartender that I wanted to show it to some drinking buddies of mine, for a laugh.

April 1983

"Taxi!"

I wonder now whether that story really was funny, intentionally or unintentionally. Anyhow, I lost it and never thought of it again — consciously — through the next two and a half years of fierce alcoholic drinking. During that time, I took a geographical cure, seriously believing that if I moved to New York from Fort Worth, my drinking would somehow get straightened out. It was a severe and scary setback to find myself drinking even worse around Times Square than I ever had back in the old corrals of Cowtown.

One morning, sweatily trying to decide which shoelace to tackle first, desperately trying to remember what horrors I had perpetrated the night (or nights) before, I found myself crying and saying, "I've got to get out of this hell, some way." Then I suddenly remembered that old Forth Worth newspaper clipping about Alcoholics Anonymous.

Two general ideas from that gossip column had apparently lodged themselves in the collection of throbbing cavities I called my head. One was that AA had something to do with people known to be very heavy drinkers. The other impression was that AA didn't ask for more than your first name, so they could never tell anyone that you had joined their club.

That promise of privacy, that pledge — implied in the name Alcoholics *Anonymous* — to keep my shameful record absolutely confidential made it possible for me to show up at the local AA office a few days later. The Traditions were still unwritten, but the spirit of trustworthiness and anonymity which pervaded our Fellowship enabled me to sneak through the door on a clear, cold January day of 1945 and find at long last not only that I was at home, that I was wanted, but that no one would tell on me.

Already, I was the beneficiary of both halves of Tradition Eleven. Fort Worth members had cooperated with that Texas columnist back in 1942, so he could carry the message of AA in his newspaper. They had given him *information* about AA — not boastful promotion material. By that action, they had acknowledged that AA *itself* could not be anonymous; it could not be a secret society if it wanted to carry the message. And in their message that problem drinkers could recover, they also conveyed the AA promise of privacy, or confidentiality.

Because their behavior saved my life, I have ever since been glad to see our public information committees helping to get more and more publicity for AA in newspapers, on television, in magazines, books, and movies. It may not always be the kind of publicity I like; but when I am tempted to criticize, I just remember that all it has to do is to plant the twin seeds of (1) hope for the problem drinker and (2) anonymity — the conviction that he can trust us never to betray him. I'm sure such publicity has saved many other lives, and I hope we get cleverer and cleverer at figuring out ways to keep AA constantly being mentioned in the public media.

Once I had joined AA, I found there was something I could do, personally and privately, to help spread the message. Rather soon after starting to sober up, I told my friends and family about this wonderful new thing I had learned: that alcoholism is a disease, not a moral failing. It wasn't my fault that I had been such a bad drunkard for so long; it was the disease's fault. But I quickly

added that now I was going to be all right, it wouldn't happen again, because I had joined this marvelous organization called Alcoholics Anonymous.

I also told my doctor and employers, when it seemed appropriate for them to know. My friends in AA did, too. Whenever we told of our own membership, we knew that it might help chip away at the cruel stigma which still kills too many alcoholics. Sometimes, of course, the message was carried to other alcoholics, indirectly, through these doctors and employers.

Since we also told of our AA membership when we made amends, when we spoke at open meetings, and when we did Twelfth Step work, the notion of keeping our membership secret, or being furtive about it, just never occurred to most of us, I guess. After all, why should we be ashamed of recovering from a disease?

We did not tell any outsiders the names of other members, of course. That promise of confidentiality in our name was precious to me, and still is; I certainly would not break it.

But I have always loved to gossip, and it wasn't easy to keep from telling last names and other identifying facts about members to other AAs. I have learned my lesson on that one, I hope, the hard way — through embarrassment. It happened to me twice. Having told one member about another member, I learned that the two were old acquaintances and each wanted particularly to keep the other from knowing he was in AA! Clearly, I had violated confidences. It was unforgivable, and I am still ashamed when I think of it.

Now I consider my knowledge of people in AA to be very much like the privileged information confided to a doctor, lawyer, or priest. I have absolutely no right whatever to disclose anything about a member to anyone else, in AA or out, without that member's explicit permission. Respecting this privileged information is not a matter of professional ethics, specifically sanctioned by law, but I think the AA promise of confidentiality is a sacred one, and I must do my part to keep it.

Within the Fellowship, I prefer to speak of another member — and be spoken of — only by the first name. I like this practice simply because it is extra insurance against letting slip things told me privately, and because it is an effective symbol, making the point — particularly to outsiders and newcomers — that we mean it when we say we're anonymous, we're trustworthy, we don't tell.

Few of us in AA, I guess, have much occasion to worry about that part of the Tradition cautioning against the use of our names or faces in mass communications media. Not long after sobering up, I discovered that neither Winchell, *Life*, the New York *Times*, nor anyone else was standing outside the meeting doors every night to announce to a breathless world that I was just leaving an AA meeting, sober. As far as I know, the network anchormen and their TV cameras have let practically all the rest of us alone too. By and large, the record is remarkably good on that part of Tradition Eleven. Even if as many as seventy-five "anonymity breaks" accidentally occur in, say, one year, that's only about .00015 percent of our membership.

One particular set of AA members does run into that problem, however, and I especially admire the way they handle it. I refer to the many good AAs who work professionally in the field of alcoholism and are always being interviewed by newspapers and on television and radio. They just say they are "recovered alcoholics," without saying that they are AA members. It seems to me that this device is honest, adheres perfectly to the Tradition, and at the same time may carry a message of hope. Certainly, the old stigma fades when good-looking, smart-sounding, respectable folks like that are not ashamed to say in public that they are recovered alcoholics, and when they say it as casually as they would state any other fact about themselves.

In my opinion, anonymity in the mass media is still very important, to all AA members and to all potential members. It signals to sick alcoholics: Come on in — we won't tell. And it guards us against the temptation to start bragging about ourselves. . . but I'm ahead of myself again. That's Tradition Twelve.

And I still have a long way to go in getting Number Eleven under my belt. Doesn't "attraction rather than promotion" have a personal meaning for me? Yes, I am supposed to make AA life look so attractive that drunks will want the kind of sobriety they see in me more than they want to go on drinking. Rather than promote AA with the hard sell or with bribes (a cup of coffee, a flop , a job, or other favors), it's up to me to make AA seem very attractive.

The members I met in 1945 did just that for me. I don't find it so easy.

B. L., Manhattan, N.Y.

Sponsor Your Doctor

by John L. Norris, MD

January 1976

ALL OF US INTERESTED IN alcoholism and the problems of alcohol have been puzzled, frustrated, and at times angered by the lack of understanding or even of interest on the part of the helping professions, especially medicine. A few pioneers in medicine — Silkworth, Tiebout, Kennedy, Gehrmann, Seixas, Block, Gitlow, among others in the United States — have understood and done much to soften the prejudice that has been a major handicap to alcoholics' recovery.

Many members of AA have gone back to the physician, clergyman, or other person who tried to help them, and have told of their recovery. This has opened many doors, and I continue to urge AA members, in every way I can, to identify themselves as individuals recovering from alcoholism wherever and whenever the disclosure seems opportune.

When AA members and others who have recovered from alcoholism do this, it is my hope that they will talk about the part of their experience most difficult to talk about — the way they *felt*, as people, while they were trying unsuccessfully to "handle" their drinking. Rarely, if ever, is this mentioned. How can professional people understand the disease unless those who are the victims will honestly and completely describe their symptoms and their feelings? — describe, for example, how they hated themselves for breaking their promises to themselves and to their families, their employers, and their friends. I can think of nothing that will help as much as this to create the understanding, working relationship we all desire between the "caring professions" and people who are in trouble with alcohol.

Sponsor your doctor, your clergyman, your lawyer, your boss, a social worker, a policeman. They need the knowledge and understanding that only you can give as you tell them honestly your own experience. Let us stop criticizing each other and get on with the job of meeting our common problem, alcoholism.

Are You Powerless Over Money?

August 1967

MY HUSBAND AND I MET and married in AA four and a half years ago. I now have six years of sobriety, and my husband almost ten. A while ago, taking a look at our situation, it seemed to us that our sobriety, which AA built, was in fine shape, but our financial "house that Jack built" was crumbling into ruins. In other words, our money affairs were in sad shape.

$$\$\ \$\ _\$\ \$\ ^\$\ \ \$\ \$\ _\$\ \ \$\ \$\ ^\$\ \ \$\ \$\ _\$\ \$\ ^\$$$

It seemed to us, on reflection, that if we really were applying AA principles in all our affairs, all our affairs ought to show it. Our finances didn't. We know that AA is for getting and staying sober, but we believe that AA's Steps are for the whole of life.

What was the trouble with us and money? We decided it wasn't the money, it was us, our defects of character: lack of foresight, not saving for a rainy day (it seemed to rain every day), attitude toward our jobs, and so on. We were getting deeper and deeper into debt, and not because we hadn't had any breaks financially since sobering up in AA. We had had plenty of breaks.

We decided it was time we took another kind of inventory. We came to the conclusion that we were powerless over money and that our lives were very, very unmanageable, still.

We also discussed the situation with other AA members and found that the condition was a common one. We began to notice references to it in AA talks. One speaker said, "When I was drinking, I owed five thousand people one dollar. Now, sober many years, I owe two people ten thousand dollars."

Another said, "I seem to have lost my drive to make money and haven't gained any abilities to use wisely what I do earn. Where is the wisdom I need?"

And yet another: "Debts, debts, debts, and seemingly no way out. I never seem to learn. Why do we keep getting ourselves trapped like this?"

"Are we still drunk when it comes to handling money?"

"I certainly don't think it's God's will that we live beyond our means, but . . . . "

"Well, I've got my credit rating back since I sobered up, but I was better off without it."

Someone suggested that perhaps we could substitute the word money for the word alcohol in Step One and take it from there. We might admit we were powerless over *money*, and that our lives consequently have become unmanageable; and then work the rest of the Steps accordingly.

Step Two: Came to believe that a Power greater than ourselves could restore us to sanity in handling our financial affairs.

Step Three: Made a decision to turn our will and our lives and our financial affairs over to the care of God as we understood him. We would ask him for help in better controlling our desire for things we can't afford; we would put this area of our life in God's hands and keep it there.

Four: Our inventory can help us to determine just what is at the root of our financial condition; we can face the situation openly.

Five: We must admit to ourselves, and another person and to God, the nature of our past financial behavior. This will help us to discover the truth of the situation, and possibly get a few suggestions about how to correct it.

Six: We must be ready and willing to have God remove the cause of our being in bondage, in debt. Unless we sincerely desire to be rid of debt and the cause of it, we cannot hope to be free. God always knows when we want to have our cake and eat it, too. Our circumstances will remain unchanged until we want what we pray for, and are willing to go to any lengths to get it, whether it be freedom from debt (or rather, the character defects that led us into debt) or any other problem.

Seven: We must humbly ask God to remove the cause of our indebtedness. Asking is an open display of willingness and sincerity of purpose. In this state we accept all the help we can get.

Eight: We make a list of all our debts, and become willing to pay in full no matter what the cost or sacrifice to our pride, ego, pocketbook, or worldly goods. We really try to be ready and willing to take right action.

Nine: We pay off as much as we can as soon as we can, and let our creditors know our intentions. We ought not evade or put off setting things in order.

Ten: We continue to take inventory daily so as to remind ourselves of our purpose, and be on guard against new extravagances or negligence. We must ask ourselves before we become obligated, if we really need or merely want this *thing*. Will it breed more trouble and debt, or will it really help solve the problem? (Now, no kidding. Have we talked this thing over with another person; with God? Have we examined our motives honestly and sincerely? Have we considered a more practical solution? Are we being impatient, and can we admit it?)

Eleven: We must try in our prayers to ask God for guidance — knowledge of his will. Ask ourselves if we have prayed for the power to carry out whatever we have to do to get out of debt. Have we dared to turn our problem over to God completely and to rest in quiet trust for the outcome?

Twelve: Are we now truly aware of our problem, believing we can and will get help if we sincerely ask? Do we believe that AA's Twelve Steps really do apply to all our affairs? Are we then willing to apply them to a specific real problem? Do we believe that even the tendency to indebtedness in our lives can be reversed? Could we not attempt to pass along this approach to others with the same problem, showing our experience?

Some observers of contemporary affairs claim that financial problems bring on more unhappiness and mental and emotional upsets, especially between husbands and wives, than any other cause. We believe that overwhelming debts can indeed jeopardize serenity, even sobriety; they take away some of the happiness that our wonderful sobriety through AA has given us.

We're working on it!

M. U. and R. U., Boulder, Colo.

The Heart Attack

March 1975

I LIKE TO THINK THAT A BASIC KEY to good, solid sobriety is acceptance of two facts — not only that I am an alcoholic, but also that I am me and have certain limitations and abilities with which to work.

The Serenity Prayer begins by requesting our God, as we understand him, to give us the serenity to accept that which we cannot change. In the beginning, I applied this only to my alcoholism, forgetting other areas. But many sober experiences have taught me to try to accept other parts of myself and not try to be that which I cannot be.

I remember, in my first year in the Fellowship, agreeing with everybody so they would like me. If John was a Republican, I'd support his views. With Ed, a Democrat, I'd be a Democrat. My sponsor came quickly to my rescue on this matter by reminding me that it was important to be myself instead of falsifying my opinions for the sake of agreement. He suggested that I try a simple prayer for a while. It said, "Dear God, let me be me."

My life changed as I began to try to follow the AA way of life. I found, through the Steps, that my horizons slowly expanded. I could leave the security of my home group and travel, going to AA meetings in other areas. Very slowly, I grew up. I found I could remarry and raise children. I also grew in the business world by leaving my first job sober, as a cab driver, and eventually reaching a position of responsibility whereby I was in charge of maintenance of an international airport.

By staying close to AA and the Twelve Steps, I discovered a new me. This took me time, a lot of time. The process was sometimes painful, but always rewarding.

Then I experienced an event that has taxed my ability to accept almost to the limit. At the ripe old age of thirty-eight, and with seven years of continuous sobriety under my belt, I had a massive coronary. The heart attack nearly took my life, and the subsequent recovery period was long. Limitations were again placed on me. For a while, doctor's orders confined me to one AA meeting a week. I still cannot risk speaking at an open meeting or getting too active in Twelfth Step work. Those things, which I had so depended upon for my sobriety, were taken from me.

Many of my AA friends have had similar experiences that necessitated changes in their AA activities, and their counseling has been a great comfort. Also, this experience gave me a chance to practice the principles I had heard about in Step discussion meetings throughout my AA life. I was unable to run to an AA meeting every night as I once had, to recharge my batteries.

I found it more difficult to accept my new limitations at work. No longer was I placed in a position of responsibility. I was given an office job, and my physical and mental activities were cut down drastically.

In short, I had to renew my feelings about accepting the things I could not change. I had overworked the Serenity Prayer in my early days of AA, and now I had to overwork it again. I had to go back and redo or retake the Steps to fit them into my new set of circumstances. I realized that I'd done this before, as have many others I know. We change as time goes by, and the full meaning of the Steps, the Traditions, and all that is AA must change within us to keep us on our happy road to recovery.

First, I had to quit resenting the changes in my life and accept them for what they were. Amazingly, as I did this, many restrictions were lifted. Today I live a full life, with an equal balance of AA, work, and recreation. I enjoy my family, my AA friends, and my business associates a whole lot more than I ever did before the heart attack.

Finally, I appreciate and need AA much more today than I did on that October day in 1964, when I had nothing to lose and everything to gain by joining the Fellowship. I still have everything to gain by following in the footsteps of my successful AA friends. But now I also would have an awful lot to lose by leaving the Fellowship. Today I can compare the sober life with my drunken existence. I like what I've got, and I believe I'm willing to go to any lengths to keep it.

W. H., West Palm Beach, Fla.

Charming Is the Word for Alcoholics

by Fulton Oursler

July 1944

DOWN AT THE BOTTOM OF THE social scale of AA society are the pariahs, the untouchables, and the outcasts, all underprivileged and all known by one excoriating epithet — relatives.

I am a relative. I know my place. I am not complaining. But I hope no one will mind if I venture the plaintive confession that there are times, oh, many times when I wish I had been an alcoholic. By that I mean that I wish I were an AA. The reason is that I consider the AA people the most charming in the world.

Such is my considered opinion. As a journalist, I have found it my fortune to meet many of the people who are considered charming. I number among my friends stars and lesser lights of stage and cinema; writers are my daily diet; I know the ladies and gentlemen of both political parties; I have been entertained in the White House; I have broken bread with kings and ministers and ambassadors; and I say, after that catalog, that I would prefer an evening with my AA friends to an evening with any person or group of persons I have indicated.

I asked myself why I consider so charming these alcoholic caterpillars who have found their butterfly wings in Alcoholics Anonymous. There are more reasons than one, but I can name a few.

The AA people are what they are, and they were what they were, because they are sensitive, imaginative, possessed of a sense of humor and an awareness of universal truth.

They are sensitive, which means that they are hurt easily, and that helped them become alcoholics. But when they have found their restoration, they are still as sensitive as ever — responsive to beauty and to truth and eager about the intangible glories of life. That makes them charming companions.

They are imaginative, and that helped to make them alcoholics. Some of them drank to flog their imagination on to greater efforts. Others guzzled only to black out unendurable visions that rose in their imaginations. But when they have found their restoration, their imagination is responsive to new incantations, and their talk abounds with color and light, and that makes them charming companions, too.

They are possessed of a sense of humor. Even in their cups, they have been known to say damnably funny things. Often, it was being forced to take seriously the little and mean things of life that made them seek escape in a bottle. But when they have found their restoration, their sense of humor finds a blessed freedom and they are able to reach a godlike state where they can laugh at themselves — the very height of self-conquest. Go to the meetings and listen to the laughter. At what are they laughing? At ghoulish memories over which weaker souls would cringe in useless remorse. And that makes them wonderful people to be with by candlelight.

And they are possessed of a sense of universal truth. That is often a new thing in their hearts. The fact that this at-oneness with God's universe had never been awakened in them is sometimes the reason they drank. The fact that it was at last awakened is almost always the reason that they were restored to the good and simple ways of life. Stand with them when the meeting is over and listen as they say the Lord's Prayer!

They have found a Power greater than themselves which they diligently serve. And that gives a charm that never was elsewhere on land and sea; it makes you know that God himself is really charming, because the AA people reflect his mercy and his forgiveness.

THREE

MEN AND WOMEN WHO SHARE

You and I Need Each Other

May 1977

DEAR JOHN:

I could almost begin this letter "Dear Newcomer." The only problem with that is, I want you to know how close I feel to you at this moment in our lives. Watching new people grow renews my sobriety, and I hope I never lose interest in the personal joy of sponsorship in the years ahead.

You asked me a question at our meeting last night. You asked why coming close to your first AA anniversary, you felt a bit down and angry. When I asked whether you thought you were getting to enough meetings, you avoided a direct answer. I have seen this before in newer people — the technique of not answering a pertinent question. The other way of avoiding honest answers is to mumble about "being tired" or "busy with work." Well — all these things may be true, but meetings are how you and I met.

The questions made me reflect on the ways of newcomers and my sponsor relationship with them over the years. God surely knows, I have made mistakes. I have tried not to repeat the same mistake. I have noticed this rebellion against a proper number of meetings in almost all the younger people I have sponsored. In fact, I have observed certain recurring habits with several of them.

I didn't tell you about this last night. I have my own need to be loved and did not want to bully you. Let me correct this character defect somewhat with this letter. I won't be likely to rationalize too much in print, because I will not have your searching face smiling at me, asking to be told there *is* a softer, easier way. If there is one, John, I don't know it and would not be interested anyway.

My lack of discipline almost killed me before AA. Yours did also; you attempted to snuff out your young life a few short months ago. The discipline of digging into the AA program pays off in peace of mind. Being undisciplined is not cute or clever. Drunks do as they please; sober adults make plans and stick to them. You wouldn't miss an appointment with a doctor who was going to charge you $150. Why miss your appointments with AA, which are free?

You say you don't read AA literature but will eventually. When? Don't wait until you are sober twenty-five years; you need it now. There is material in our books, written in the language of the heart, that you should know. You should be getting the program from every available source, not just from me. If you don't get it now, you will have to do it later. It may be more expensive later. I should not be your only source of basic AA. After all, I may get drunk.

You say you are not sure you are ready to hold group office, even though they asked you. If the group conscience asked you, they think you are ready, and you are. Maybe they are hinting gently that it is time for you to open up to others more and stop being so self-centered. You have much love to give, John; please don't hoard it. Some shaky newcomer who desperately needs your strength, hope, and experience is being directed to a meeting tonight by our Higher Power. A meeting you may not be at.

You told me you were very shy when you first tried AA, and AA did not work. I think sometimes shyness, or being introverted, disguises itself after a time as a desire to be super-comfortable. I went to many uncomfortable meetings in the beginning. The discomfort was within me. I am comfortable at all meetings now. This took practice. I broke the ice of shyness, and I resist when it occasionally tries to freeze over again. Isolation is bad for new people, old people, and in-between people if they are alcoholic people.

Isolation sneaks up on us. We can mask it with familiar props that are not in themselves bad. We can isolate ourselves in an attempt to clean up our apartments (and then not do the cleaning); we can isolate ourselves in churches or in sleep; we can use family, sweethearts, compulsive working, television. The list is long. The nicest way to end it is the way you and I do: together. Reach out — people can't read your mind. Say *ouch!* Someone hears. Always.

I think you know that alcohol is no answer. You would not have made the attempts to help yourself that you have if you wanted to go on as you were. You would not have given me the marvelous opportunity you did when you said, "Will you be my sponsor?" You have not exactly come this far on dumb luck. You worked hard.

I found that I had to stop misusing the AA slogans after a time. I clung to their simple logic at first. As the days went by, however, I found that the Higher Power wanted me to think, at least partially, for myself. I had to explore with the mind God gave me.

You quickly learned that it is pointless to allow yourself to be hungry, angry, lonely, or tired. I don't believe that this means we can go into a swoon and nod our way through life. I go to meetings when it snows even if my feet hurt. Guess what? — I feel a lot better afterward. I also read AA literature every day, and I have read it all many times before. Rereading it makes me feel good. It doesn't take too much thinking to know it's better to feel good than bad.

You move either away from a drink or toward one. People never stand still. Life is not arrival at a destination; life is travel to many destinations. You must reach your potential in sobriety. Enjoy the journey, bumpy roads and all.

Our friendship is a two-way street. I try to give, and I know I receive. As we become partners, I get more and more from you. You renew my faith and make my journey more joyous. Never think there is a superior-inferior relationship in any way. If I ever give that impression — tell me. You may be refreshingly surprised at how quickly I admit I am wrong.

I learned to do this in the Tenth Step. The Twelve Steps are my absolute guideposts for living. My old guides directed me into bars; our Steps brought me to AA and you. Is there any doubt which path is better?

When you reentered the program, you were smart enough to allow yourself to be sponsored by an energetic guy who is superb with brand-new people. His enthusiasm buoyed you up and really worked wonders. Then you asked me, because you were wise enough to know your sponsorship needs had changed. I keep growing, and the people around me change constantly. I hope you continue to exhibit this common sense.

You worry a lot about your past defects. Don't, please, thrash around too long in guilt. Learn what you can from past negative experiences, and move on. Guilt is insidious and counterproductive. You are a perfect child of God. It shines through in your sobriety. I see it, and so do others. Make yourself see it.

Past liabilities can be turned around and become our strongest points. Childishness can become childlikeness or freshness; stubbornness or self-will can turn into energy to do good things; radical attitudes can help us empathize with the downtrodden or with still-drinking members. No need to feel guilt; simply get rid of the thing you feel guilty about. A wonderful way to do this is to reverse your shortcomings by reaching out to another drunk. It works.

You asked me to be your sponsor. Everything I believe and know best is contained in the Big Book. Chapter Five explains the program perfectly. It begins, "Rarely have we seen a person fail who has thoroughly followed our path." Then it goes on to explain the path. Of course, you must have read it by now — no, that's right, you told me six months ago you would read it eventually, and you haven't yet. Oh well, I hope you will some day soon.

John, you are too young to remember World War II and the Korean conflict. It just occurred to me that a lot of soldiers received letters from their spouses or sweethearts in those days informing them that the marriage or the romance was over. These letters were called "Dear John" letters. It was ghastly for the poor guys. Now I write you, and I want you to know I will be around whenever you need me. We never lose each other in AA. Never.

I want you to think of this as a "hello letter" rather than a "good-bye letter." I will continue to make suggestions based on my own journey. Let's go on it together. It's easier for both of us that way. Thanks forever for being new in AA.

Hello,

Your Sponsor

E. S., Manhattan, N.Y.

Leadership in AA: Ever a Vital Need

by Bill W.

April 1959

N O SOCIETY CAN FUNCTION WELL without able leadership in all its levels, and AA can be no exception. It must be said, though, that we AAs sometimes cherish the thought that we can do without any leadership at all. We are apt to warp the traditional idea of "principles before personalities" around to such a point that there would be no "personality" in leadership whatever. This would imply rather faceless automatons trying to please everybody, regardless.

At other times we are quite as apt to demand that AA's leaders must necessarily be people of the most sterling judgment, morals, and inspiration; big doers, prime examples to all, and practically infallible.

Real leadership, of course, has to function in between these entirely imaginary poles. In AA, certainly, no leader is faceless and neither is any leader perfect. Fortunately, our Society is blessed with any amount of *real* leadership — the active people of today and the potential leaders for tomorrow, as each new generation of able members swarms in. We have an abundance of men and women whose dedication, stability, vision, and special skills make them capable of dealing with every possible service assignment. We have only to seek these folks out and trust them to serve us.

Somewhere in our literature there is a statement to this effect: "Our leaders do not drive by mandate, they lead by example." In effect we are saying to them, "Act for us, but don't boss us."

A leader in AA service is therefore a guy (or a gal) who can personally put principles, plans, and policies into such dedicated and effective action that the rest of us want to back him up and help him with his job. When a leader power-drives us badly, we rebel; but when he too meekly becomes an order-taker and exercises no judgment of his own — well, he really isn't a leader at all.

Good leadership originates plans, policies, and ideas for the improvement of our Fellowship and its services. But in new and important matters it will nevertheless consult widely before taking decisions and actions. Good leadership will also remember that a fine plan or idea can come from anybody, anywhere. Consequently, good leadership will often discard its own cherished plans for others that are better, and it will give credit to the source.

Good leadership never passes the buck. Once assured that it has, or can obtain, sufficient general backing, it freely takes decisions and puts them into action forthwith, provided, of course, that such actions be within the framework of its defined authority and responsibility.

A politico is an individual who is forever trying to "get the people what they want." A statesman is an individual who can carefully discriminate when and *when not* to do this. He recognizes that even large majorities, when badly disturbed or uninformed, can once in a while be dead wrong. When such an occasional situation arises, and something vital is at stake, it is always the duty of leadership, even when in a small minority, to take a stand against the storm — using its every ability of authority and persuasion to effect a change.

Nothing, however, can be more fatal to leadership than opposition for opposition's sake. It can never be "Let's have it our way or no way at all." This sort of opposition is often powered by a visionless pride or a gripe that makes us want to block something or somebody. Then there is the opposition that casts its vote saying, "No, we don't like it." No real reasons are ever given. This won't do. When called upon, leadership must always give its reasons, and good ones.

Then, too, a leader must realize that even very prideful or angry people can sometimes be dead right, when the calm and the more humble are quite mistaken.

These points are practical illustrations of the kinds of careful discrimination and soul-searching that true leadership must always try to exercise.

Another qualification for leadership is give-and-take — the ability to compromise cheerfully whenever a proper compromise can cause a situation to progress in what appears to be the right direction.

Compromise comes hard to us all-or-nothing drunks. Nevertheless, we must never lose sight of the fact that progress is nearly always characterized by *a series of improving compromises*. We cannot, however, compromise always. Now and then it is truly necessary to stick flatfooted to one's conviction about an issue until it is settled. These are situations for keen timing and a most careful discrimination as to which course to take.

Leadership is often called upon to face heavy and sometimes long-continued criticism. This is an acid test. There are always the

October 1969

"We're sober. . . it was a good day."

constructive critics, our friends indeed. We ought never fail to give them a careful hearing. We should be willing to let them modify our opinions or change them completely. Often, too, we shall have to disagree and then stand fast without losing their friendship.

Then we have those whom we like to call our "destructive" critics. They power-drive, they are politickers, they make accusations. Maybe they are violent, malicious. They pitch gobs of rumors, gossip, and general scuttlebutt to gain their ends — all for the good of AA, of course! Well, in AA at least, we have at last learned that these folks, who may be a trifle sicker than the rest of us, need not be really destructive at all, depending entirely on how we relate ourselves to them.

To begin with, we ought to listen very carefully to what they say. Sometimes, they are telling the whole truth; at other times, a little truth. More often, though, they are just rationalizing themselves into nonsense. If we are within range, the whole truth, the half-truth, or even no truth at all can equally hurt us. That is why we have to listen so carefully. If they've got the whole truth, or even a little truth, then we'd better thank them and get on with our respective inventories, admitting we were wrong, regardless. If it's nonsense, we can ignore them. Or we can lay all the cards on the table and try to persuade them. Failing this, we can be sorry they are too sick to listen, and we can try to forget the whole business. We can think of few better means of self-survey, of developing genuine patience, than the workouts these usually well-meaning but erratic brother members can afford us. This is always a large order, and we shall sometimes fail to make good on it ourselves. But we must needs keep trying.

Now comes that all-important attribute of vision. Vision is, I think, the ability to make good estimates, both for the immediate and for the more distant future. Some might feel this sort of striving to be a sort of heresy because we AAs are constantly telling ourselves, "One day at a time." But that valued maxim really refers to our emotional lives and means only that we are not to repine over the past or wishfully fantasy or daydream about our future.

As individuals and as a Fellowship, we shall surely suffer if we cast the whole job of planning for tomorrow onto a kind Providence. God has endowed us human beings with considerable capability for foresight, and he evidently expects us to use it. Therefore, we must needs distinguish between wishful dreaming for a happy tomorrow and today's use of our powers of thoughtful estimate —

estimate of the kind which we trust will bring future progress rather than unforeseen woe.

Vision is therefore the very essence of prudence — a sound virtue if ever there was one. Of course, we shall often miscalculate the future in whole or in part. But even so, this will be far better than to refuse to think at all.

The making of estimates has several aspects. We look at past and present experience to see what we think it means. From this, we derive a tentative idea or policy. Looking first at the nearby future, we ask how our idea or policy might work. Following this estimate, we ask how our policies and ideas might work under the several differing conditions that could arise in the longer future. If an idea looks like a good bet, we try it on — always experimentally, when that is possible. Somewhat later, we revalue the situation and ask whether our estimate is, or may soon be, working out.

At about this stage, we may have to take a critical decision. Maybe we have a policy or plan that still looks fine and is apparently doing well. Nevertheless, we ought to ponder very carefully what its longtime effect will be. Will today's nearby advantages boomerang into large liabilities for tomorrow? The temptation will almost always be to seize the nearby benefits and quite forget about the harmful precedents or consequences that we may be setting in motion.

These are no fancy theories. We have found that we must use these principles of estimate constantly, especially at world-service levels where the stakes are high. In public relations, for example, we must estimate the reaction of both AA groups and the general public, both short-term and long-term. The same thing goes for our literature. Our finances have to be estimated and budgeted. We must think about our service needs as they relate to general economic conditions, group capability, and willingness to contribute. On many such problems we must very often try to think many months and even years ahead.

As a matter of fact, all of AA's Twelve Traditions were at first questions of estimate and vision for the future. Years ago, we slowly evolved an idea about AA being self-supporting. There had been trouble here and there about "outside gifts." Then still more trouble developed. Consequently, we began to devise a policy of "no outside gifts." We began to suspect that large sums would tend to make us irresponsible and could divert us from our primary aim. Finally, we saw that for the long pull "outside" money could ruin us utterly. At this point, what had been just an idea or general policy hardened firmly down into an AA Tradition. We saw that we must sacrifice the quick, nearby advantage for long-term safety in the future.

We went through this same process on anonymity. A few public breaks had looked good. But then the vision came that many such breaks could finally raise havoc among us. So it went — first a gleam in the eye, then an experimental policy, then a firm policy, and finally a deep conviction — a vision for tomorrow. Such is our process of estimating the future. Our responsible world leadership must be especially and constantly proficient in this vital activity. This is an ability much to be desired, especially among our trustees, and I think most of them should be chosen on the basis that they have already proved their aptness for foresight in business or professional careers.

We shall continually need many of these same attributes, insofar as they can be had, among our leaders of AA services at all levels. The principles of leadership will be just about the same, no matter what the size of the operation.

This discussion on leadership may look, at first glance, like an attempt to stake out a specially privileged and superior type of AA member. But this is not really so. We are simply recognizing that our talents vary greatly. The conductor of an orchestra is not necessarily good at finance or foresight. And it is even less likely that a fine banker could be much of a musical success. When, therefore, we talk about AA leadership, we declare only that we ought to select that leadership on the basis of obtaining the best talent we can find, making sure that we land that talent, whatever it is, in the spot where it will do us the most good.

While this article was first thought of in connection with our world-service leadership, it is quite possible that many of its suggestions can be useful to everyone who takes an active part in our Society.

Nowhere could this be more true than in the area of Twelfth Step work itself — something at which nearly all of us most eagerly work. Every sponsor is necessarily a leader. The stakes are huge. A human life and usually the happiness of a whole family hang in the balance. What the sponsor does and says, how well he estimates the reactions of his prospect, how well he times and makes his presentation, how well he handles criticisms, and how well he leads his prospect on by personal spiritual example — well, these attributes of leadership can make all the difference, often the difference between life and death.

Thank God that Alcoholics Anonymous is blessed with so much leadership in each and all of its great affairs!

It's What Happened to <u>Me</u>

April 1967

THE SIGN "THINK" is often seen on the walls of our AA meeting places. Although I seldom hear speakers hold forth specifically on the importance of thinking as an aid to recovery, I have noticed that during the first stage of sobriety there is likely to be a period lasting for some months (or, with some people, forever) when the neophyte is bursting with thoughts upon which he will talk endlessly. He has ideas, theories, speculations about the nature and causes of alcoholism, about the reasons why and the ways in which the program of Alcoholics Anonymous works, about Life and Society and the Meaning-of-It-All.

In a veritable explosion of thought set off by recognition of previous stupidity, old philosophical concepts are revived or new ones acquired. Often a note of preaching, of advice-giving creeps into the talk of those so affected.

I first became aware of this phenomenon when I found myself inexplicably impatient with certain speakers. Slowly I began to detect what it was that produced a deadening effect, and what, on the contrary, held my attention and lifted my spirits. The speakers who left me feeling stronger and calmer were those who simply and earnestly told their own personal experiences, either of drinking, or of how they happened to come to AA, or of the problems they had since encountered in daily living. The more the speaker seemed simply to be reporting the facts about himself as best he could see them, without embellishing them with general conclusions and moral judgments that the rest of us had better profit by if we knew what was good for us, the better was the effect on me.

It was the simplest little things people told that lightened and cleared the air inside me. For instance, a fellow named John hap-

pened to remark one evening in his talk that he had been upset about the previous day's events and hadn't been able to get to sleep that night. He said, "In the old days, I'd have been drinking and stamping around the house all night, telling my troubles to my wife."

This made me smile with an inward glow that comes even now from remembering. I used to stamp, too; and my husband's chief complaint about my drinking was that it interfered with his sleep. John is a big man, and I felt a light moment of envy at the thought that, although I stamped as hard as I could, he must have been able to do so much more resoundingly.

Slowly it dawned on me that in speaking I, too, was inclined to share great thoughts, about Life and Love and Humility and responsibility and — you name it. In short, I had a tendency to Talk Big.

I also began to notice that I constantly used the word "you" — not meaning a definite other person as when one asks, "Are you ready to go?" but as one would say (meaning "any of us"), "You have to quit drinking if you want to live." I was always saying things like, "You feel just terrible when you realize how you behaved when you were drunk," instead of, "I felt terrible. I was drunk."

I talked about myself enough, God knows; I dodged the "I," hiding among "we" or this catch-all "you."

Lifelong social conditioning accounts for some of this. In social gatherings, it is not considered good form to talk exclusively about oneself. The worst bores are people who never get off the personal and on to general concepts and objective consideration of facts or ideas.

It took me a while to realize that AA is different. This is not a tea party or an intellectual discussion group (which are excellent and enjoyable and have their place). An AA meeting is something else again.

Egotistical as it seems, and distasteful as such conduct would be at a dinner party, when I speak in AA I must learn to tell what I did, what I was like as far as I can see it, what happened to me, and what I think I am like now, without even unconsciously implying, "You'd just better learn something from my experience and do likewise." I must try to forget about "we" and "you" and "them," not even being concerned about whether what I say is going to help "You." If I speak about what I think, my opinions, my philosophical views, I should do so as one reporting events of a particular nature that pertain only to me, not to you, just as some people will report, "I was in jail thirty-six times" or "I spent six months in a mental hospital."

Contradictory as it seems, and whether I fully understand it or not, I escape my own egocentricity by the inevitable identification that takes place with someone else when he talks about himself. So when I get up and talk about myself, others are finding release from their own self-centeredness in observing mine, with the result that all of us will go out feeling better, and therefore perhaps with less need to drink in order to escape the intolerable tyranny of our own egos.

Anonymous, Calif.

Tradition Two

*For our group purpose there is but one
ultimate authority — a loving God as He may
express Himself in our group conscience.
Our leaders are but trusted servants,
they do not govern*

December 1969

S HORTLY AFTER I RETURNED to the office from lunch, the phone on my desk rang. It was a late autumn day during my first sober AA year.

"Did you know J—— B—— got drunk?" asked the AA acquaintance on the line.

Such momentous news overwhelmed me. J —— was the chairman of our group. I had considered him Mr. AA. Now I felt that the whole movement would soon totter under this disastrous blow, unless someone rushed to the rescue. A brilliant new leader would have to be found, quickly.

Well, how about me? I had been a club president a couple of times in school. Surely, my ability would be a great boon to the Fellowship.

"But he's so young!" I could hear someone exclaim. (I was chronologically twenty-seven, emotionally minus one.)

"Yes, but he's really brilliant," a wiser voice would reply.

By this time, I had tidied up my desk, made some excuse to the boss, grabbed my briefcase, hat, and coat, dashed to the subway, and ridden halfway to the old church building we used as a clubhouse for AAs in Manhattan in 1945. I carried with me about as much sense as a flea plotting to run a kennel.

Surprisingly, everything seemed calm when I arrived. No doubt some committee somewhere was already, privately, trying to find someone who could save AA. How could I let them know I was willing? Even if it was a tough job, with low salary, I'd make the sacrifice out of gratitude and love for AA. I could already hear my inaugural address after the swearing-in ceremony: plenty of laughs, plus enough heart stuff to bring tears to the eyes of the old folks (everybody over thirty); then a ringing peroration of rededication that would bring 'em to their feet roaring, as I turned modestly from the rostrum to take my seat of honor. (Just as in drunken days, I could still out-Mitty James Thurber's Walter M.)

At the clubhouse, though, all I could do was smile graciously at everyone around, cheerily reassure some new wretch from my lofty eminence of ten sober months, and chin a bit with other seedy statesmen. I even, for the first time, sprang for several cups of coffee.

Throughout the afternoon and evening, however, no one mentioned the vacant chairmanship. So, finally, I brought it up over coffee after the meeting. "Isn't it too bad about J ——?" I brightly blurted.

Only one old-timer paid attention. His look seemed to probe uncomfortably close to my deepest secrets, but his voice was kind as he said, "Well, just because J —— got drunk doesn't mean *you* have to drink."

The idea was so breathtaking, I just shut up.

But my mentor continued, "You see, we'll get somebody else to do J——'s job. We rotate chores around here, you know. There's really no honor connected with AA offices or titles, just work. And it's often dirty work at that."

Although our Twelve Traditions had not yet been put into words, the truth, the spirit, and the sense of our Traditions was guiding those who helped me.

The shattering of my fantasy of eminence in AA was one lesson in what was to become our Second Tradition: that AA has no bosses. And that fact, only slowly learned, even more reluctantly accepted, but finally embraced, is greatly responsible for my sobriety. To stay sober, I had to learn that I could not be a boss in AA, no matter how much I wanted to or tried to.

There had been an earlier lesson on the obverse of that truth: that no one in AA could boss *me*, either. Upon discovering, my very first day in AA, that there was no place to sign up, no formal rite to initiate or mark me as a "member," I had asked with puzzlement, "But how will you know if I stay sober?"

"We won't," I was told. "But you will."

My first AA conversation had been an ever-increasing series of shocks, but this was almost too much. No one would check up on whether I had a drink or not! I felt relief, coupled with mild twinges of panic (Was it possible for me *not* to get drunk unless something or someone forcibly prevented it?) and wry anger (Dammit, this was a dirty trick! Why wouldn't "they" give me some magic thing to keep me safe?).

"No one in AA tells us what to do, or scolds us for not doing it," my first AA friend had explained.

Now, twenty-five years later, I am convinced that, as much as anything, that truth about AA heated up my determination to belong to the Fellowship.

But appreciation of the truth did not spring forth full-grown. To whittle down an egotism like mine takes years (It still sprouts unexpectedly, sneakily) and many experiences similar to my short-lived dream of the AA "presidency." If I never became a power and a glory in AA, it wasn't for lack of trying.

Just a few months later, I actually did become chairman of a new, small group. I summoned "my" other officers to a meeting and informed them of the new organization and the new rules that I was setting up. And in a few days I got drunk.

In fact, I remember the preparation of written bylaws for four separate groups in New York City in the 1940s. We just did not trust each other or our successors. Each of those "business" sessions for framing such documents, as you no doubt suspect, was a comedy that could have been titled *Full Moon Over the Madhouse*. The records of our labors have long since disappeared, but the groups did survive and now flourish beautifully without such appurtenances. Also surviving is a lesson that can be drawn from this experience: Those who did not get their way in the squabbles over laws frequently got drunk, and some of them did not survive.

I truly believe that our Second Tradition, like all the others, is important for my individual survival, as well as for that of every AA group and our Fellowship as a whole.

I truly believe that our Second Tradition, like all the others, is important for my individual survival, as well as for that of every AA group and our Fellowship as a whole.

At still another time in my life, I was again chosen to be chairman of a group, after serving some apprenticeships. On the night of the election (no one else wanted the job), despite my previous experience as a chairman, I was enormously moved. I felt very happy and even proud to receive from my group something that felt like an honor.

July 1984

"They've asked him to pick up ashtrays."

Big deal! At the very next meeting, the entire group turned on me. It was not personal, you understand. It was just that the coffee was too weak that night and the meeting had run overtime.

In every single AA job, I have received gripes and criticism; yet it has been rewarding to learn to listen to criticism, to evaluate it, to use it or reject it, and then to go on doing the job the best I could. In all honesty, I can say there were some pats on the back, too. But I did learn that, no matter what AA title I might briefly hold, I had absolutely no authority over any AA member. And, of course, no AA member, group, committee, office, or board has any authority whatsoever over me or any other member. (It has to be love, not government, that keeps AA stuck together.) This has the effect of keeping us all on one level in AA, and makes brotherhood easier than it would be if some of us were higher, others lower. I have at last come to like the fact that for AA purposes the final authority is a loving God (whatever concept of a benign Greater Power that word may represent to each of us) as expressed in the consensus of us all.

Suppose it were otherwise. Suppose we had layer upon hierarchical layer of drunks scrambling for higher and higher rungs of AA power and fame. Suppose we had to elect representatives to sit in some *governing* body (instead of our strictly *advisory* councils – intergroup committees and the General Service Conference). Or what if we had to choose a national president!

Can't you just hear the nominating speeches and electioneering slogans? Can't you just hear the debates? Can't you just hear sobriety groaning under the strain, then the ice in the glasses, the cans and corks popping, and the sound of mass DTs that would surely result?

Fortunately, AA never puts us under such stress, thanks to our Second Tradition. Two things about the group conscience, however, still bother me. One is the fact that the Tradition does not say an *informed* group conscience. Once, we discussed all evening just what kind of quarters our central office should move into. Not one of us had ever searched out or tried to lease office space. Another time, we went on and on about procedures for electing regional members of AA's General Service Board, but only two people in the room had ever read *The Third Legacy Manual* (now revised and titled *The AA Service Manual*). If we had been better informed, our group decisions would probably have been wiser.

The other thing about group conscience that has given me

trouble is the discovery that it does not always agree with me. After quite a few such ego-wounding differences, I had to admit that the group conscience could manage without me, but that I needed it — just as we say about AA.

Finally, one more thing about this Tradition troubles me, and that is the word "trusted." I cannot do all the Twelfth Step jobs that I'd like to do and that need doing in my town and around the globe. But surely I can support, with loving trust, those at Intergroup and GSO who do help to make AA's reach citywide and worldwide. The committees that arrange conventions or banquets, meeting programs, or group anniversaries also deserve confidence. If I am not doing any of the work, the least I can contribute is trust in those who are.

Vice versa, if any AA job is entrusted to me, especially a Twelfth Step call, I will do the best I can, especially if the person is a sick newcomer who has just come to us. For in this way I maintain my own recovery. If we cannot trust each other, as our Second Tradition suggests, who on earth can we trust?

B. L., Manhattan, N.Y.

The Whisper of Humility

March 1955

ONE PART OF OUR GREAT program — the Twelve Traditions — has come to mean life itself to me. The Traditions, as written by our co-founder Bill, define for me clearly and precisely how to get well and stay well. They tell me who God is, what he does, and where he functions. They show me what sprirituality is and how I can seek and find it. They clarify what anonymity means.

Perhaps most important of all, they point out the path toward humility. It is helpful that this path is not described bluntly; rather, it is whispered to me in each Tradition.

Tradition One tells me, "Our common welfare should come first..." Not second or fourth or tenth, but *first*. Why? Because "personal recovery depends upon AA unity." So I learn that after the Twelve Steps have been digested, my group, my AA, *comes first;* not myself, you understand, but my AA group or groups. My own recovery — my most prized possession, since it means life itself — depends upon my group's unity.

I am told how to stay well in Tradition One, and to my surprise, it dawns on me that I have received the first gentle whisper nudging me along the path of humility.

Tradition Two tells me who God is, where he is, and what he does. It says, "for our group purpose there is but one ultimate authority — a loving God as He may express Himself in our group conscience." God expresses himself in a specific location — my conscience. This is good news to me. I have wondered for over forty years where and who God was and what he did. Now I understand what was meant, long ago, by the command "Be still and know that I am God."

I read on in the last half of Tradition Two, and I find the second gentle whisper toward humility: "Our leaders [you and I] are but trusted servants; they do not govern." I love the clarity and force of that simple word "but." As a leader, I am *but* a trusted servant; I need not govern. Thank God! For too long, I have been a dubiously trusted leader who felt that he *must* govern; now I can be relieved of all that. As God may express himself in my conscience, I am his and your trusted servant, who governs only me!

Tradition Three tells me, "the only requirement for AA membership is a desire to stop drinking." To have a *desire to stop* anything is new to me. So I receive the third gentle whisper toward humility. As I hear and feel these gentle whispers, I settle more and more each day to life size, and as a Los Angeles member has said, "Life comes to be for free and for fun."

Tradition Four brings me clearly and simply into my own right. It says, "Each group should be autonomous except in matters affecting other groups or AA as whole." You and I are autonomous. Individually and collectively, we may do as we wish; we are unrestricted — except when we step on someone else's toes or when we step on a group's toes. Thus the fourth gentle whisper toward humility says to me, "Brother, the common welfare comes first for the truly spiritual selfish reason that your own recovery depends upon its continued existence."

Tradition Five defines in clear terms my only reason for existence. There is no other for me. "Each group has but one primary purpose — to carry its message to the alcoholic who still suffers." There is my answer. I need purpose — and I have it! I must carry the message to the alcoholic who still suffers. So I say to myself, "Thank God for alcohol and for the unrecovered drunk!" And I hear a fifth gentle whisper toward humility deep within me that says, "At long last, you have come to realize that service to others is all you have to offer in this life!"

Tradition Six clarifies the spiritual side of this program. It says, "An AA group ought never endorse, finance, or lend the AA name to any related facility or outside enterprise, lest problems of money, property, and prestige divert us from our primary purpose." I'm glad to know this, because now I can be on guard. I have a primary spiritual aim that money, property, and prestige can bust wide open and devour. I hear a sixth gentle whisper toward humility that says, "*Your* primary purpose is to carry the message to the alcoholic who still suffers!" In the role of a trusted servant, I must follow the instructions of a loving authority who lives in the depths of my soul. It says, "In all reverence, carry to the sick alcoholic the message that I have given you."

Tradition Seven tells me how to obtain peace of mind. It shows me how to regain my self-respect. At long last, I understand the inner peace that comes from being responsible for myself and to myself. Tradition Seven says, "Every AA group ought to be fully self-supporting, declining outside contributions." What a relief that is! No longer do I need to *wait* for contributions." I am now free to *give* contributions.

Tradition Eight gives to me, a professional man, the very keynote of humility: "Alcoholics Anonymous should remain forever nonprofessional, but our service centers may employ special workers." I know the professional life; I am in it up to my very ears; I love it. But I know one other thing, too: In my life of service, there is absolutely no room for professionalism. In AA, I am an ordinary human being with no more skills than anyone else.

Tradition Nine astonishes me by stating, "AA, as such, ought never be organized; but we may create service boards or committees directly responsible to those they serve." You see, in the past I have been so well organized (or so I thought) that I almost died from it! I was frightened at first to find that I needed to be in a group that wasn't organized. But in AA I am free to be myself as I find myself at the minute, and here I find another whisper toward humility: I can be on service boards or committees, and I can be a trusted servant who is directly responsible to you, my fellow AAs.

Tradition Ten pleases me very much. I read it daily with a joy-

ful smile. "Alcoholics Anonymous has no opinion on outside issues; hence the AA name ought never be drawn into public controversy." Just think, as an AA I need never be drawn into public
controversy. I don't have to worry about being right. Never again!
I don't have to fight any more. I've had enough of controversy.

God love our good co-founder Bill for taking it easy on my
befuddled brain. He held off giving me Tradition Eleven until I
could hear and digest Tradition Ten. I read: "Our public relations
policy is based on attraction rather than promotion; we need always maintain personal anonymity at the level of press, radio, and
films." Never again do I have to promote a single thing. I am now
free to be myself. I am free to believe what I believe. I am free to
say what I believe in my own way. And I hear a whisper (number
eleven) deep within that says, "The way to humility is to realize
that you *need* to maintain personal anonymity!" It doesn't say
that I have to, or that I should, or that I must; it says I *need* to
maintain anonymity, as I need the very food and water and air that
keep me alive.

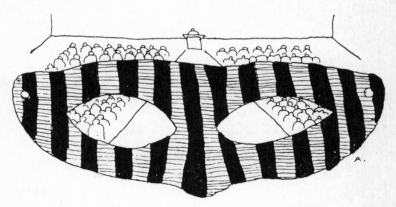

And so Tradition Twelve comes into view: "Anonymity is the
spiritual foundation of all our Traditions, ever reminding us to
place principles before personalities." I've been wondering about
this anonymity business. Now I know. Anonymity means that I am
only Earle. I am just a guy like you. You and I are equal. There are
no class distinctions. I am not a professional man; I am just Earle.
The weather way up there on the peak of prestige and gain was bitter cold; but down here in the world of anonymity, it is warm and
balmy. I can shake hands with you and look you straight in the eye

and say, "Hi, My name is Earle." I am just one guy. No more. No less. I am one of the grains of sand that go to make up our great beach of AA. Without me as a grain of sand, without each of you as a grain of sand, there would be no AA beach. Without the beach of AA, there would be no you and no me.

So I hear the last and best whisper of all. It says: ". . . ever reminding us to place principles before personalities." I smile a deep inward smile. Day after day, I come to know that our common welfare comes first, that my God is a living authority located inside me, that I am his ungoverning, trusted servant who is dedicated to the spiritual activity of carrying the message without fanfare to the alcoholic who still suffers.

I smile because in my organization I am unorganized. I smile because I need not be a professional who has opinions he must cram down your throat. I smile because I can at last be myself, and if I don't attract anyone, at least I won't promote anyone.

But mainly, I smile because you — all of you in AA — have given me the opportunity to fight for your principles rather than my personality.

E. M., San Francisco, Calif.

Tradition Four

Each group should be autonomous except in
matters affecting other groups or AA as a whole

April 1970

D URING MY FIRST SOBER YEAR in AA, I heard that a group in the next state was awarding poker chips to members who stayed sober for various lengths of time. They even gave a party at the end of a newcomer's first year, with a candle on a cake, and everybody singing "Happy Birthday."

I was horrified. Scandalized! I declared that such childish behavior led people to stay sober only for rewards, rather than for their own lives' sake. Besides, it violated the 24-hour plan of trying to stay sober one day at a time, not for a month or a year. I shook my head and muttered, "Something ought to be done."

Soon after that, a speaker at our meeting told some off-color stories. (Like many "reformed drunkards," I had become quite a puritanical prig.) He also revealed that he had been drinking the day before. This was too outrageous to be ignored, of course. So I went to an older member, who had patiently listened to me before, and I complained again, "Something ought to be done!"

"Well, do it then," he declared, grinning, and walked away. (No Traditions had been written down yet. It was 1945.)

Shortly thereafter, through the Grapevine, I began to learn shocking facts: In Chicago, Minneapolis, St. Louis, and Miami, lots of groups did things "wrong" — which meant, of course, not the way we did them in my group.

And yet those faraway, seemingly benighted AAs seemed to stay sober just as well as we did. Besides, with their anniversary parties and sobriety tokens, they seemed to have a lot of fun that my group missed out on. And those exasperating old-timers I talked to didn't seem to mind one bit. They just kept on serenely staying sober. Apparently it bothered them not at all that other groups and other members were going their own independent ways. I didn't know then what the old-timers realized: that getting distressed about other members and groups was dangerous, not to those others, but to the AA who got upset about them.

There was the rub: If I was unwilling to grant autonomy to others, the one likely to get drunk was *me*. So finally I had to learn, once more, that there are no bosses in AA (as our Second Tradition says) and that nobody in the outfit would take orders anyway.

In my opinion, there is additional, specific guidance on this in the now-written words of our Fourth Tradition: *Each group should be autonomous except in matters affecting other groups or AA as a whole.* And I don't think I am distorting the spirit of those words when I say to myself that not only each group, but also each member, deserves autonomy. Besides, respect for the independence of others is to my own advantage.

If there were no Fourth Tradition (first in the old-timers' experience, then in written words), what would my own AA story be?

If, during my first AA months, *one* way of doing things had been forced on all groups, I might not have stayed around to get well. If the poker chips and anniversary parties had been mandatory in my group, all of us who shrank from such sociability could easily have found AA not for us, and gone away to drink again and to die.

On the other hand, if some AA laws had absolutely forbidden such practices (as I had wanted to do), many AAs who have found sobriety tokens or key chains, birthday cakes and anniversary parties helpful in their recovery would have been deprived of these aids in staying sober.

I think the autonomy Tradition means that *any* help — whether it is a poker chip, a piece of jewelry, a book, a prayer, a cake and candle, a slogan, a clinic, one particular kind of meeting, a psychiatrist, a sponsor, or any other means of staying sober — is wonderful.

If each of us is expected to arrive at his own understanding of a greater power, I cannot believe that any other member — or a committee of us — is meant to decide how he shall do it. But I have found that grudging tolerance of others' ways is not enough. Learning to respect the positive values of these different ways has contributed much to my recovery.

As AA now grows into its thirty-fifth year, I feel that our Fourth Tradition has grown in value. Because of it, we are helped to avoid a rigidity which might destroy the usefulness of AA and hinder its ability to take in more and more kinds of sick alcoholics.

Early in my own AA life, I was fortunate enough to encounter members who wanted to try daring AA experiments. They started types of meetings that no one in AA had heard of before: closed discussions, open discussions, and Step meetings, among others. Some even persuaded a general hospital to open a ward for alcoholic patients, run in close cooperation with our AA Central Office, and to allow meetings on the premises.

You can guess what a ruckus these innovations kicked up. "Heresy!" one faction cried. Because a certain approach had never been used before, they said, it would not work. It might even ruin AA!

Of course, thousands of us now know that different kinds of meetings give us the different kinds of help we need at various stages of our sobriety. Thousands of us have had our lives saved by such hospital arrangements. (Mine was, twice.) Who says the Fourth Tradition does not apply to sobriety for an individual?

So I am glad that group autonomy gives us the right to experiment if we wish. Otherwise, all meetings would be alike, all held at the same time, and every one of us who has ever benefited from a daytime discussion or a midnight Eleventh Step meeting would just be out of luck.

Quite recently, I found myself back on a group steering committee. I had been chairman of the group many years before, but no one else on the committee knew that. I sat in quiet horror as the Young Turks discussed what kind of sandwiches seemed to go best at the beginners meeting. *Sandwiches?*

I smirked inwardly. They couldn't get anybody to make them, I was sure. Besides, the group treasury would be depleted by such fancy food, and our rent would go unpaid until our church landlord was heard from.

At our beginners meetings, we now have the biggest crowds ever, happily munching away, sober. Instead of barely scraping up the rent, we now have a treasury full enough to pay it and then make generous monthly gifts to our local intergroup and the AA General Service Office as well. Thanks to that Fourth Tradition, my group could be independent of me and my rigidity. And who knows what wonderful new ideas are yet to come if members like me will be flexible enough to accept them and use them?

The closing words of our Tradition do suggest, however, that the autonomy is not unqualified. My group has the right to run itself any way it pleases, but only so long as it does not mess things up for other groups, or hurt our beloved Fellowship as a whole.

Each time I recognize the value of my group's autonomy, I am reminded of my personal responsibility. For example, when those all-important newcomers arrive at a meeting where I am present, whatever I do or fail to do may indeed affect other groups. If I am not friendly, if I am overzealous, if I am hypocritical, if I am dogmatic, if I am frivolous, if I am humorless, any one of these may be the quality which a newcomer ascribes to *all* AA. He may go away saying, "Those AAs are clannish" or "fanatical" or "dreary," and he may never come back to that group — nor try any other.

What can I do about it? Well, whenever I lead or speak at an open meeting or participate in a discussion meeting, it is probably important for me to say clearly that no one member speaks for AA as a whole or for any AA group, that each speaker expresses his own opinion only. In AA, we seek diversity of opinion, not uniformity, because in that way we can help more and more people. (I especially need to remember this, of course, when opinions I do not like are voiced.)

But I am not sure that such announcements are totally effective. In fact, as an AA member, I can do very little that does not reflect on my group or on AA as a whole, whether I like it or not. To the non-AA world, we individuals *are* AA. It is an awesome responsibility. Once I spoke sharply to a fellow worker, not in AA, and he responded acidly, "All you AAs are so damn rigid!" Since I was the only AA he knew, I represented to him our entire Fellowship.

My AA freedom to do or say as I please does indeed need to be watched.

On the group level, the widespread autonomy so fiercely practiced and cherished sometimes brings with it a severe handicap to our Fellowship overall — or at least a disadvantage which we have to work hard and ingeniously to overcome. I mean that autonomy sometimes can make free communication and free exchange of experience somewhat difficult.

If we had the kind of chain of command most organizations have, helpful information might travel better or more quickly. If we had echelons of authority, ideas could be forcefully passed down to all units. News of a new pamphlet would automatically be disseminated by governing units to those being governed. Results of new kinds of meetings could be instantly transmitted to all groups and members.

As it is now, thousands of AA members are deprived of knowledge which they would happily use. For example, fewer than half the AA groups in the world take the Grapevine. And, because each group is autonomous, no one can force on them the knowledge that this wonderful (in my opinion) magazine exists. I am continually being surprised, as I visit various groups, to learn that many members have never heard of Bill's book *As Bill Sees It*; some have no idea that there is an AA Anniversary International Convention every five years; and some, to be sure, have not been told about any of the Traditions, only about the Steps; and at a meeting I attended last night, I met one young man who had been around AA more than three years before anyone suggested to him, "Have you tried the Steps? They were helpful to me."

This seems a heavy, if not a dangerous, price for AA to pay for group autonomy. Is it worth such a risk?

The answer, I believe, is yes, since the alternative would be rigid, doctrinal uniformity imposed on all groups and members. That alternative would threaten my sobriety, dangerously.

Instead, I am free to continue learning and growing at my own rate (or to stand still). That Fourth Tradition offers true independence to me, the individual, as well as to every AA group, so long as we accept some responsibility along with it. But I don't mind. Who ever said that freedom was for free?

B. L., Manhattan, N.Y.

Real Rotation — or 'Back Seat' Indispensables?

May 1953

T HERE MAY BE TOO MUCH GRISTLE in this soliloquy for many to chew through to the meat, but in spite of inept pens, two of us would like to discuss the underlying cause of a general feeling in many groups, as we see it, of lengthy frustration.

We have been asked too often lately in too many places: "why doesn't this group grow?" and we have only shrugged our shoulders with a cheering word to the leader, instead of giving the answer that "Something may be wrong with your group, and you're the only one who can change it."

This is an unaccusing attempt to spread out on the bar the increasingly common occurrence of one or two stable members of a group becoming its most dependable nucleus and never letting go their leadership and experienced guidance. Almost all groups we have known change secretaries and chairmen regularly. Too often the newly chosen become only the nominal leaders of the group, without a single member recognizing the underlying cause. Of course it is suspected, but suspicion for us is always one of the three little steps to degenerative hate.

The situation usually begins when "the best secretary or chairman the group ever had" steps down, and does not go through the difficult process of turning over *everything* to the new leaders, including his intangibles — pride in the job and the group's dependence upon him. The tricks of indispensability are instinctive to us "dipsoenthusiacs" — rather than purposefully thought out.

A couple of concrete examples may clarify the matter. We refer not to the group that merely thinks it isn't doing so well, but to the many groups that have been traveling backward for *a year or more.* (From here, we will take turns in the first person singular.)

Last year I found myself in the position of having to start a group or not having meetings to go to. When all my so-called experience did not avail, I gave up; then God started the group. It grew like wildfire for four months and then leveled off in a beautiful fellowship. At our half-year party, someone mentioned that there were no brand new men, in spite of the increasing death rate from alcoholism in the locality. Something reminded me of a hotel room session long ago, when one of the "First Ten" stated that he did not believe that *anyone* could stay "in the saddle" over AAs for more than six months without the "governed" beginning to develop saddle sores. (We believe he meant "guided" instead of "governed.")

At the next meeting, I attempted to turn over the leadership to a lad whose new serene enthusiasm could be an extra asset to any group. He squawked and was a little frightened, and for three weeks the group fought my stepping down, even to the extent of an accusation about shirking my duty. But I stepped down.

The new leader was still a little lost at his second meeting, and on seeing why, I found it a real task to turn over to him *everything* that had been useful in my chairmanship: contacts with outside key members and AA events; my mental fingers on the group's Twelfth Step work; personal notes of group value; and writing to request the leaders of other groups to contact him directly instead of secondhand through me. And then before long, the group took on a second spurt of growth, better than the first.

But here's the catch. I have to admit not giving up my sense of possessiveness toward the group. Our correspondence with the New York office and our area secretary had become a steady flow. I was on the inside of any Twelfth Step work involving group mail

VICTOR E.

and all the other group matters so dear to an AA heart. I notified the various secretaries and event chairmen of our new leader's name and address, but it didn't take. And second notices didn't change our file cards in most of those places. Then, to put it mildly, I found myself "judging"; not turning an occasional piece of mail over to him because I thought it time wasting, or not good for the group, or because I wanted to handle that particular matter myself. Of course *I* had the experience to do it best! Best for whom?

There are three cases in my book where the "unofficial chairman's" permanent slip caused the group to have its first growing pains. And several related occurrences that can't be mentioned because they are individual enough to point an accusing finger, however humorous.

Every densely populated area has its pair of mighty swell paternalists, trying to garner a larger group under their alternate chairmanships by moving their meeting place into a more AA-populated region about once a year. But we give them a pat on the back because they are out in the open with their possessiveness.

To quote an old Grapevine: "The background boss who never lets the group forget about the two who became secretary and chairman and promptly slipped, or about the member who never had enough spare cash to get drunk on until he was put in charge of the kitty."

The steering committee of one, who says he prefers a small group. (It's easier to control by soft suggestion.) This is not as common as we thought we first recognized, so be careful not to hurt a right guy who *completely* lets the group have its will in spite of his well-founded fears.

May 1965

In several very real instances, we have found the control to be the nonalcoholic wife of the seemingly background boss. She wants to maintain the prestige of their position in a major group, never understanding just how the new person is the most important situation within any group function. These are the wives who answer the phone in the daytime and make it nicely difficult for the stranger to find a certain meeting place on the right day.

And the rare area or intergroup secretary who almost forces groups to keep the oldest hands on the reins by subtle intonations, to ensure his or her own reappointment, and since "younger representatives to local headquarters are not so cognizant of great things in the past."

For one so-called intergroup, including several counties at that time, two persons actually chose by invitation the more than fifty representatives. For a long time in that district, the rank and file heard little about outside AA, with exceptions of course. Interesting contingent matters formerly discussed at regular meetings were saved for special interest at the privileged little conclaves. The entire assembly seemed to feel that its information was something to be guarded for the proper cliques. I was guilty, too. Any one of us has the traits to get that way.

On the other hand, one finds in some groups at the closed meeting, on the literature table, a blank loose-leaf notebook, up to date with Headquarters bulletins and data for all members to refer to — usually unnecessary, but just another thing to make the post-novice feel that he really belongs.

Both of us were once the lower power behind the scenes for a period, in adjacent groups by coincidence; we need not tell our sins to active paternalists.

We will not discuss the small "captive group" that, through the unintentional instinctive defense mechanisms (wow) in the minds of its founders, prevents the formation of other AA gatherings in counties where actually hundreds of willing prospects have attended meetings during the past decade. Most of the private excuses for maintaining "background directorships" are as valid as those we used for taking the first drink.

It has taken us several years to realize that background chairmanship or secretarism causes a state of affairs whereby the fledgling AA does not acquire quite as many close friends as he may need. Can you fathom it? Maybe the yearlings need a freer opportunity to make minor changes for the worse in your old small group so that it will grow.

Too often, some members don't make the grade in the splitting of a small group. If your group has been consistently not holding new members for too long a time, and you are the "guiding light," it might be time for someone to do more praying, and less thinking, working and smooth directing, even though the latter seems impossible to avoid and, when accused of shirking, hurts to the core.

J. K. and J. B., U.S.A.

How Group Conscious Are You?

January 1961

I BELIEVE THAT IF A GROUP has "a group conscience" it can take an inventory, and I am part of that inventory. My inventory includes my own behavior toward my group and each individual member, toward other groups, and toward AA as a whole.

I first ask myself: Am I a good AA member?

Then: What is my inventory as part of my group?

Do I . . .

1. Attend meetings only when "I need a meeting"? or feel like it?

2. Always refuse to hold any office at any time, even when I could? Shun responsibility, refuse to run errands, make coffee, wipe a cup, empty ashtrays, set up chairs, and ignore *anything* that needs doing by refusing to notice — always manage to "let somebody else do it"?

3. Neglect to talk to newcomers or, worse, listen to them? Drift off to certain little cliques of personal friends after meetings — or just "beat it," always with good reasons, too tired, too busy — TV more often than not?

4. Turn down, or over to someone else, all Twelfth Step calls, when I could have gone? Refuse to speak or to find someone in my place, before non-AA groups or students, without good reason?

5. Give up after a time or two recontacting the sick alcoholic? Use the "not ready," "not honest" routine? Try to carry the alcoholic instead of the message? Forget that I go to see the sick

alcoholic not because he is an alcoholic (only he can say he is or isn't) but because I am?

Do I . . .

6. Make no effort to attend other meetings, help other groups get started, or give a lift to an older group? Encourage other groups to visit us, or am I (pardon the expression) a tight little island?

7. Show no interest in our Traditions, General Service, or worldwide AA? Have I grown tight with my money when I do not have to be, not realizing that the pamphlets and other services to help other alcoholics "grow not on trees"?

8. Indulge in criticism, resentment, or self-pity toward the group, a member, or members? Complain of boredom, repetition, the speakers, the chairman? Am I becoming part of the problem instead of part of the solution?

9. Criticize a member to other members behind his back with no chance for him to defend himself? Criticize slippers? Take people's moral inventory?

10. Do these things behind the group's back without trying to help the situation in any way?

. . . Do I?

M., Fort Collins, Colo.

Tradition Seven

*Every AA group ought to be self-supporting,
declining outside contributions*

October 1970

O N MY FIRST APPROACH to AA, the movement was just ten years old. The Traditions had not yet been written, but already AA had effectively declared itself independent of all handouts, thank you. It was managing, somehow, to pay its own way, and I was very glad to learn that.

If it had turned out to be a government-financed project or a charitable branch of some church, my feelings about it could not have been so instantly warm and comfortable. The fact that it was just us drunks, paying our own way, lessened my shame at having to ask for help.

I did, though, feel embarrassed the first few times the collection hat came my way. I was so ashamed to have not even a dime for it that I might have stayed away if the leader had not made a little speech one night. He said it was perfectly all right for those of us with no dough at present to let the hat pass by, since everyone there understood being broke. Visitors were also asked not to contribute because AA wanted to be self-supporting, he said, and we needed only a little money for our purposes.

Later, as treasurer of a group, I understood more clearly those purposes: paying rent for the meeting room, providing AA literature to carry the message outside the meeting room, and putting coffee into the pot. In addition, we sent a certain percentage monthly to our local central office (intergroup) and another portion to keep the big world central office (the General Service Office) going.

Interlocking with Tradition Seven, Five and Six do suggest that we have no other enterprises to finance, don't they? The conclusion seems so simple that since then it has always taken me by surprise when financial disagreements hit the fan in AA groups. Yet I have joined my most mature, serene AA friends time after time in acting positively demented over the clubhouse cost of a cup of coffee.

In fact, years ago here in New York, almost all groups had an unspoken rule: Finances were too inflammatory to be mentioned at a regular meeting. I suppose we were afraid we were too immature to stay sober if we took the dangerous risk of mixing talk about, say, the moral inventory with that dirty word "money."

Instead, before the regular meeting time each group had a separate business meeting, usually monthly (when the moon was full, I guess). Then we could madly and happily screech at each other about bills and cash with no mention of "prayer and meditation" or being "restored to sanity" to mix us up.

It was as if we were supposed to be safe, protected somehow from getting drunk over financial pettiness, from 7:30 to 8:30 on one Tuesday each month, but never after 8:30 and never on Sunday or Monday.

At stake in those long-ago verbal battles were usually such paltry sums that a visitor would have thought us truly beyond help, even from a greater power. Maybe we thought so, too; prayers were often absent from business meetings, as I recall.

The results were not all bad, however. Instead of disagreeing with each other about the truly important business of helping each other not take the first drink today, we worked off our tempers by arguing over trivial bookkeeping details, and little harm was done.

Indeed, one hung-over fellow attended his very first AA meeting, by mistake, on the night we were stomping all over a new little baby budget for the group, shyly proposed by a new treasurer. We started at 7:30, waxed wackier and wrother than usual, and by 10:30 never had gotten around to mentioning alcoholism at all, much less recovery. As soon as the meeting was over, however, this new prospect rushed up to the somewhat wrung-out, harassed chairman and pumped his hand joyously. "I want to join!" he exclaimed. "I can tell you're my kind of people, all right!" And he never took another drink.

I have sat in on many such group donnybrooks which were, or could have been, halted by judicious study and prayerful application of the wisdom of our Seventh Tradition. Such as:

Members had to sit on boxes and a bench at meetings of a small group I used to attend near skid row. So the state's tax-supported alcoholism clinic offered them some fancy chairs. (They declined gracefully, and proudly salvaged some secondhand ones for themselves.)

In another group, the meeting place badly needed a coat of paint, and a rich woman member, who had never stayed sober, insisted on footing the whole bill. (Instead of giving in, they waited until the treasury could buy the paint, and all pitched in to do the work. She helped — and started staying sober.)

A church told a big group that met there that AA's money was not needed, so the group collections just piled up for several years. (Free use of the space was, of course, really the acceptance of an outside contribution. Subsidized by the church, the group was not autonomous; the church treated it as if it were just another church activity, canceling its meetings during Christmas and other holidays, moving it from attic to basement, and so on. When the group treasury reached $700, quarreling broke out, and the group died.)

In one small town, local AA life centers around a club, known locally as "the AA club." Its officers wanted to pay off the club mortgage with raffles and benefit dances — selling tickets to the public. (As any Traditions lawyer can explain, technically a club is not a group and is therefore free to do such things. But is that the *spirit* of AA? What impression would this give the townsfolk — and prospective members?)

Another group I used to visit meets in a charitable institution which does not allow a collection at *any* meeting on its premises. One year, the institution wanted to send, *from its own funds*, a donation to GSO, to be credited to the AA group concerned. (That year, I was general service committee member for the district in which that group meets, so the group's GSR (general service representative) and I had many discussions about this!)

In the last case, I do not know what the final decision was. But I learned that there is far more to this Tradition than I had seen at first reading.

The lessons kept coming. One small group in the district I served had a GSR who made sure everyone in the group understood the nature of the message-carrying done at GSO, and the fact that there was (as there still is) no one but us to foot the bills. That group sent in a whopping donation to GSO each year, plus paying all its other obligations, while much bigger groups sent in only one-fifth as much. That bugged me. Somebody wasn't paying his fair share, pulling his own weight. On my podium of self-importance, as the righteous committee member, I prepared to speechify about it.

Fortunately, I looked at my own record first.

Thanks to AA, I was earning enough of a steady salary to throw a buck into the hat twice a week. That was my share, wasn't it? But wait a minute. Some newcomers were not able to afford giving anything yet. When I was new, obviously someone had, without my knowing it, put in enough to make up my share, as well as his own. And before that, how much had I spent annually on booze?

For the first time, I took a serious look at my group treasurer's report and at the GSO financial statements printed in the annual Conference Report, to see where I myself fitted in. I looked at my group's total contribution to our intergroup office and to GSO. I discovered there was a limit, then $100, now $200, [in 1984, $500] set on the amount any one individual could give to such offices in one year. Apparently, some people had been privately making direct gifts for years to help keep those places going.

To say I began doing the same is not immodest, because it had taken me so long to get around to it. And guess what! That year, for the very first time in my life, I found a faint glimmering of what self-respect means.

Of course, from the realization of my financial responsibility for seeing that the AA message got carried, it was only a short step to a sharp look at my other behavior with money. Technically, since sobering up in AA I had been almost completely self-supporting, declining outside contributions. But I often acted as if I somehow deserved special financial consideration.

For example, when I first got sober, I had rather promptly paid off most debts, and it felt wonderful being able to hold up my head, debt-free for a change. Except...loans a brother and a cousin had made to me remained unpaid a long time. I let them

June 1963

"Our children — Gordon, Harper, Overholt, Schenley, Faith, Hope, and Serenity."

wait until last (and paid no interest), vaguely feeling that they didn't need the money as much as I did. They never asked me for it, so I was buying new suits and other things I enjoyed (telling myself that I owed these to myself), long before I got around to paying these two legitimate debts. Hardly mature, responsible behavior!

My analyst and I tussled with this problem for many dreary months, ending in a draw. I am still at it, with only occasional, thin patches of success. I still find it too easy to rationalize postponing payments of my American Express bill this month if there is something else I'd rather do with the money.

That's what I meant when I said that AA principles are hard for me to practice in all my affairs. But our Seventh Tradition has shed light and pointed a direction for me to follow, when I will and can.

Our Traditions have always made it possible for me to stay sober. But they also teach me lessons for the other parts of my life. In this instance, an AA path of service (being a committee member) led me right into the inside core of me, where broad roads of self-improvement had never been traveled. When I then began to try to behave responsibly in financial matters, to act as if I really were self-supporting, my new feeling about myself was quite different from any I had ever known before.

At last I was starting to grow up, I felt. I was forty years old at the time.

B. L., Manhattan, N.Y.

Beginnings in Beirut

April 1984

T OWARD THE END OF MAY 1983, a letter requesting literature arrived at the AA General Service Office from J. O., a U.S. marine stationed with the International Peacekeeping Force in Beirut, Lebanon. At just about the same time, two nonalcoholics — a woman student at the American University in Beirut and a priest — were working along with an American AA member in Beirut trying to start a group there.

Shortly after J. O.'s first letter arrived, the student wrote asking for literature. At her suggestion, the clergyman visited GSO during a trip to the U.S. and took a supply of literature back with him. GSO staff members put these two in touch with J. O.

Through their joint efforts, public information announcements appeared on radio and TV and in Beirut newspapers. The first newspaper article concluded: "As Lebanon is striving to gain sovereignty and recover from war, we know there are countless individuals who have had wars within themselves. Countries all over the world have Alcoholics Anonymous, and now so does Lebanon."

The letters that follow, with one exception, constitute J. O.'s correspondence with various GSO staff members.

18 May, 1983

To Whom It May Concern:

I am writing this letter concerning your resources on AA. I would like to order some resources from you so I may use them for our group in Beirut, Lebanon. (I am a U.S. marine serving with the International Peacekeeping Force.)

Would you please send me order forms for all the AA resources you have on hand, or a catalog? I am deeply interested in speakers' tapes, since we may not have many speakers at our meetings.

I'll be looking forward to hearing from you very soon. Thank you.

Sincerely yours,
J—— O——

21 June, 1983

Dear P——,

I want to thank you and your friends for the letter and other information you sent to me. The pamphlets were useful in providing me and my friends with important information about AA.

At the present time, our group consists of two devoted AAs and one possible. We hope to grow in numbers day by day. It has been difficult getting started here at Beirut International Airport, but we're being patient.

We haven't set a schedule for our meetings yet. At present, we just get together when we can make the time. When we get started, we'll contact you with more information concerning our progress.

I've already contacted one man from the list you sent me, and I hope to order tapes and correspond with him by cassette tapes.

I brought along some books and information on AA when we left the States in May. I've got a Big Book, a "Twelve and Twelve," *As Bill Sees It, Living Sober,* and *Came to Believe.* These are the essentials that I can take with me everywhere I go, even to the bush on field operations.

I got sober one year and two months ago, and I've been a member of a group in North Carolina since then. My unit deployed to Beirut for six months, and I'd like to begin a group within my unit here. So far, I've got two others besides me.

I really appreciate the concern you show in your letter, and I hope we can keep in touch. Please feel free to write back with any information or experiences you would like to share with us. We wish you all the best.

Sincerely,
J—— O——

7 July, 1983

Dear P—— and friends,

I was very glad to receive your letter of hope and support. Yours are some of the kindest people I've had the pleasure of becoming acquainted with.

There have been no developments in our small group. We are two people who are supporting each other in sobriety. My friend is a beginner and is not anxious to completely surrender his alcoholic dilemma. I am busy trying to convince him of the futility of self-discipline and willpower when it comes to King Alcohol.

Hopefully, if it is God's will, we will get our group started here.

I am busy working and writing my inventory at present time. So my Twelfth Step efforts have been premature but, I hope, helpful. Who says you can't help another alcoholic because you haven't worked Steps Five to Eleven? It would be a mistake to let the man slide deeper into a miserable world.

Send advice and literature if you please. I'll keep in touch.

Baffled in Beirut,
J—— O——

20 July, 1983

Dear P——,

Our group has grown here in Beirut. We now meet every Sunday at 4:30 PM. There are eight members. Our group name is the Peacekeeping AA Group.

Please return another order form for us to use in future orders. Thank you very much for your service.

Very truly yours,
J——— O———

25 July, 1983

Dear L———,

Our group is now meeting at the Peacekeeping Chapel in the BLT [Battalion Landing Team] Marine Building Headquarters each Sunday. There are about five members. We've held two successful meetings there so far.

No wonder we call our group the Peacekeeping Group. We are all marines, with the exception of two ladies who drive over from the far side of Beirut when they feel it is safe to come here. I'm sure you've heard how dangerous this airport is. We were shelled on Friday.

Now I don't need to join with the Loners/Internationalists, since our group is meeting regularly. But thank you for your help when I needed you.

I hope to hear from you again soon, and send my hope for you in search of your dreams.

Beginning in Beirut,
J—— O——

2 September, 1983

Dear AA Friends,

Thank you for the much-needed literature you have so generously supplied for us. We are continuing our growth progress in our group and holding meetings whenever circumstances permit them. You understand it is very difficult to attend meetings and fight a war at the same time, but we are struggling on.

I have made changes or filled in blanks on the opposite side of the group information form. I hope this will help in recording information for our file there.

We are very grateful to be able to attend meetings here in this ravaged city and will continue to hold meetings as often as we can to help carry the message of AA to newcomers. Our thanks to you for your letters and gifts of sobriety tools.

Gratitude from Beirut,
J—— O——
and the Peacekeeping Group

21 September, 1983

Dear S——,

I'm sorry I haven't written back to you sooner, but we have been very busy doing other things, like trying to stay alive.

We have had meetings as often as possible (two or three a week) since July. Some of our members have difficulty leaving their field positions to get to Battalion Headquarters, so our meetings have only four people, with four other members on the front lines in the field.

We've been successful in carrying the message to three newcomers, and the other five of us were already members of AA when we left the States in May.

Two civilians from Beirut were very much the beginners of our group as we know it. They have been at our meetings often and even during a bombing attack one Sunday afternoon. (Since then, they have not returned.) I haven't contacted those two girls for weeks because of the extremely dangerous situation we've been in. I will try to contact one of them again real soon.

We are very grateful for the chance to begin our AA group here, and we thank you for your extra help in this project. We hope that when we leave in November our following marines and sailors will continue the group as it is now. Though they will be a new bunch of servicemen, we think it's possible there may be an alcoholic in the bunch who'll continue the Peacekeeping Group.

God bless and goodwill to you good folks in New York.

Sincerely yours,
J—— O——
Peacekeeping Group

On Sunday, October 23, 1983, the Battalion Landing Team headquarters building in the marine Amphibious Unit compound at Beirut International Airport was destroyed by a bomb, taking the lives of 241 U.S. military personnel.

This letter was written to GSO by the Lebanese student who had requested literature the preceding summer.

December 6, 1983

Dear S——,

Thank you very much for your thoughtful letter of October 27. I received it one month late due to the situation here and to the fact that the airport is closed. I am sending you this letter through the American Embassy.

As for the marines, the young man who was in touch with you was killed by the explosion. The others have left, and a new company was brought in. All of the AA literature was lost, because we used to meet in the library, located in the basement of the same building that was blown up. [GSO sent more literature, which was returned because of mail problems.] I want very much to be able to start AA again for the men in the new company, but at the moment, this is impossible. The base is located right next to the airport, and there is a lot of shelling and fighting in that area. Also, it would be very difficult for me to get on base, because new precaution measures have been taken since the explosion. I hope that things will change soon. Keep them in your prayers. Also pray for the AA group in Beirut.

Best regards from the AA members here, and they all thank you for your concern.

Sincerely,
S—— M——

FOUR

EXPERIENCE, STRENGTH, AND HOPE

The Steps Are the Program

July 1975

T HE WORD "HEAL" MEANS "make whole." The aim of AA is to help a shattered, fragmented human being find wholeness, direction, and freedom. This begins with release from our compulsion to drink and, through our use of the Twelve Steps, gradually moves into growing freedom from fear, depression, anxiety, and the overwhelming self-concern that characterized life before AA.

Ecologists hammer persistently at the theme that destroying the natural balance anywhere will have an effect, frequently adverse, somewhere else. Nothing stands alone. Our lives are not compartmentalized. Pollution in one segment of my life will poison another, seemingly unconnected area of my life. Failure to work *all* of the Steps will eventually create problems such as depression, anxiety, fear, hostility, boredom, and finally drunkenness.

While the scientific method has generated sweeping advances in technology, it has also created the trend toward fragmentation and reductionism that continues today. Our ecological crisis is only one example of this unhappy legacy, which has resulted in a persistent inability to see the connection of one thing with another.

Dr. Barry Commoner, in his widely acclaimed book *The Closing Circle*, describes the problem this way: "There is indeed a

specific fault in our system of science, and in the resultant understanding of the natural world. This fault is reductionism, the view
that effective understanding of a complex system can be achieved
by investigating the properties of its isolated parts." Commoner
goes on to say: "[reductionism is] the dominant viewpoint of
modern science as a whole. Reductionism tends to isolate scientific
disciplines from each other, and all of them from the real world."

Commoner etches a disturbing picture of human technology,
which provides power without purpose, means but no meaning.
Incapable of seeing the connection of one thing to another, its
hyperspecialization tries to solve problems without seeing either
the real causes or the necessary solutions.

Loren Eiseley, an anthropologist who writes with a prophet's
insight, carries the same unsettling message in *The Unexpected
Universe*. Describing man's talent for creating difficulties for himself, Eiseley points out that each time science solves a problem, it
creates two new ones. Like Commoner, he indicts reductionism
and its accompanying fragmentation as the culprits.

In the 1950s, I worked on overseas construction jobs in Thule,
Greenland, and Point Barrow, Alaska. I got to know some of the
Eskimos in Thule and Barrow and spent some time studying their
cultures. Like all nonliterate groups, they originally saw everything
as a unity. Their families, friends, and work, the animals, the land,
the sea, and God as they understood him were all one. To the degree that they have been influenced by our technology and culture,
that sense of unity has been shattered, and problems similar to
ours have been created. As their culture fragmented, they became
fragmented. Like many peoples in transition between two cultures,
the Barrow Eskimos seemed to adopt the worst aspects of both.

During those years, my AA came primarily from the Big
Book. Many times, I've seen in Chapter Five: "Those who do not
recover are people who cannot or will not completely give themselves to this simple program. . . " Is recovery simply not drinking?
Not at all. Those early AAs, who understood so well the need for
thoroughness, wrote on page 82: "We feel a man is unthinking
when he says that sobriety is enough." With precise clarity, these
same sober drunks defined our objective on page 77: "Our real
purpose is to fit ourselves to be of maximum service to God and the
people about us."

In AA, we find some conventional wisdom that has flourished
through the years, but on examination is seen to have absolutely no

connection with the program. "There are no musts," for example. Despite the frequency of such phrases in the Big Book as: "If we are planning to stop drinking there *must* be no reservation of any kind" and "We *must* not shrink at anything," we hear AAs declare there are no musts at all. In my experience, "There are no musts" only for those members who never bothered to find out what the program is really about.

Each Step of the twelve is connected to every other Step, and they work as a unity. With deafening consistency, we hear that these are "suggested" Steps. Again, nowhere do we read this in the Big Book. "Here are the steps we took, which are suggested as a program of recovery:" (page 59). Totally different. What's suggested is a program of Twelve Steps. Used honestly and thoroughly, they provide precise results.

Certainly it's my privilege to use part of them, none of them, or all of them. Regardless of my approach, I'm still a member of this Fellowship. Tradition Three guarantees this. It seems to me that considerable confusion arises on this point, however. I don't have to do anything to be a member of AA. On the other hand, to follow the program and get the results it guarantees, there are a number of things I *must* do.

It's my right to use six of the Steps, three of them, or none at all, but what I have then is something other than the AA program. At that point, what I have is my own invention. It's a product of

November 1973

my own arrogant stupidity and my unwillingness, once again, to pay attention and follow directions. It's the kind of blindness T. S. Eliot must have meant when he observed, "Many people think they're emancipated when, in reality, they're only unbuttoned."

A fragmented program will leave me fragmented. Using part of the prescription produces inadequate results. "Those who do not recover are people who cannot or will not completely give themselves to this simple program. . ." My life is a totality, and long ago it became obvious that it can't be compartmentalized. Dishonesty in one area creates problems in another area. Healing in one segment provides better health in another. It *is* all connected. Each Step blends with another in an integrated, comprehensive program designed to transform you and me into human beings capable of willingly and joyously doing God's will.

One of the worst bits of advice I ever got was to work the first nine Steps *once* and then try to subsist on the last three for the rest of my life. That is simply another form of fragmentation. Redoing every one of the Steps provides results I never experienced with the other method. The demands of the program are simple, precise, and specific. The guarantees are equally precise and specific. Viewing each of us as a totality, rather than a collection of slightly related parts, the program speaks to our conditions wherever we are in sobriety. The Steps enable us to move from where we are within ourselves toward the place we belong.

Loren Eiseley once wrote of a Brazilian fish with a two-lensed eye. The upper lens examines the world of sunlight and air, while the lower inspects the water depths in which the fish swims. Said Eiseley: "Now the fish, we might say, looks simultaneously into two worlds of reality, though what he makes of this divided knowledge we do not know. In the case of man, although there are degrees of seeing, we can observe that the individual has always possessed the ability to see beyond naked reality into some other dimension, some place outside the realm of what might be called 'facts.'"

Seeing my life with the "two-lensed eye" created by persistent work with the Steps, I can be at ease in the swiftly changing society where I make my living because part of my vision is focused on the timeless world opened to me by AA's eternal truths. AA works, but it does *not* work on my terms. A fragmented, "individual" program is destined to bring only partial recovery and leave me as bewildered and lost as my Eskimo friends in Point Barrow.

On the other hand, with lives grounded in eternal principles, "We will comprehend the word serenity and we will know peace. ...Fear of people and of economic insecurity will leave us. We will intuitively know how to handle situations that used to baffle us" (pages 83 and 84 in the Big Book). What happens outside me is far less important than what's happening inside. My being *does* attract my life; repeated work with each of the Twelve Steps generates changes within me that are reflected in improvements around me. Simple, but not always easy, the AA program gives me everything needed to become what I should be. Finally, there is no you or me or them. Everything *is* connected to everything else, and the salvation of each of us is linked to the salvation of all of us.

P. M., Riverside, Ill.

When the Big 'I' Becomes Nobody

by Harry M. Tiebout, MD

September 1965

T HE AA PROGRAM OF HELP is touched with elements of true inspiration, and in no place is that inspiration more evident than in the selection of its name, Alcoholics Anonymous. Anonymity is, of course, of great protective value, especially to the newcomer; but my present target is to focus on the even greater value anonymity has in contributing to the state of humility necessary for the maintenance of sobriety in the recovered alcoholic.

My thesis is that anonymity, thoughtfully preserved, supplies two essential ingredients to that maintenance. The two ingredients, actually two sides of the same coin, are: first, the preservation of a reduced ego; second, the continued presence of humility or humbleness. As stated in the Twelfth Tradition of AA, "Anonymity is the spiritual foundation of all our Traditions," reminding each member to place "principles before personalities."

Many of you will wonder what that word ego means. It has so many definitions that the first task is to clarify the nature of the ego needing reduction.

This ego is not an intellectual concept, but a state of feeling —
a feeling of importance — of being "special." Few people can recognize this need to be special in themselves. Most of us, however,
can recognize offshoots of this attitude and put the proper name to
it. Let me illustrate. Early in the AA days, I was consulted about a
serious problem plaguing the local group. The practice of celebrating a year's sobriety with a birthday cake had resulted in a
certain number of the members getting drunk within a short period
after the celebration. It seemed apparent that some could not stand
prosperity. I was asked to settle between birthday cakes and no
birthday cakes. Characteristically, I begged off, not from shyness,
but from ignorance. Some three or four years later, AA furnished
me the answer. The group no longer had such a problem, because,
as one member said, "We celebrate still, but a year's sobriety is
now a dime a dozen. No one gets much of a kick out of that any
more!"

A look at what happened shows us ego, as I see it, in action.
Initially, the person who had been sober for a full year was a stand-
out, someone to be looked up to. His ego naturally expanded; his
pride flowered; any previous deflation vanished. With such a re-
newal of confidence, he took a drink. He had been made special

January 1967

"You're kidding! Practice these principles a day at a time?
Remember, our days are six months long!"

and reacted accordingly. Later, the special element dropped out. No ego feeds off being in the dime-a-dozen category, and the problem of ego build-up vanished.

Today, AA in practice is well aware of the dangers of singling anyone out for honors and praise. The dangers of reinflation are recognized. The phrase "trusted servant" is a conscious effort to keep that ego down, although admittedly some servants have a problem in that regard.

Now let us take a closer look at this ego which causes trouble. The feelings associated with this state of mind are of basic importance in understanding the value of anonymity for the individual — the value of placing him in the rank and file of humanity.

Certain qualities typify this ego which views itself as special and therefore different. It is high on itself and prone to keep its goals and visions at the same high level. It disdains what it sees as grubs who plod along without the fire and inspiration of those sparked by ideals lifting people out of the commonplace and offering promise of better things to come.

Often the same ego operates in reverse. It despairs of man, with his faults and his failings, and develops a cynicism which sours the spirit and makes of its possessor a cranky realist who finds nothing good in this vale of tears. Life never quite meets his demands upon it, and he lives an embittered existence, grabbing what he can out of the moment, but never really part of what goes on around him. He seeks love and understanding and prates endlessly about his sense of alienation from those around him. Basically, he is a disappointed idealist — forever aiming high and landing low. Both of these egos confuse humbleness with humiliation.

To develop this further, the expression "You think you're something" nicely catches the sense of being above the crowd. Children readily spot youngsters who think they are something, and do their best to puncture that illusion. For instance, they play a game called tag. In it, the one who is tagged is called "it." You've heard them accuse each other saying, "You think you're it," thereby charging the other with acting as though he was better than his mates. In their own way, children make very good therapists or head-shrinkers. They are skillful puncturers of inflated egos, even though their purpose is not necessarily therapeutic.

AA had its start in just such a puncturing. Bill W. always refers to his experience at Towns Hospital as a "deflation in great depth" and on occasion has been heard to say that his ego took a "hell of a licking." AA stems from that deflation and that licking.

Clearly, the sense of being special, of being "something," has its dangers, its drawbacks for the alcoholic. Yet the opposite, namely, that one is to be a nothing, has little counter appeal. The individual seems faced with being a something and getting drunk, or being a nothing and getting drunk from boredom.

The apparent dilemma rests upon a false impression about the namely, that one is to be a nothing, has little counter-appeal. The selves as nothing is not easily developed. It runs counter to all our desires for identity, for an apparently meaningful existence, one filled with hope and promise. To be nothing seems a form of psychological suicide. We cling to our somethingness with all the strength at our command. The thought of being a nothing is simply not acceptable. But the fact is that the person who does not learn to be as nothing cannot feel that he is but a plain, ordinary, everyday kind of person who merges with the human race — and as such is humble, lost in the crowd, and essentially anonymous. When that can happen, the individual has a lot going for him.

People with "nothing" on their minds can relax and go about their business quietly and with a minimum of fuss and bother. They can even enjoy life as it comes along. In AA, this is called the 24-hour program, which really signifies that the individual does not have tomorrow on his mind. He can live in the present and find his pleasure in the here and now. He is hustling nowhere. With nothing on his mind, the individual is receptive and open-minded.

The great religions are conscious of the need for nothingness if one is to attain grace. In the New Testament, Matthew (18:3) quotes Christ with these words: "Truly I say to you, unless you turn and become like children, you will never enter the kingdom of heaven. Whoever humbles himself like this child, he is the greatest in the kingdom of heaven."

Zen teaches the release of nothingness. A famous series of pictures designed to show growth in man's nature ends with a circle enclosed in a square. The circle depicts man in a state of nothingness; the square represents the framework of limitations man must learn to live within. In this blank state, "Nothing is easy, nothing hard," and so Zen, too, has linked nothingness, humbleness, and grace.

Anonymity is a state of mind of great value to the individual in maintaining sobriety. While I recognize its protective function, I feel that any discussion of it would be one-sided if it failed to em-

phasize the fact that the maintenance of a feeling of anonymity —
of a feeling "I am nothing special" — is a basic insurance of humility and so a basic safeguard against further trouble with alcohol. This kind of anonymity is truly a precious possession.

Truth

August 1973

THE WORDS "YE SHALL KNOW the truth and the truth shall
make you free" have echoed through time for two thousand
years. Hands to ears, humanity has fled them ever since they were
spoken.

If you don't believe me, hold a discussion meeting on the subject of truth or honesty or communication, and see what happens.
Unless your group is highly unusual — and you are highly deter-
mined — within minutes the discussion will bog down in the comfortable rut of cash-register honesty.

"...Seven years later, I sent that bartender a check," someone will proudly say in concluding an anecdote.

"Not me!" another will reply. "The liquor industry got
enough out of me — I'm not repaying a cent!"

Unless the discussion is reined in sharply, it will canter lazily
back to the barn without much benefit to anyone, you realize. So
you suggest more emphasis on truthfulness per se, rather than fis-
cal responsibility. Immediately, someone will point out that truth
must be used discreetly; someone else will offer, as an illustration,
his anger over a truthful but harsh remark; and — presto! — you
are not discussing truth anymore, but resentment.

You try once again. "But don't you think being honest in *all*
our dealings is important?" you ask desperately.

The clamorous response to this even awakens the drunk sleeping it off in the back row. Everyone is furious, the assumption
being that you have demanded a mass orgy of public confession
during which their darkest sins will be revealed for group vilifica-
tion. If you are lucky, someone will bring up the Fifth Step or the
anonymity Traditions before you are lynched.

I have only gradually come to view truth as the most beautiful and accessible aspect of Harmony, or It, or God. This mass fear of it would surprise me more if I had not once felt the same way. Before AA, I had a go-around with psychiatry. I frequently complained that, although I arrived at the doctor's office with green eyes and pink cheeks, after a tearful bout with truth I left with pink eyes and green cheeks. "And for this, I'm *paying* you!" I would conclude furiously.

I felt then, as many of us do, that the full revelation of "the real me" could result only in total rejection by those who saw it. I remembered a film version of Oscar Wilde's "The Picture of Dorian Gray," the story of a man who makes a pact with the devil, in return for which he lives on unchanged forever, while his shrouded portrait bears the visible ravages of time and depravity. At the conclusion of the black-and-white film, Dorian draws back the curtain and the picture of a monstrous, barely human creature is revealed in color, unbelievably horrible.

Although Dorian presumably practiced every form of evil for a long period, and I was barely thirty, I was convinced that I, too, harbored within me a Dorian Gray who, once displayed publicly, would end forever my chance for acceptance. Gradually, however, in the course of therapy, the curtain began to slip aside, until finally the truth of "the real me" was revealed. When I mustered up the courage — and it took a lot — to look fully at the self I had run from all my life, I saw, not Dorian Gray, not Ilse Koch, not even Madame Defarge, but an average American housewife! My relief was overwhelming. True, as I began to look more closely, I noticed serious flaws: I was an alcoholic; I was neurotic; I was brimful of character defects. But these were things that, in time and with help, could be dealt with. No longer did I have to run with nightmarish terror from an inner monster. I had seen the truth, and the truth had freed me to do less hiding and more seeking.

The effort to escape from truth is the father of anxiety. Consider the man who lies awake at night wondering whether his chest pains are the result of indigestion or heart trouble. If he fears going to a doctor to find out, he is carrying a burden he may not have to carry at all. Even if he finds that it *is* his heart, he is free to deal with reality and take precautions that may save his life. Truth has not hurt, but healed.

A world where truth does not shine is a world filled with fog and cobwebs, a gray miasma through which we run blind and lost and terrified, tripping over roots we do not see, dodging the threat of looming shapes, remaining separated from our fellows in the dripping, fear-filled darkness.

The world of truth is the world of what is, the world of the Spanish lime tree outside my window, wearing sunshine like a halo. It is the room I sit in, the sleeping kitten, the job that must be done, the pleasure to be had or planned for. It is here. It is now. It is what is. It is my world, my truth, my reality, and in it I am no longer "a stranger and afraid/In a world I never made."

True, this world of mine contains ingredients I do not like — pain, grief, anger, fear, tragedy, But these are the things I must accept, because they are part of the totality and I cannot change them. I wasted years escaping into the unreality of alcoholism. Until I faced the truth that I could not drink, I was alone in the fog and the silence.

Before I learned to love truth, I had to learn to recognize it. Truth is not an immutable absolute, a granite peak, eternal, unmoving, hiding its head in a nimbus of clouds. Truth is a ballerina tracing arabesques in a pattern of color and music, ever-changing, harmonious.

Truth is totality: question-and-answer, nail-and-hammer, inside-and-outside. It is never narrow or sectarian. It is not blind, because its own radiance banishes obscurity.

Truth is multifaceted, because it is reality. Your truth and mine are different, because we are different. Your beliefs are your truth, as mine are mine. When that is accepted, any cause for conflict between us is resolved. Neither of us is right or wrong. We simply hold different pieces of the incredible jigsaw puzzle of life, and each piece has its place.

Truth is immediate. What was true yesterday is no longer true today, and tomorrow is not born yet. Today — now — is truth. What is happening all over the world at this moment is truth, and no part is "truer" than any other part. We are all equal shareholders in reality. For an individual or group to believe he or it has captured the whole of truth is absurd.

When truth is so beautiful, why do we embrace the lie? As a practicing alcoholic, I escaped into nontruth because I felt ill-equipped to cope with reality. And yet the "reality" I perceived was a lie, too. I was escaping from one lie to another, seemingly more pleasant. Because I felt, sober, that I was unlovable, ugly, awkward, and flawed, surrounded by hostile strangers who were devoting their entire attention to spotting my inadequacies, I got drunk. Then, for a while, I felt confident and safe enough from others to enjoy them and myself. Is it any wonder that I fought against returning to the ugly "reality" that sobriety seemed to offer?

When I finally accepted the fact that I couldn't drink, that the solace and fun I had found in alcohol were no longer there for me, I turned to AA to show me how to live in that hostile, terrifying, sober world I had deserted many years before. Having found the first truth, I now had to find others: that people were not hostile; that they were not looking for my flaws, but were much more concerned with their own; that, though reality presented many challenges, it had also provided me with the means to deal with them; and that the rewards of dealing with them were multifold — self-respect, a sense of accomplishment, ability to accept responsibility, tolerance, and, most of all, a feeling of being in step with my world. I had begun to grow up. I had found more truth.

Now I search for truth — for the reality I can deal with, rather than the nightmare I cannot. If a snake is coiled in my living room, I want him out where I can see him — not hiding in the shadows, waiting, while I reach for another drink and pretend he isn't there.

What we really fear is not truth, but the lie, as I did when "reality," *as I mistakenly viewed it,* chased me into alcoholism. I have found that it is not wise to accept everything at face value — it is often lazy or stupid.

The concept that a little truth goes a long way, that truth hurts, never ceases to surprise me, since I have found that truth protects. Suppose a "friend" comes up to you at a party and asks, "Why did you ever buy that dress? It's a horrible color for you." Is that the truth? It may or may not be. Only other opinions will help determine that, and you can get them from people whose opinions you respect. If everyone agrees with the "friend," you have been spared looking unattractive — get the darned thing dyed, and look pretty! If no one agrees with her, don't stop there — recognize that your "friend" may be spiteful, cruel, or jealous, and if she is, you are better off without her.

If someone at the office brings you a rumor that a cutback is impending and you will be the first to go, don't just stand there getting ulcers — find out the truth while there is still time to seek another job. Don't agonize over truth or turn your back on it — use it!

When it comes to telling others the truth, I have a few simple

rules. First, I ask myself whether telling it is necessary and whether it will help. Truth is not a bludgeon to be used indiscriminately. If the truth is unwanted, speaking out is often premature. When I am *asked* for an opinion or advice, I give it to the best of my ability with as much gentleness, understanding, and tolerance as I can scrape up. I do not misuse the request by unloading a backlog of resentment and criticism, and I never, never use the confidence as ammunition against the person in the future, in talking either with him or to others about him. I have been honored with a confidence, and I must treat it as the precious thing it is.

On the rare occasions when I feel I *must* offer unsolicited advice, I try to remember that I am paying a compliment. I am saying, in effect, "You have a serious problem that must be dealt with, and I am taking the liberty of pointing it out to you because I am sure you have the wisdom and ability to deal with it. I have confidence in you." Truth presented in this way is reinforcing and seldom resented for long. Honesty in dealing *kindly* with oneself and others does not backfire.

In one way only is truth an absolute: *Without it, there can be no growth.* Truth is to inner space what sunshine is to a garden. In its absence, fear flourishes and imagination runs riot, conjuring up pursuing monsters where there are only paper dragons. I wonder why it takes so long to realize that nightmares can never be outdistanced, simply because *they do not exist.* Unreality cannot be coped with precisely because it is unreal. Only when we open our minds and hearts to the truth can we expose our paper dragons for what they are — a child's forgotten toys.

Truth liberates. Truth heals. Truth unlocks the door to the glory of reality, and gives us the means to live in harmony with reality. In return, it asks only that we surrender all lies and illusions and love what is. Why do we wait so long?

J. W., Key West, Fla.

Action and More Action

January 1978

T HE ONE THING THAT POPS INTO my mind most often when I think of the Big Book of Alcoholics Anonymous is the incredible number of times it mentions giving this program away to keep it.

This month, I am celebrating my sixth AA birthday, and I've made a decision to pick up the Big Book daily and read something to strengthen my sobriety. The treasures that I'm finding are very rewarding.

I like the way Bill and Dr. Bob, co-founders of AA, carried the message to the third member. On page 186, they say, "We have a program whereby we think we can stay sober. Part of that program is that we take it to someone else, that needs it and wants it." This cleared up a misconception that I've heard at several AA meetings: "AA is for those that want it, not for those that need it." In fact, I was guilty of saying that a number of times until I read Dr. Bob's story. He says on page 180, "I spend a great deal of time passing on what I learned to others who want and need it badly."

Twelfth-stepping has always been one of AA's attractions to me. When I bought the Big Book, my first week in AA, I remember turning to the chapter "Working with Others," reading and rereading it, and dreaming that some day I might be able to help someone with an alcoholic problem. I am aware that not too many members care to go out on Twelfth Step calls. One of the reasons I hear is "I gave up after a few tries. I guess they weren't ready yet." What if Bill and Dr. Bob had given up? Where would we be now? The chapter "A Vision for You" tells how the early AAs experienced a few distressing failures, but knew they must help other alcoholics if they wanted to remain sober.

I'm so grateful to know that God has chosen me to help carry the message to alcoholics. When I was drinking, I was in a wreck that totaled my car. The damage was so bad that my right front wheel wound up next to me in the front seat. There was no room in the car for anyone else to survive, yet my life was spared. I am another miracle among many in this beautiful Fellowship of miracles.

I keep involved in the AA program, trying to give back a little of what I have received so freely. Whenever I go to a meeting, I like to arrive early and stay late. I like the face-to-face sharing before and after the meetings. That way, I get to meet the new members and give them a warm welcome, a handshake, and a smile.

Both in and out of meetings, some of the promises the Big Book makes on pages 83 and 84 are beginning to come true. I found another one on page 100: "You. . . must walk day by day in the path of spiritual progress. If you persist, remarkable things will happen." I read things like that, and I keep hearing that it gets better and better the longer I stay sober, and I'm not kidding — if it gets much better, I'll bust! When I was sober two years, I was told, "You ain't seen nothin' yet!" Then, this month, after six glorious years of sobriety, one of my sponsors said, "You have barely scratched the surface!" All of the rewards that I'm receiving are much more than I'm giving. I'm so very grateful for Alcoholics Anonymous.

By looking into the Big Book daily, I am learning how to stay on that path that the first one hundred members cleared for me. Whenever I get down in the dumps, or feeling low, I think of "Bill's Story," on page 15, when he was full of self-pity and resentment during his trying times: "When all other measures failed, work with another alcoholic would save the day."

One of the ways I stay active is on our local H&I (hospital and institution) committee of AA. We carry the message to those who are confined. When I share my story at a jail or hospital, I talk about how AA has helped me stay sober, how I couldn't do it alone. I read the beginning of Chapter 3 — they always seem to identify with that. In many cases, I've found people who want help and honestly don't want to drink any more. In our book *Twelve Steps and Twelve Traditions,* on page 109, it says, "The joy of living is the theme of AA's Twelfth Step, and action is its key word."

The Big Book's chapter "Working with Others" says (on page 89), "Carry this message to other alcoholics! . . . Life will take on new meaning. To watch people recover, to see them help others, to watch loneliness vanish, to see a fellowship grow up about you, to have a host of friends — this is an experience you must not miss." It is these things that keep me going back for more, because each one of them has happened before my eyes.

I see a lot of sick alcoholics just coming off one in detox centers. Most of them say that they have tried AA but it didn't work for them. A doctor in AA told me to ask them, when they say that, if they have attended thirty consecutive AA meetings and at half of those gotten active with emptying ashtrays, stacking chairs, helping to clean up after the meeting, etc. Usually, that questions rings a bell when I ask it at a meeting. Afterward, one man will come up to me and say he thinks that's the reason he slipped — he hadn't been active. "How can I help?" he will ask.

If you really want to get into action, and you have already taken Steps One, Two, and Three, and you honestly know that you should do Step Four, but you keep putting it off (the way I did), I suggest that you get moving right now. Open the Big Book and start at the bottom of page 63: "We launched out on a course of vigorous action." For those who say, "Oh, I've taken the Steps": turn to page 88, where it says, "But this is not all. There is action and more action." For me, that's what this program is all about. That's the magic word — *action!*

June 1977

"Do I have time to run below and get my copy of the Big Book?"

One of the best suggestions that I received early in my program, I'd like to pass on to others. I heard this from an old-timer in AA with lots of good sobriety. He held up four fingers and said, "AA is a simple program. There are four things you should do. One, put the plug in the jug. Two, go to plenty of AA meetings. Three, ask for help in the morning, and four, say thank-you at night." I'd like to add one more thing to that list to make it five: Get into action as soon as possible.

H. R., Millbrae, Calif.

The Big Book: One-Shot Deal or Constant Companion?

March 1972

SOME AA MEMBERS VOICE THE OPINION that the book *Alcoholics Anonymous* can be sufficiently absorbed at the first reading, that the Big Book contains little or nothing to repay later reference or study. This may be true for geniuses gifted with instant comprehension and total recall. Yet capable nonalcoholic attorneys must refer frequently to basic source books. The same is true of engineers, navigators, editors, and surgeons. Is it possible that alcoholic brains, only recently groggy and confused with malnutrition, resentment, anxiety, and disastrous convictions, can permanently retain the essentials of a 575-page volume after only one exposure?

One thing is certain: I do not have such a powerful learning capacity as that. I frequently find it necessary to refer to our Big Book. Like many others, I often get the impression that changes have been made in the text since I last referred to it. Sentences have been added, meanings have been altered, and other statements that I recall with great clarity have somehow been deleted without a trace.

There are two possible explanations for this:

1. While I am asleep, gnomes sneak into my house and cleverly make revisions on their tiny Linotype machines and printing presses, even duplicating the marginal notes which I put there months before in my own handwriting! Or...

2. My memory is fallible, and also — if I am being restored to sanity, as the Big Book promises in Step Two, and if the program is giving me spiritual progress (page 60) — I may actually be aware of meanings that escaped me on my previous reading.

The gnome theory has its appeal. It is less damaging to the ego to believe privately in elves than to entertain the possibility that I could be wrong.

Prankish though the gnomes may be, they are invariably benevolent. So far, all their changes have been helpful. And the gnomes who tamper with *my* book seem to make identical changes in the Big Books of other members who constantly refer to *their* copies.

In addition to correcting my own erratic memory, there is another reason I must occasionally reread the Big Book. I hear statements from AA speakers that confuse me. For example, in our area we often hear it said, "There are no musts in AA."

Such speakers evidently have a copy of the Big Book that has not yet been "defaced" by the gnomes. All through my copy, I find musts, sometimes three or four on a page. Here are a few (the italics are mine):

"If we are planning to stop drinking, there *must* be no reservation of any kind, nor any lurking notion that someday we will be immune to alcohol" (page 33).

". . . We *must* find a spiritual basis of life — or else" (44).

"Above everything, we alcoholics *must* be rid of this selfishness. We *must*, or it kills us!" (62)

". . . We *must* be willing to make amends. . ."(69)

". . . We ask that we be given strength and direction to do the right thing, no matter what the personal consequences may be. . . We *must* not shrink at anything." (79)

These are only a handful of the scores of musts scattered through the Big Book. Along with them are hundreds of other phrases containing words like "absolutely," "necessary," "completely," "essential," and "without fail." These words imply musts to any mind not looking for a loophole or an escape hatch.

Admittedly, these musts are not forced on the newcomer by any "big shots" in AA or by any manmade law or regulation. In that sense, there *are* no musts; we alcoholics are free to drink, free to disregard the Twelve Steps. For doing so, we will not be fined or kicked out of the Fellowship. All that will happen to us is that we will go mad or die.

If we don't try to make this consequence clear to new men and

women, we are cheating them.

A few years ago, a fairly successful Los Angeles businessman, sober a few weeks, had to go back to Detroit on a company matter. There, he would meet some of his old drinking pals. At an AA meeting one night, he triumphantly told a friend of mine that he had read the Big Book and discovered there was no reason why he couldn't have a few highballs with the boys. His proof? "It doesn't say in the Big Book that you can't drink in Detroit!"

True. For that matter, neither did it say he couldn't drink right here in Los Angeles. Or Dallas. Or Pine Gulch. But he had found what he was looking for: a loophole.

Another statement I sometimes hear from AA speakers is that, since *they* have never taken an inventory, Step Four isn't necessary. Others say it isn't necessary to write out our inventories. Some cite themselves as living proof that Step Five can be skipped.

If I don't consult the Big Book, I might assume their statements were gospel. But the book says, "If we skip this vital step [Number Five], we may not overcome drinking. Time after time newcomers have tried to keep to themselves certain facts about their lives... Almost invariably they got drunk."

Contrary to the advice given from the podium by some speakers, the Big Book repeatedly stresses the importance of *writing* the inventory: "making a list"... "setting it down on paper"... "We consulted our list of names."

From my own experience, I know I need the Big Book, not only to correct errors innocently planted by other members, but to bring into line my own misconceptions about what I *thought* the speakers were saying.

In listening to tapes of my own AA talks, I am often horrified at my incoherence and at the discovery that I did not say what I intended to say or what I *thought* I was saying. Then I pray that newcomers will not judge the AA program by what I have told them. God, how I hope they will read the Big Book! — not once, but many times.

Often, at meetings, I'll hear a member tell a newcomer, "All you have to do is keep the plug in the jug."

The Big Book (pages 82-83) says, "We feel a man is unthinking when he says that sobriety is enough. . . There is a long period of reconstruction ahead. . . The spiritual life is not a theory. *We have to live it.*" (Another implied must.)

Does one reading of the Big Book equip us with enough information to judge the validity of statements tossed out in an informal conversation or an extemporaneous talk?

The newcomer sometimes hears this statement from people that he, in his innocence, may consider experts: "Take what you like in AA, and forget the rest."

Does it make sense to tell a newcomer, devoted to the alcoholic principle of "self-will run riot," that his own sick, confused mind (which repeatedly got him drunk and into trouble) is the mind capable of judging what is good for him?

The Big Book suggests (page 98), "Burn the idea into the consciousness of every man that he can get well regardless of anyone. The only condition is that he trust in God and clean house."

The new person may be looking for a way to drink without disaster and to get family, employer, creditors, and the law off his back. With that goal in his boozy brain, is one reading of the Big Book, or any part of it, likely to convince him of the nature of his illness, or to make clear the requirements of the AA recovery program?

Rereading of the book may be of great value even beyond maintaining personal sobriety. Because of the success of Alcoholics Anonymous, members are invited increasingly to participate in the activities of other organizations and agencies in the field of alcoholism. Some of these worthy organizations have as their proper goal the providing of housing, food, and other material assistance to various unfortunate persons, including alcoholics. Of necessity, these agencies must be supported by outside contributions, including tax subsidies. Unless AA members keep the AA name out of the operation, and serve the organization as individuals, they will create public misunderstanding as to the policy and purpose of AA.

Further, they will render it easy for the recipient of such services to assume he is receiving them as part of the AA program. Is this bad?

The Big Book, on page 98, says: "The minute we put our work on a service plane, the alcoholic commences to rely upon our assistance rather than upon God. He clamors for this or that, claiming he cannot master alcohol until his material needs are cared for. Nonsense. . . We simply do not stop drinking so long as we place dependence upon other people ahead of dependence on God."

The Big Book helps us explain to others where other aids leave off and AA begins. If that distinction is not observed by members, AA could become diluted and powerless to help the alcoholic.

As a writer, I am often amused at the reaction of other writers when they come to AA. When first sober, the writer frequently announces that he intends to donate his talent in a magnificent service to the Fellowship: He will rewrite the Big Book!

Unfortunately, his professional eye is focused more on achieving terse, flowing prose than on understanding AA principles. So the writer gets drunk before finding a better way of saying, "We admitted we were powerless over alcohol — that our lives had become unmanageable."

For some reason, those writers who remain sober get very busy in their own outside work and in various AA activities at the level of group, institutions, or general service. They seem never to have time to *rewrite* the Big Book. These sober writers do, however, seem to have time to re*read* it.

L. H., North Hollywood, Calif.

Promises, Promises

May 1981

I LOVE THE SO-CALLED PROMISES in the paragraph that begins at bottom of page 83 and continues at the top of page 84 of the Big Book. I frequently quote one or another of them. I often mention them in an AA qualification.

That's why I was pleased recently to receive a scroll containing "The Promises," inscribed in beautiful calligraphy, as a souvenir of an AA dinner I attended. And then, as I admired the scroll, it set me to thinking. We are certainly hearing more about "The Promises" these days. I've seen them printed in AA newsletters and bulletins and AA convention programs. I've heard members ask, "Why doesn't AA offer 'The Promises' as a wall plaque like the Steps and the Traditions? And maybe on a wallet card?"

Is this a trend in our Fellowship — this lifting the promises out of context and inscribing them in bronze? Are we sanctifying the promises?

If so, it troubles me. I view such a trend with alarm. Why?

Because, first of all, if we go back to the source and read the paragraph of the Big Book containing the promises, it is immediately clear that they were not intended to be set apart. They are not written as a separate element as are the Steps (page 59) or the Traditions (beginning page 564).

They are buried in the text (and within the context), and for a reason: *They are part of a discussion of how to work the Steps.* Not even all the Steps, really, but specifically the first nine. The paragraph in question follows a *long* description of the mess our alcoholic lives are in and advice on how to work our way out.

Second, these are not *unconditional* promises as they seem to be when set apart. Quite the contrary. They are a spontaneous, almost euphoric expression of the experiences of the authors with the rewards that can be expected "if we are painstaking about this phase of our development." What phase? The working of the first nine Steps as described in the preceding twenty-four pages!

And how many of us have actually worked the Steps that way? How many of us, for example, in doing our Fourth Step inventory, have followed the example in the Big Book? — a written "grudge list" in three separate columns, analyzing the causes of each resentment and how it affects us. Not I. How many of us took Steps Eight and Nine with the diligence and thoroughness recommended in detail from page 76 to page 83 in the Big Book? Not I. Yet we must recognize that that is what is meant by being "painstaking."

What the Big Book is saying on page 83 is that *if* we have bared our souls, *if* we have completely reconstructed our shattered relationships with others, *then* we "are going to know a new freedom...," *then* "we will not regret the past," and so on through the rest of the promises. In fact it says "they will always materialize *if we work for them*" (the italics are mine). And the rest of that chapter is devoted to telling us how to continue *to work for them* by practicing Steps Ten and Eleven.

Finally, it seems to me that when I quote the promises so glibly and smugly (as I am inclined to do), I may actually be playing down the Steps. Am I glorifying end results while ignoring the footwork necessary to get there? Is it easier and more comforting to take refuge in the promises (lifting them out of context, of course) than to go through the purging and the pain of taking the first nine Steps — which are clearly the prerequisites of the promises? The alcoholic seizes upon the promises, consciously or unconsciously, as "an easier, softer way."

So let's read and reread Chapters Five and Six (along with the rest of the Big Book, naturally!). And when we get to the beautiful section on pages 83 and 84, let's cherish the promised rewards set forth there. Let's carry them in our minds and hearts as a joyous and inspiring part of our program of recovery.

But let's not sanctify the promises.

R. P., Riverside, Conn.

What About This 24-Hour Plan?

January 1968

"THIS 24-HOUR PLAN IS THE slickest package of intellectual dishonesty and self-deception I've ever encountered! You tell me all I have to do is stay sober for one day — when I know darn well you expect me to give up drinking for life. Who's

kidding whom? And as to the 24-hour plan applied to 'all my affairs,' how the hell can I do a job if I don't plan ahead?''

These were the words I would like to have shouted at one and
all when I first came around AA. I didn't shout them only because
I didn't have the nerve. But I did mutter them to myself — angrily
and often.

In the intervening years, I have come to believe that the 24-
hour plan is the most exquisite prescription for productivity, serenity, and therefore happiness that man has ever devised. So let's, for
a few minutes, examine its whats and whys and hows and where-
fores.

First off, what does the 24-hour plan say? It says, ''Take your
life one day at a time. Whether it be staying away from a drink or
conducting any other activity in life, don't let yesterday or tomorrow distract you from what you can do today.''

In my drinking days, I had to live in the past or the future. I
wallowed alternately in the glow of yesterday's glories (mostly
imagined), and in remorse and resentment over yesterday's failures. Or I shored myself up with dreams of what I would do tomorrow, or tortured myself with fears of what I might fail to do.
But I couldn't live in today. That would have demanded more
action and accountability than I could marshal.

The 24-hour plan has been my key to escape from this limbo.
It is the art of living where we can act, of focusing our energies
down to the only pinpoint of time in which we can perform — this
living instant. This is the only instant in which I can do anything
about drinking or refusing to drink, the only instant in which I can
do anything about carrying the message or, for that matter, do
anything about any activity in my life.

VICTOR E.

Does this mean that I can't plan for the future? Assuredly not. It means that I can plan my actions, but not project the result. It means that if the most important thing I can do this instant (First Things First) is to plan something for tomorrow, next month, or next year, I should apply myself this instant and plan for tomorrow, next month, or next year.

Why does the 24-hour plan work? It has worked for me because it breaks life down into manageable segments — one at a time. You recall the old horse operas where the hero, beset by Indians, always retired to a narrow defile where he could take them on one at a time. And I recall that in my schooldays the rowing coach used to tell us, when we came to the *last* quarter-mile sprint, that we should forget about the quarter-mile still to go and just concentrate on getting that oar forward and back one more time.

The quarter-mile, the tribe of Indians, the span of life are not manageable. But the one stroke, the one Indian, the one day we can act on at this instant in time.

Another reason the 24-hour plan has worked for me is that it offers emotional rewards for success. If I say that I shall never take another drink as long as I live, I shall have to be on my deathbed before I know whether I made it. And if I get hit by a truck, I'll never know. So life has become an endless reaching for a goal which I may never have the satisfaction of knowing I reached. But if I decide I will not have a drink today, I know at the end of the day that I made it. This is an achievement and, like all achievements, yields satisfaction. I do the same day after day after day, and I am piling achievement on achievement and building an equity that becomes more precious — and therefore one I am less likely to give up — with every passing day.

February 1966

And achievement can be as addictive as alcohol. A little achievement feels good, so we stretch for a little more. The more we get, the more we want, and pretty soon we're hooked — hooked into a habit that's constructive, not destructive.

I had to make the 24-hour plan a habit. When I went at it haphazardly, it neither worked nor made sense. I didn't know the old truism that, with a recovering alcoholic, action has to come before understanding and faith. I hadn't learned that we have to act our way to right thinking, rather than the reverse.

In the last days of my drinking, I had no faith — no faith, at least, in the existence of a benevolent Higher Power. If there was any Higher Power at all, it had to be malevolent, else why would it have singled me out for deprivation of the most relaxing activity in life — drinking?

Thus, when my sponsor told me to thank God every morning for the preceding day and to ask help for the day ahead, I told him I didn't believe in God. His answer: "Do it anyway."

So I finally decided to put the 24-hour plan on a habitual basis. I would tie it to something I did every day — taking a shower, for instance. Every morning in the shower, I would set the structure for the 24-hour plan of that day. Gradually, this has evolved into quite a program. It probably wastes a lot of water, but at least water is cheaper than vodka.

The program goes something like this:

1. First, I thank God for my sobriety during the preceding day.

2. Next, I search my mind for something in the preceding day that I did better than I would have done before. Some little victory over a character defect — some little application of something I have learned in AA. And I thank God for it. This is part of the business of building an equity and making success addictive. But more than that, it is a specific for my most crippling handicap when I came to AA — lack of self-respect. The fact of making myself aware of something I did right each day has imperceptibly fertilized the very roots of my ailing self-respect.

3. Third, I say to myself that I am an alcoholic. I know that the human mind reflexively dims down unpleasant memories, and I am resolved to counteract this reflex, lest I should ever think I can safely drink again. So I picture a drink in my mind (usually a frosty martini) and then consciously recall some horrendous drinking incident. Now I have locked together in my mind the drink and the inevitable result. Having done this for several thousand mornings,

I believe it would not be possible to reach for a drink without at the same time seeing a full-color picture of the result. I have built my own counter-reflex.

4. Fourth, I decide not to take a drink during the coming day and ask God's help in carrying out that decision. In the early months and years, I would actually picture situations in the upcoming day where I knew I would be exposed to a drink — a business lunch with a group of heavy drinkers or an hour to kill in the Cleveland airport. I would visualize the forthcoming situation in detail, and say to myself, "I am deciding now (in the shower) that I will not have a drink when the situation occurs."

5. Last, I decide on "Today's Special." I came into AA with so many faults and character defects that I couldn't even count them. I still have a good portion of them. While intellectually I yearn to be rid of them, emotionally I still find them kind of fun. With this conflict going on, the problem of working on them is like trying to shake hands with an octopus. So each morning I pick one fault or character defect that I am going to concentrate on for that day, and I ask God's help in making progress.

Naturally, this daily program did not arrive on my doorstep prefabricated. It evolved through doing.

Within a few months, it proved to me the existence of a benevolent Higher Power.

On the day in question, I knew I would be working late in the evening and have time to kill in Grand Central Station waiting for

a late commuter train. So, in my morning shower, I pictured the
situation in Grand Central, made the decision not to dash for my
usual row of doubles at the bar, and asked for help to stick to the
decision. The following morning, I was stunned to realize that I
had killed an hour reading the newspaper in the station without the
thought of a drink having entered my mind.

I might have been able to prevent a thought's turning into an
urge, or an urge's turning into action, but it took a Power far
greater than myself to bar even the thought from my consciousness.

From that day on, I believed.

These five "morning shower" steps may sound rather complex. All they really amount to is thanking God for sobriety and
growth, admitting to being an alcoholic, and asking help for further sobriety and growth — for just one day. Simple, yet if you will
examine the process, you will see it embodies every one of the
Twelve Steps except for the "carrying the message" part of the
Twelfth — for just one day.

Perhaps this is a slow way of gaining sobriety and growth.
But, after all, sobriety is a pretty recently planted sprout. If I act
impatient and tug at the topmost shoot to make it grow faster, I
may pull the whole thing out of the ground. But If I nurture the
roots day by day by day, I am likely to promote secure and healthy
growth.

Or, to put it another way, getting away from the pull of the
first drink is like putting a space vehicle in orbit. It takes a lot of
thrust to overcome the initial pull of gravity and get the vehicle off
the ground. But once it gets in orbit, all that's required is a small
correction from time to time. That's how the 24-hour plan works
— a small daily checkup and correction to keep us away from the
pull of that first drink.

The 24-hour plan is a discipline whose yield is freedom.

In my own efforts to apply the 24-hour plan, I have been so
bold as to do violence to the Serenity Prayer. I have added seven
words — and they are all the same word — "today."

God grant me
The serenity *today* to accept *today* the things I cannot change
today,
Courage *today* to change *today* the things I can *today*,
And the wisdom *today* to know the difference.

So this is the prescription for productivity, serenity, and therefore happiness that AA has given me. And this is the reason I can say from the bottom of my heart, "Thank God I am an alcoholic."

Religions and sects, other movements and fellowships have their codes of behavior. Their members can take them or leave them alone. Application is not a matter of life or death. But we in AA have our 24-hour plan, and our incentive to apply it is life itself.

B. P. Manhattan, N.Y.

A Selfish Program?

November 1963

HOW MANY TIMES HAVE WE HEARD this expression and perhaps wondered how anything selfish can be good for us? How can we acquire humility, gain sincerity, overcome resentments, be strictly honest with ourselves and others, and be selfish?

I believe we associate selfishness with meanness, thinking of one's self in terms of material advantages, and living for one's own comfort and desires. Also, we have abused ourselves so much during our drinking careers that to give ourselves some real earnest thought and attention is hard to comprehend at first.

Actually, being selfish in the AA sense is an entirely different matter, and here is the writer's opinion of it, after being sober long enough to think things through and able to remember enough not to take that first drink.

There is an old saying, "Self-preservation is the first law of Nature." To paraphrase this, I should say, "To be selfish about our AA program is life itself" for us. If we preserve ourselves, we are not being selfish at all. Everyone associated with us, our family, friends, employer, employees, the community as a whole benefits accordingly, and we regain our rightful place in society. We are thoughtful of others, take care of our obligations, assume our proper responsibilities, and become respectable human beings instead of walking zombies or vegetables, as we were when we drank.

Yes, this is a selfish program, because it brings us back to "First Things First" one-day-at-a-time living, so fundamental to happiness.

I need to remind myself that I was always equivocating and procrastinating when I drank, about what I was going to do tomorrow, next week, or next year. I was a world-beater at a bar or over a bottle, but I know now I actually did very little about today, or any other day for that matter.

Being selfish about AA for ourselves restores our dignity as individuals. It makes many of us realize that in being married or in trying to give to family, job, or community, we many times subjugated our own personalities to meet the requirements of these social and worldly obligations. Too often we tried to fortify ourselves with alcohol to overcome our feelings of inferiority or inadequacy, but the result in time was just the reverse, and we became in effect more inadequate and definitely inferior.

Being selfish in AA means using our normal minds to think objectively and constructively about the things around us, something we could never do with our brains paralyzed by liquor.

Being selfish in AA further helps us to be big enough to overcome resentments, humble enough to overlook fancied slights and

October 1967

"It's his story, and he's telling it in his own way."

wrongs, honest enough to evaluate things in their true perspective, serene enough to accept the things we cannot change, and sensible enough to judge what the finer things of life really are, instead of chasing myths and material things!

Being selfish in AA also means taking a look at our environment, and the people we associate with. We no longer want to be argumentative and full of self-pity. Somehow, we slowly but surely cut loose from this sort of thing. It is time-consuming, it is destructive, it could lead to "stinking thinking." It is not the way we want to live anymore, and we do something constructive about it.

Gone are the fears, the tensions, the self-pity, the apprehensions. We become imbued each new day with vigor and hope, a clear conscience, a renewed strength of both body and spirit, and, last and most important, we receive the greatest gift of all, *peace of mind.*

It is simple, it is selfish, it is AA, and it works wonders.

F. R., Moorestown, N.J.

How AA Works

May 1972

CONTRARY TO THE ADVICE of the AAs who say, "Don't bother to find out why," I have always been curious as to why AA has had the success it has. As a man who's been around AA for a long time, I understand that AA cannot and does not help everybody. But it does offer the greatest help to the largest number of alcoholics of any system that has been offered to date. Why?

My friends ask, "What goes on at an AA meeting? How does it happen that a guy who was just throwing everything away has suddenly started to come back and is well and happy and is carrying his weight in the world?"

If I say, "Well, we meet together, we alcoholics," he says, "Yeah, yeah." So I say, "We have some speakers, and one of the speakers will get up and talk about his experiences and how AA helped him. Another guy will tell his experiences, and often we have a third fellow who sums up what the other two have said, and we say the Lord's Prayer, have coffee and doughnuts, and go home."

The guy says, "And *that* keeps you sober?"

Obviously, there's a great deal more at work to enable us to overcome the obsession with alcohol and the compulsion to drink. I offer you my own analysis, for what it's worth. You know there is no party line in AA; this analysis represents a distillation of what I've learned about myself and what I've heard at countless AA meetings.

It's this simple, I think: AA meets the needs of the alcoholic in a way that satisfies him. Let's examine these needs. They're no different, by the way, from the needs of all humanity; but by the time AA sees the alcoholic, these needs have become acute and hence are often more urgent, more present, more demanding than they are in the ordinary run of mankind.

The first of these needs is hope. If one word had been used to describe the alcoholic more often than any other, I suspect it is "hopeless." "John is a good guy, he's smart enough, he's able, he's bright, he's capable. But he can't stay sober; he's hopeless."

If that is repeated over and over again — John and other alcoholics do not live in a vacuum — we hear what is said. We shrug it off for a while, don't we? "A lot of bluenoses!" we say. We seek explanations outside ourselves: It was raining; it was clear weather; the team won; the team lost; Republicans won; Republicans lost; I made a lot of money; I lost a lot of money.

Always, there's the same delusion in the back of our minds: "I can quit." Finally, we get tired of this constant repetition, and we try to stop. We can't. Anxiety gives way to panic, panic to depression, depression to hopelessness. And we reach the point where we drink simply because we can't see any other way out, and we can't stand what is happening to us. Until that little flicker of hope is lighted in the alcoholic's heart, nothing is going to happen.

The greatest sin that one alcoholic can commit against another is to perpetuate the idea of hopelessness. Even if you find that *you* aren't the man or woman to help, never let him feel that he's hopeless. Let him feel that you haven't been the one who's able to supply the answers. If we turn our backs on the alcoholic, who in God's name — and I say this reverently — who in God's name is going to help him? You and I are the people who know from our own experience that there *is* hope, that alcoholics *can* come back from the very depths. This hope is the priceless ingredient for recovery. This, AA gives, most frequently not in mere words. Upon the alcoholic's first contact with AA, as he looks around the room and sees men and women respectably clothed and in their right minds, enjoying themselves, that flicker of hope begins to burn. And he says to himself, "If these jokers can do it, I can." The first need, beyond any other, is hope. Without it, there is nothing.

The second need — and this is almost as desperate, because it accompanies the first — is the need to be welcomed back into the human race. The alcoholic has experienced universal rejection. Every man's hand is against him; the doors of employment are closed; his friends do not invite him around anymore because he's a nuisance; sometimes the door of his own home is closed to him. And he begins to feel that horrible sensation that he is insignificant to every other living human being.

There are a few rare souls who can live in total solitude, but they are very rare. Most of us need some significance and importance in the eyes of others. We must have some meaning, be it only to one other person. And yet we often reach the point where we think nobody cares whether we live or die, except for the people who wish we *would* die.

Couple that feeling of utter loneliness with the feeling that you can't do anything about it, and you begin to understand the depths to which alcoholism reduces the individual. He becomes a man of no importance to anybody, in a situation from which he can find no escape. This is why the outstretched hand of AA is so vital.

In my work at the clinic, I heard hundreds of men tell about their first AA experiences, and over and over again it went something like this: "I told these guys I'd go to this meeting, and one of them came around to pick me up. We went, and they met on the second floor somewhere, and I stumbled up the steps and came into this room, and some guy was up front talking, but I couldn't hear what he said. A couple of guys shook my hand. Another one put his arm around my shoulder, and a third one gave me a cup of coffee. These guys had never seen me before — they didn't know me from a bag of beans — but all of a sudden I felt they liked me."

An elementary thing, you say? Of no importance? Nonsense! When you've been lost, lonely, forgotten, rejected, it's the most important thing in the world to have somebody shake your hand.

So we have first, hope; second, acceptance as a human being. Third, as we all know from our First Step, the alcoholic desperately needs to admit what's wrong with him. To us in AA, it isn't surprising that the drinking alcoholic doesn't know what's wrong with him, though everybody else does. But this is the nature of the disease, isn't it? It blinds us to what we're doing and what's happening to us. Oh yes, we know we're having some sort of trouble with alcohol, but we blame it on others; we look outside ourselves.

The Grapevine Through the Years

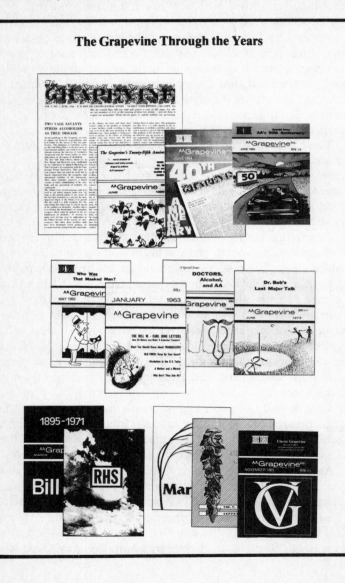

Here's another priceless gift that AA provides: frank, sometimes brutal, but loving confrontation with our problem. We give all our excuses, and the AA guys laugh at us. Even if your wife was as beautiful and loving as Venus (they say in effect), even if your boss was the most wonderful guy and was going to give you a raise, even if the Democrats were going to win next year, it wouldn't make any difference. You still couldn't drink! Over and over again, they tell us. The evidence is too strong to withstand, and finally they get us to admit that we are alcoholics.

We've got to begin here — but admission is just a cerebral function. When I was a reporter in Philadelphia, I often wrote about Joe Blow, who was arrested by the police beside the open door of a store, with a lot of stolen goods on him. But only after questioning would he admit the robbery. And that's what frequently happens in the case of the alcoholic. AA members back him into a corner he can't get out of. They use every argument until he finally says, "Okay, okay, I admit it — I'm an alcoholic."

The admission is not enough. Down inside, something is saying, "Yeah, but *if* I get my job back, my health back, *if* I get my wife back" — *if* this, *if* that — "I'll show these guys!" We talk a lot about resentment in AA. Here is the basic resentment of all we've got to deal with, the resentment that "I'm an alcoholic. Who am I that God should point his finger at me and tell me that I can't drink? My wife can drink, the kids can drink, the stupid guy next door who hasn't got enough sense to come in out of the rain can drink, and I can't. It's unfair. It's un-American!"

After admission, the alcoholic needs to learn acceptance. I first heard this beautiful word from Harry Tiebout, when he talked about surrender in AA. Acceptance is a different process — not a cerebral, but an emotional response to alcoholism: "Okay, I quit. I can't help it. There's nothing I can do about it."

Now the Serenity Prayer begins to take on a new meaning for this guy. This is one of the things he can't change. This is what he's asking serenity for — the basic serenity, to accept alcoholism and stop battling it. All of us who have gone through this move from admission to acceptance know the enormous weight that rolls from our shoulders when we can stand up and say, "I don't have to worry about being an alcoholic anymore. It's just the way I am. Like the color of my eyes." The alcoholic desperately needs to accept his own alcoholism.

Now there's another act of acceptance that has to take place, I think, and AA helps with this. The alcoholic has to accept himself. As you think back on your own life, as you think of the alcoholics with whom you've talked, haven't you discovered that all of us have a very naive conception of what it means to be a human being? At an AA meeting, I heard a guy say, "Before I came to AA, I used to be an idealist." The implication is that once he got into AA he threw all his ideals away. Well, this is not what he meant at all. He meant, "Before I got into AA, I was a Utopian." A Utopian is one who believes that human beings can be perfect. The speaker thought he could be perfect himself, so other people should be perfect. He found out they weren't, and so he settled for being a junior-grade cynic.

I often think of this in terms of William Steig's wonderful cartoon showing a dour old man sitting inside a box, with a caption saying, "People are no damn good." This is the attitude of many drinking alcoholics: People are no damn good, because they're not perfect.

AA teaches us the truth about people by letting us rub shoulders with it. For example, the newcomer soon finds out that his sponsor, perhaps idolized at first, puts his pants on one leg at a time — that he's a human being. The newcomer finds that the finest members still do make mistakes. He reads Step Ten and sees that the AA program isn't written for Utopians. It's written for human beings who are going to make mistakes over and over again. We make mistakes; we admit them; we try to clean up the mess we made; and we go on.

Finally, the alcoholic comes to the point where he can accept himself as a human being, with all his strengths and weaknesses — that mixture which we are — and live with himself, and once he is

VICTOR E.

tolerant of himself, he can be tolerant of other people. Now this, I say, is something that happens in AA. I'm convinced it's a vital part of growing up in AA.

Another of the alcoholic's needs is pointed out in the AA program strongly and emphatically: the need to accept God as each of us understands him. To somebody like me, born in a preacher's house, brought up on the Bible and church, it isn't very difficult to conceive what God is like. But for many alcoholics, it's a tough row to hoe. When I talk about the Twelve Steps, I counsel newcomers not to be surprised if Steps Two and Three do not happen overnight. We have to work into them and through them. For many of us, God is a somewhat threatening figure. To turn life and will over to a figure like that takes either courage or desperation.

A friend of mine is now about as spiritual-minded a man as I know. I heard him tell an AA group about his first efforts. He said, "I heard these other guys talk about it. I had to stay sober, so I said I'd give it a whirl." In the morning, he told us, he would get up and say, "Oh God, if you're there, help me stay sober." At night, when he got home, he'd say, "God, if you're there, thank you."

My own feeling is that this is the kind of approach God understands perfectly, and which he welcomes. But that isn't the end of the story. Hank went on with his prayers until one night, when he said, "Thank you," he swears he heard the answer, "You're welcome." He can't prove this. But you'll never make Hank believe it didn't happen.

Fortunately, AA never discusses theology, never talks about creeds, and never formulates any concept of the nature of the Deity to be forced upon anybody. But, whether we realize it or not,

July 1972

we in AA are practical theologians — we learn by doing. The first
inkling comes when we try to understand what AA is talking about
in the sign that hangs in countless meeting rooms all over the country — "But for the Grace of God." New members come to feel
that it isn't just the empty repetition of ritual. When a member
stands before a group and says, "I'm here tonight thanks to the
grace of God and AA," the first part of that phrase means something. What is it?

He begins to think back. When he first came up that flight of
stairs, he didn't know any of these guys. They didn't owe him anything. And yet he was welcomed. They did what they could for
him; they nurtured him, sustained him, criticized him, told him
where he was wrong, told him where he was right. Why? Some
people have waited three months for someone in AA to send them
a bill. This is natural. The motto of America is "Nothing for nothing. You pay for what you get." And yet we have been given life,
the most precious thing of all, which all the money in the world
cannot buy — nor all the intelligence, all the education, all the
position.

Why did these AAs do it? I think we all find an unavoidable
association between what AA does and the grace of God. AA re-
flects, in an limited, human sense, the way God works with us. AA
people love us when we're newcomers, not because of what we've
done, but in spite of it, not because we've earned love, but because
we need it. And so, I think, comes the final great acceptance of the
AA member: the realization that I have been accepted by God —
that, when I staggered up those stairs for the first time, God was
there waiting for me.

J. L., Santa Fe, N.M.

NOT ALLIED WITH ANY SECT OR DENOMINATION

The Bill W. — Carl Jung Letters

January 1963

HERE IS a vital chapter of AA's early history, first published in the Grapevine in January 1963, and reprinted in January 1968 and November 1974. This extraordinary exchange of letters revealed for the first time not only the direct historical ancestry of AA, but the bizarre situation wherein Jung, deeply involved with scientists and with a scientific reputation at stake, felt he had to be cautious about revealing his profound and lasting belief that the ultimate sources of recovery are spiritual. Permission to publish Dr. Jung's letter was granted to the Grapevine by the Jung estate.

January 23, 1961

My dear Dr. Jung:

This letter of great appreciation has been very long overdue.

May I first introduce myself as Bill W., a co-founder of the Society of Alcoholics Anonymous. Though you have surely heard of us, I doubt if you are aware that a certain conversation you once had with one of your patients, a Mr. Rowland H., back in the early 1930s, did play a critical role in the founding of our Fellowship.

Though Rowland H. has long since passed away, the recollection of his remarkable experience while under treatment by you has definitely become part of AA history. Our remembrance of

Rowland H.'s statements about his experience with you is as follows:

Having exhausted other means of recovery from his alcoholism, it was about 1931 that he became your patient. I believe he remained under your care for perhaps a year. His admiration for you was boundless, and he left you with a feeling of much confidence.

To his great consternation, he soon relapsed into intoxication. Certain that you were his "court of last resort," he again returned to your care. Then followed the conversation between you that was to become the first link in the chain of events that led to the founding of Alcoholics Anonymous.

My recollection of his account of that conversation is this: First of all, you frankly told him of his hopelessness, so far as any further medical or psychiatric treatment might be concerned. This candid and humble statement of yours was beyond doubt the first foundation stone upon which our Society has since been built.

Coming from you, one he so trusted and admired, the impact upon him was immense.

When he then asked you if there was any other hope, you told him that there might be, provided he could become the subject of a spiritual or religious experience — in short, a genuine conversion. You pointed out how such an experience, if brought about, might remotivate him when nothing else could. You did caution, though, that while such experiences had sometimes brought recovery to alcoholics, they were, nevertheless, comparatively rare. You recommended that he place himself in a religious atmosphere and hope for the best. This, I believe, was the substance of your advice.

Shortly thereafter, Mr. H. joined the Oxford Group, an evangelical movement then at the height of its success in Europe, and one with which you are doubtless familiar. You will remember their large emphasis upon the principles of self-survey, confession, restitution, and the giving of oneself in service to others. They strongly stressed meditation and prayer. In these surroundings, Rowland H. did find a conversion experience that released him for the time being from his compulsion to drink.

Returning to New York, he became very active with the "O.G." here, then led by an Episcopal clergyman, Dr. Samuel Shoemaker. Dr. Shoemaker had been one of the founders of that movement, and his was a powerful personality that carried immense sincerity and conviction.

At this time (1932-34), the Oxford Group had already sobered a number of alcoholics, and Rowland, feeling that he could especially identify with these sufferers, addressed himself to the help of still others. One of these chanced to be an old schoolmate of mine, named Edwin T. ["Ebby"]. He had been threatened with commitment to an institution, but Mr. H. and another ex-alcoholic "O.G." member procured his parole, and helped to bring about his sobriety.

Meanwhile, I had run the course of alcoholism and was threatened with commitment myself. Fortunately, I had fallen under the care of a physician — a Dr. William D. Silkworth — who was wonderfully capable of understanding alcoholics. But just as you had given up on Rowland, so had he given me up. It was his theory that alcoholism had two components — an obsession that compelled the sufferer to drink against his will and interest, and some sort of metabolism difficulty which he then called an allergy. The alcoholic's compulsion guaranteed that the alcoholic's drinking would go on, and the allergy made sure that the sufferer would finally deteriorate, go insane, or die. Though I had been one of the few he had thought it possible to help, he was finally obliged to tell me of my hopelessness; I, too, would have to be locked up. To me, this was a shattering blow. Just as Rowland had been made ready for his conversion experience by you, so had my wonderful friend Dr. Silkworth prepared me.

Hearing of my plight, my friend Edwin T. came to see me at my home, where I was drinking. By then, it was November 1934. I had long marked my friend Edwin for a hopeless case. Yet here he was in a very evident state of "release," which could by no means be accounted for by his mere association for a very short time with the Oxford Group. Yet this obvious state of release, as distinguished from the usual depression, was tremendously convincing. Because he was a kindred sufferer, he could unquestionably communicate with me at great depth. I knew at once I must find an experience like his, or die.

Again I returned to Dr. Silkworth's care, where I could be once more sobered and so gain a clearer view of my friend's experience of release, and of Rowland H.'s approach to him.

Clear once more of alcohol, I found myself terribly depressed. This seemed to be caused by my inability to gain the slightest faith. Edwin T. again visited me and repeated the simple Oxford Group formulas. Soon after he left me, I became even more

depressed. In utter despair, I cried out, "If there be a God, will he show himself." There immediately came to me an illumination of enormous impact and dimension, something which I have since tried to describe in the book *Alcoholics Anonymous* and also in *AA Come of Age*, basic texts which I am sending to you.

My release from the alcohol obsession was immediate. At once, I knew I was a free man.

Shortly following my experience, my friend Edwin came to the hospital, bringing me a copy of William James's *The Varieties of Religious Experience*. This book gave me the realization that most conversion experiences, whatever their variety, do have a common denominator of ego collapse at depth. The individual faces an impossible dilemma. In my case, the dilemma had been created by my compulsive drinking, and the deep feeling of hopelessness had been vastly deepened still more by my alcoholic friend when he acquainted me with your verdict of hopelessness respecting Rowland H.

In the wake of my spiritual experience, there came a vision of a society of alcoholics, each identifying with and transmitting his experience to the next — chain-style. If each sufferer were to carry the news of the scientific hopelessness of alcoholism to each new prospect, he might be able to lay every newcomer wide open to a transforming spiritual experience. This concept proved to be the foundation of such success as Alcoholics Anonymous has since achieved. This has made conversion experience — nearly every variety reported by James — available on almost wholesale basis. Our sustained recoveries over the last quarter-century number about 300,000. In America and through the world, there are today [1961] 8,000 AA groups.

So to you, to Dr. Shoemaker of the Oxford Group, to

William James, and to my own physician, Dr. Silkworth, we of AA owe this tremendous benefaction. As you will now clearly see, this astonishing chain of events actually started long ago in your consulting room, and it was directly founded upon your own humility and deep perception.

Very many thoughtful AAs are students of your writings. Because of your conviction that man is something more than intellect, emotion, and two dollars' worth of chemicals, you have especially endeared yourself to us.

How our Society grew, developed its Traditions for unity, and structured its functioning, will be seen in the texts and pamphlet material that I am sending you.

You will also be interested to learn that, in addition to the "spiritual experience," many AAs report a great variety of psychic phenomena, the cumulative weight of which is very considerable. Other members have — following their recovery in AA — been much helped by your practitioners. A few have been intrigued by the *I Ching* and your remarkable introduction to that work.

Please be certain that your place in the affection, and in the history, of our Fellowship is like no other.

Gratefully yours,
William G. W——

January 30, 1961

Dear Mr. W.:

Your letter has been very welcome indeed.

I had no news from Rowland H. any more and often wondered what has been his fate. Our conversation which he has adequately reported to you had an aspect of which he did not know. The reason that I could not tell him everything was that those days I had to be exceedingly careful of what I said. I had found out that I was misunderstood in every possible way. Thus I was very careful when I talked to Rowland H. But what I really thought about was the result of many experiences with men of his kind.

His craving for alcohol was the equivalent, on a low level, of the spiritual thirst of our being for wholeness, expressed in medieval language: the union with God.*

How could one formulate such an insight in a language that is not misunderstood in our days?

*"As the hart panteth after the water brooks, so panteth my soul after thee, O God." (Psalm 42:1)

The only right and legitimate way to such an experience is that it happens to you in reality, and it can only happen to you when you walk on a path which leads you to higher understanding. You might be led to that goal by an act of grace or through a personal and honest contact with friends, or through a higher education of the mind beyond the confines of mere rationalism. I see from your letter that Rowland H. has chosen the second way, which was, under the circumstances, obviously the best one.

I am strongly convinced that the evil principle prevailing in this world leads the unrecognized spiritual need into perdition if it is not counter-acted either by real religious insight or by the protective wall of human community. An ordinary man, not protected by an action from above and isolated in society, cannot resist the power of evil which is called, very aptly, the Devil. But the use of such words arouses so many mistakes that one can only keep aloof from them as much as possible.

These are the reasons why I could not give a full and sufficient explanation to Rowland H., but I am risking it with you because I conclude from your very decent and honest letter that you have acquired a point of view above the misleading platitudes one usually hears about alcoholism.

You see, "alcohol" in Latin is *spiritus*, and you use the same word for the highest religious experience as well as for the most depraving poison. The helpful formula therefore is: *spiritus contra spiritum*.

Thanking you again for your kind letter, I remain,

Yours sincerely,

C. G. Jung

After the Fall

August 1969

SOME OF THE COMMONLY EXPRESSED opinions about Jewish people are: All of us are rich; all are doctors, lawyers, storekeepers, or pawnbrokers; not one is an alcoholic.

In my case, all three opinions are wrong. For over thirty years of my adult life, I've never been above the near-sinking point financially, and actually sank into four skid-row sessions during those decades. I've been a farmer, soldier, laborer, bartender, jail trusty, and social worker during my dry spells. And I'm an alcoholic.

At my birth, two of my best friends were Jews — my mother and father. Both were sensitive, kind, and loving parents. As of today, I have not seen or written to my mother in five years. I have been unable even to commence my amends to her. I'm sure my father, who died five years ago, died unhappily wondering why the behavior of his promising only son was so defective and without honor.

One popular conception of my ethnic group is true: Our families, from time immemorial, have stressed the value and worth of higher education for their children — often above all else. I was not the best example of this philosophy, but an example nonetheless — and, in a way, a victim. I came out of the early molding process overeducated, underskilled, and guilt-ridden, among other major inadequacies. Not a pretty record for one who would be referred to biblically as one of "God's chosen people."

With all these misfit qualities, I finally came to Alcoholics Anonymous eleven months ago. Being a long-time sufferer, con artist, and debtor to the psychiatrists' couches, I arrived at my first meeting with all my disbelief, intellectual arrogance, and surface security intact.

My beautiful wife-to-be, an AA for some years, had introduced me to active members of the group in our area. The day before this meeting, I had been released from seven days in the local drunk tank. Being broke and feeling suitably humble, I was naturally eager to please my fiancee and my new acquaintances with my repentance and my desire to rejoin the human race. I felt sure that I was concealing my customary con artistry and omnipotent wisdom about all things, so that my waiting saviors would believe I really had hit the bottom of my ego structure.

But Cloud Nine supported me anyhow. For ten months after that meeting, I did not take that first drink. Momentary compulsions that assailed me were quickly overcome. Most of the time, I was dry mentally as well as physically. Though I didn't consciously think of how I was doing it, or think much of the Twelve Steps, which I had read and spouted about many times, I was staying sober a day at a time, and my life was assuming some evidences of manageability.

For a guy who in adulthood had never gone ten days without a drink, it was something to find I'd gone ten months! I had it made!

For those ten months, at numberless meetings, I found myself verbalizing well and knowingly about AA principles and doctrine. Of course, throughout my life, drunk or sober, I could orate fairly well about many subjects of which I knew little or nothing. For those ten months, I was sober and articulate, attended meetings, and made friends — even became secretary of an evening group.

Then it happened. The excuse was there: ——, by that time my wife, was in the hospital and doing poorly. But today, upon sober reflection, I know the excuse was a fraud and I didn't need it to take the first drink.

Only now, beginning my day-to-day sobriety again, have I come to understand where my Cloud Nine had holes in it. I had put up a sober appearance at the meetings, but with half-effort and depthless thought. I had not opened my heart to listen. I had not geared my brain to remember what I had been like. I had not been grateful for the joy and, yes, serenity my ten months of sobriety had blessed me with. That period had been the most lucid and promising I could recall. I had forgotten that its continuance had to be earned. I didn't just have it coming to me!

The damage done by my think-stoppage, this time, was fortunately minor. I am positive, considering past performances, that some small part of the program must have penetrated my awareness during my sober AA initiation, and that it was responsible for helping me cut short my fall from personal grace. I still have my job. My wife still loves me and is with me. And I can swing the AA door of our town's club inward once again.

The most important of all lessons is one I must try never to lose — that the AA Fellowship is my only hope. I must labor at it, not with words, but with all the thought-strength I can muster daily.

Reared in an ancient religion, but having only a foggy spirituality, I've made little or no progress with AA's spiritual Steps. If my sobriety is to be enriched and firmed up, I'm aware that I must continue to seek my own kinship with whatever God is identifiable, just as relentlessly as I work to make each minute a sober one.

The biblical reference to "God's chosen people" has no reality in my life. Rather, because of the living examples and wise words of the courageous and exceptional sober alcoholics of Alcoholics Anonymous, I think that God's true "chosen people" are those who have successfully linked their lives to our Fellowship and have found for themselves, and helped countless others to find, some full measures of fulfillment and serenity in daily existence.

Only through my AA life, regardless of my "fall" or more

likely because of it, have I been able to regenerate some desire and will to conquer my enemy within. I know the right and true answers lie ahead for me if I remember that *now* is when I live or die. The lighted road and the help are there for the asking. The commandments are clear and simple. The choice is mine alone.

Y. S., Sparks, Nev.

Seeking Through Meditation

April 1969

"S OMETIMES, WHEN FRIENDS TELL us how well we are doing, we know better inside. We know we aren't doing well enough. We still can't handle life, as life is. There must be a serious flaw somewhere in our spiritual practice and development.

"What, then, is it?

"The chances are better than ever that we shall locate our trouble in our misunderstanding or neglect of AA's Step Eleven — prayer, meditation, and the guidance of God.

"The other Steps can keep most of us sober and somehow functioning. But Step Eleven can keep us growing, if we try hard and work at it continually." (*As Bill Sees It*, page 264)

When I realized that these words applied to me, I also realized that it was meditation itself that I knew least about. I had misunderstood and neglected the Eleventh Step because I did not know what meditation is. I did not know that meditation means awareness, attention, listening. During a lifetime of drinking, I had not wanted to listen, especially to the self within.

With others in the same situation, I now belong to an Eleventh Step meditation group. The general intent of our work is to increase and enrich our understanding of meditation as described in the books *Alcoholics Anonymous* and *Twelve Steps and Twelve Traditions*. We have also adopted procedures from a number of other sources, some very old, but all quite standard, well-known, and simple, if not easy. We make use of some organization and planning simply to learn to sit still and to liberate and direct our faculty of attention. Many of the great thinkers of the past and present can instruct us, particularly in the early stages of the work.

Our purpose generally is to meditate every day, mostly when alone. But by sharing our experience, strength, and hope at the meetings, we enrich our meditations and our methods with as many leads and as many viewpoints as we can, just as in any other AA meeting. Meditation belongs and grows with daily life and daily growth, for it is in daily life that analytical thought binds us into the dilemma of opposites and consequently into sorrow, pleasure-seeking, and loss of freedom. In a life that may often seem onerous, boring, and senseless, meditation can free us to its beauty, its joy beyond pleasure, its passion beyond sorrow.

Because of the vital and literally endless potential of our Eleventh Step meditation meeting, I want to emphasize that it is in no sense a religious exercise; it "is not allied with any sect, denomination. . .or institution." It is rather a training in the continuous application of mind for those who seek "to improve our conscious contact with God as we understand Him." Its methods are equally applicable for agnostic, atheist, and any believer — or for those who use AA, their AA group, health, sanity, or any other of the many interpretations and manifestations of the Higher Power.

Our meditation is divided into three phases. The first is concerned with an awareness of reality. Here we meet immediately the

February 1978

"I have this sense of impending happiness."

oldest forms of resistance: "My mind is jumping all over. I can't concentrate. I should have said this. I'd like to do that. I ought to know more. I wish I had...Why can't I...?" and so on without end. The mind is like an overactive child in its restless flight from self, from guilt and discomfort, and in its darting search for something, anything. The mind is always seeking pleasure or self-expansion and avoiding effort or danger, like an animal. When the animal rules us, thinking becomes a substitute for action while masquerading as a plan for action.

Meditation is not an attempt to solve difficulties. Planning has its place in our mental life, and the discipline and training of meditation can help us to plan more effectively. But meditation itself is not planning or managing. And it is not daydreaming.

Meditation is, in fact, the specific corrective for racing thoughts. This first phase is a lesson in healthy thinking. We no longer fight these thousand thoughts and fantasies — we experience them. We used to let the manipulating ego eternally touch up its precious image, busily denying, distorting, and hiding the truth. Now we simply experience what is happening within the self and outside the self. Fearlessly, calmly, as if watching beside a stream, we watch all thoughts and all experiences flow by us. This is the essential process beginning the meditation: the reduction of the ego.

Thoughts are quietly observed; feelings are experienced; noises are heard, all just as they really are: "I hear a taxi horn outside. I feel my left foot. I feel my breathing. I remember what I should have said, not what I did say. I feel a tightness in my stomach. What is this anger? What do I really feel? I am daydreaming. I am not paying attention. I am attached to my thoughts; I must experience them. Why do I want to be good at this? Why do I want to fail? When will this be over? I don't want to think of bad things. It ought to be different. It ought to be this way — my way."

We discover what is happening right now, within the body and outside the body, as an experience, without any attempt to enter into it, to change it, to master it. We want only to be truly aware of a new experience, the experience of the inner and outer worlds perceived with immediate, fresh contact and without memories, images, or ideologies picturing what should be. The mind will often drift away into daydreams, but patiently we turn our attention back to the truth and the reality of existence and experience, all as it is happening right now.

Adequate understanding of this first phase is essential: We

must accept reality — all of it, the self and the world — just as it is. Only this acceptance will help us to receive sanity in place of what we have called the madness of alcoholic thinking.

It is at this point that we need help and instruction, in addition to working out problems in the group. The final purpose is to apply this process in all our affairs. "Let's always remember that meditation is in reality intensely practical. One of its first fruits is emotional balance." ("Twelve and Twelve," page 104) It is in this first phase of our method that we begin to accept ourselves and life, to participate in reality in closer union with reality, to diminish the eternal bickering of escape, conquest, evasion, triumph, and injustice-collecting. It is here that study, reading, and practice will begin to open a new world of health and sanity.

The second phase of our method depends upon the use of one-pointed attention. Some like to relax by tightening the fists for a minute and then allowing the hands to open of themselves, and so let all tension drain from the body. This little exercise is not essential; it is simply a physical reminder to experience and be aware, not to try to run things, but to let them happen. It is a symbol of "letting go." As we move into the second phase, we allow the thoughts and pictures in the mind to drift or be gently led from center to side of the mental screen, often gray or dark at first before our closed or half-closed eyes.

Instead, at the center we picture an idea, an important thought, or, as in the beautiful example given in "Twelve and Twelve," a prayer. We may find one or more of the Steps or other parts of the AA program useful as a center for awareness. We can review the day to come or the day past — not analyzing, recriminating, or gloating, but experiencing and understanding. How often, for example, have I suddenly realized the deeper meanings of one of the slogans! Here is where I allow new understanding to develop: Instead of focusing on *my* idea of sobriety or growth or sanity, I learn that which is *new* to me — which was not mine until now — which comes from a source beyond me, a Higher Power (no matter how I describe it or experience it). As I can do in looking at an icon, I let ideas, experiences, and memories look back at me and teach me; I learn from them. If I try to strangle a habit or a fault, it will teach me nothing; but if I am truly aware, I can learn from it. For instance, compare controlled drinking to the First Step.

If a problem persistently comes up and will not let me alone, it is here in meditation that I learn to experience it. It is here that I

learn what I truly feel, not how I analyze it. Analyzing it is only another way of blaming someone or something else. Often just the
willingness to see a problem clearly is the beginning of its resolu-
tion. Facing something and experiencing it fully means the end of
escape maneuvers and ego domination, and these are the real
sources of anxiety and resentment. "As we have seen, self-search-
ing is the means by which we bring new vision, action, and grace to
bear upon the dark and negative side of our natures. It is a step in
the development of that kind of humility that makes it possible for

us to receive God's help." ("Twelve and Twelve," page 100) Here
in this phase I learn the meanings, for me, of many kinds of wisdom and many parts of the program. I allow the depth and impact
of these meanings to grow within and to teach me to grow from
within. In this way I can experience the joy of discovery of my true
self; such joy releases more energy for more growth and discovery
of life.

Having now prepared ourselves in awareness and attention, in
totally experiencing reality, and in willingness to learn, we are
ready to move into the third and last phase of our meditation. This
is the Eleventh Step proper. We are not managing anything. We
are not teaching anyone. We are not mentally repairing the past or
gilding the future. We are allowing all the contents of the mind to
drift to the side of the mental screen. We practice readiness to learn

— humility and teachability — the state of seeking and receptivity. And that is all we do. All the rest is up to the Higher Power.

New understandings may come now or at any time later. Our practice here is to be ready and to trust, openly and without ego or pride, as much as we can. Our contact may be in the form of healthier understanding; it may be very simple; it may be beyond anything we can imagine. There is no end to the kinds of individual experiences possible in the practice of the Eleventh Step or in the effects flowing from it.

Here, in the third phase of our meditation, we offer our preparation, imperfect as it may be, for whatever within or beyond us leads to new growth of the true self. From here on, each person follows and develops his own beliefs, outside the limits of this discussion. The meditation can then be ended with a brief review of the experience. Sometimes it is all hard, even painful work; just as often, perhaps, there is a pure and unexpected joy. Both feelings are valid and ought not to surprise or mislead us. There is only this: Awareness is all.

An AA doctor, Manhattan, N.Y.

A Gift That Surpasses Understanding

April 1970

FREQUENTLY, AROUND THE AA PROGRAM we hear a person say, "The spiritual side of the program is not for me" or "I don't go for the spiritual bit. As long as I don't drink, I'm satisfied. I leave the pie-in-the-sky stuff to other people." Any such cavalier dismissal of the spiritual side of our program makes me wince a little and feel a bit sorry for this person. This sense of pity and sorrow is the more intense and poignant the longer the person has been in the program.

In most cases, I have good reason to suspect that this man or woman is unwittingly confusing formal religion with what we call the spiritual side of the program. To my mind, he is unconsciously rebelling against the possiblity of his being soft-soaped into embracing the creed, code, and cult of some particular religious denomination and then being wheedled into a kind of dogmatic straitjacket. For him the word "spiritual" has overtones of something soft, hypocritical, less-than-virile, because it can evoke images of "church mice" with hands folded, eyes down, grim faces that seem to say, "Remember death!" And, understandably, he wants nothing to do with these creeps.

Yet I am quite sure that such a person, like the rest of us, would be quick to deny that he came into AA primarily because he had a religious problem. I have never yet met anyone who crawled into AA because he couldn't understand the infallibility of the Pope or the source of authority in the Protestant or Jewish faith. I seriously doubt, too, that any atheist has come into our program to get a definite answer to the question of God's existence.

When I first came into AA, the good people in the program told me that, if I was alcoholic, I had a very real sickness, that I was sick physically, mentally, and spiritually. I do not remember anyone ever telling me that I was sick religiously or that, because I was a priest, I could not be sick spiritually. And how right they were in refraining from saying that I was sick religiously! In my descent down the skids of booze and pills, I never had any serious difficulty with my religion or my priesthood. It is true that I was less than vigorous in the practice of both, but I sensed that my sickness was on a level much more basic than these.

Yet it was by no means clear to me what it meant for me to be spiritually sick and at the same time not to be religiously sick. Like many others in AA, I was uneasy with the word "spiritual" as it is used in the program. But when it dawned on me that the term "spiritual" is derived from the word "spirit," things started to clear up. I was comfortable with the word "spirit," because I had lived with it all my life. This spirit, this soul, this principle of life, call it what you will, was given to me long before I had any knowledge or practice of a formal religion, long before I had the slightest idea what profession or vocation I might want to pursue.

This is the spirit that was infused into me at the moment of my conception, the thing that would automatically give me membership in the human race. This spirit is the rational part of me that endowed me with dignity, nobility, and a separate identity. My spirit or soul gave me the power to think, to make judgments, to wish, to will, to love, to reach out for the infinite. This spirit of mine gave me all these wonderful powers and something more — it gave me my total personality, which in the years to come would be moulded and shaped, for better or worse, by environment, education, and circumstances.

The environment, education, and circumstances of the intervening years can be briefly telescoped. I had all the advantages of a good home, a better-than-ordinary education, a life with pleasant surroundings. My priesthood, which I loved (and still love dearly!), should have enhanced all these advantages. But life does not always work according to a definite blueprint.

Somewhere along the line, fears, self-doubt, and a sense of inadequacy began to manifest themselves. Then I discovered those two "friends," alcohol and tranquilizers, which seemed to quiet the fears and self-doubt and restore the sense of adequacy. The classical, insidious pattern started to form and continued growing over a long period: more and deeper fears, loss of interest in work and in life, gradual withdrawal from people and activities, deep-seated loneliness, panic, near despair. In this process of slow death, there was no one to whom I could turn except my two "friends."

The climax was occasioned by an enforced withdrawal from both the alcohol and the pills during hospitalization for major surgery. I went into DTs for a period of eleven days. After emerging from this pleasant interlude, I was shipped to a "special" hospital (nut factory). About six weeks after being released from this institution, I went in and out of hallucinations, a delayed withdrawal symptom, and I soon found myself in the alcoholic ward of a state mental hospital. It was here that AA came to me.

Life had taken a tremendous toll on my spirit, my soul. I came into AA broken in spirit, soul-sick. If the ray of hope that I heard

VICTOR E.

had worked for so many thousands in AA was to warm up my heart and light up my life, it would have to penetrate, not into the areas of my religion and my priesthood, but into the much deeper, more basic areas where I was really sick — into my human spirit. Had there been in the AA program any suggestion of theology, formal or otherwise, I would have picked up my weak carcass and broken spirit and headed back to the desert outside. Having formally studied theology for four years under good professors, I was, according to ordinary standards, something of a professional theologian. At that time, I needed more theology about as much as I needed a third thumb.

What I did need and need desperately was, not more knowledge about God, but, with God's help, a deep, penetrating knowledge about myself. How could I learn to live, not ecstatically or even euphorically, but with at least a modicum of peace? How could this spirit of mine find some kind of interest, enthusiasm, self-fulfillment? I was to discover that AA had the answer for this plain, ordinary, human craving of my heart.

I followed the suggestions of the AA people in the hope that I might emerge from the jungle, as they had, and enjoy a kind of resurrection. I went and still go to many meetings; I talked with many people, a newly discovered pleasure; I read a great deal of the available AA literature. These were immensely helpful and will always be necessary for me, to a certain extent. But if these techniques are to have any real meaning, body, and flavor for me, they must rest on something as substantial, vigorous, and life-giving as the Twelve Steps. When I studied and started to live these Steps, it became clear that, at least for me, the "spiritual awakening" mentioned in the Twelfth Step had to mean "an awakening of the

April 1965

spirit" — i.e., no matter how swift or prolonged the process might be, I had to come awake, alive in my spirit as a human being. From that time on, I have had a very few, if any, hang-ups with the word "spiritual" as used in the AA program.

I was greatly impressed with the order, the logic, and the thoroughness of the Steps. They seemed to be an all-or-nothing deal. If I had taken the First Step and settled for that, I would have been guilty of the "selective surrender" spoken of by that pioneer friend of AA, Dr. Harry M. Tiebout. In his wonderfully perceptive brochure, "The Act of Surrender in the Therapeutic Process," he makes this comment about one of his patients: "His surrender is not to life as a person, but to alcohol as an alcoholic."

Had I merely surrendered to alcohol as an alcoholic, this would have been good, but not nearly good enough. True, it would have meant that alcohol and pills, two deadly substances for me, would have gone out of my life — no small blessing! But the trouble with me was that everything was going out of my life — friends, activities, my sense of values, the meaning of life, love, laughter, and beauty. My human spirit was indeed desert-dry, and now, with booze and pills gone, it would seem a more arid, barren wasteland. If I was to recover the wholeness, the oneness of my personality, if I truly wanted a rebirth of my human spirit, a taste of the joy of living, then, in accordance with Dr. Tiebout's formula, I had to surrender, not only to alcohol as an alcoholic, but to life as a person.

But Chapter 5 of the Big Book, "How It Works," assured me that this awakening of the spirit was the natural, orderly result of studying and living the Twelve Steps. "Rarely have we seen a person fail who has thoroughly followed our path," it says. Here was a safe, secure, comfortable framework within which I could move forward gradually and gracefully toward a new way of life, toward something of the peace and serenity that I saw in other AA people. Here was a mode of living fashioned not from pure theory nor in the halls of academe, but from the rough, tough, raw experience in life of the first hundred members of AA, who had desperately wanted the same kind of awakening of the spirit that I was searching for.

This awakening of the spirit is set down so naturally and confidently in the Twelfth Step that it seems to carry this implicit warning: "If you are not having at least the beginnings of a spiritual awakening, it would be well to look back over the Steps and find out where you are failing." And there are no qualifying words, such as "maybe," "perhaps," or "perchance." On the other hand, there is a kind of built-in guarantee that, if you are living the Steps to the best of your ability, no matter how difficult it may be at times, you will eventually have this awakening of the spirit. What a tremendous source of encouragement!

It should not surprise us that the idea of God and our complete dependence on him for recovery should be woven into the Steps. God has many kinds of presence. He has a general presence, by which he is present at every moment in every nook and cranny of

the universe. He has many kinds of special presence, by which he is present to different groups who are trying to do something in his name. We can say that God is present with a special presence in a church congregation when its members are gathered to honor and worship him according to the dictates of their conscience and the rites of their particular denomination. God is certainly present with a special presence to the heads of governments who are honestly seeking ways and means of promoting justice and peace. He is present by a special presence to any society, fellowship, or family that is gathered together in his name to work out some problem or achieve some worthwhile goal. Should it surprise us, then, that God is present by a special presence in AA, which is "a fellowship of men and women who share their experience, strength and hope with each other that they may solve their common problem and help others to recover from alcoholism"? Indeed, since alcoholism is such a destructive, insidious, baffling disease, would it be an exaggeration to say that God is present to us in AA by a *very* special presence?

Yet this special presence of God in AA says nothing about our religious creed, code, or cult. It imposes no theology on anyone. It says one thing clear and loud: If you have a problem with alcohol, and if you wish to do something about it within AA, then you, too, can partake of this special presence of God in this Fellowship. "If a drunk, fallen-away Catholic comes into AA, and if he works the program with God's grace to the best of his ability, he will emerge as a sober, fallen-away Catholic. But the difference is infinite." Such is the astute observation of a priest friend of mine, who is very knowledgeable both in things AA and in things theological. This observation would be as true, it seems to me, whether the person was Protestant, Jewish, Buddhist, or atheist, provided that he recognized his need for a Power greater than himself.

Should a man, after attaining a length of solid sobriety, wish to return to the practice of some formal religion in a particular denomination, this would be fine with AA. But, it would seem, such a return would require another special type of God's presence, outside the ambition and concern of AA.

I feel that anyone who comes into AA wants to "get better," whatever this term may specifically mean to him. It may mean getting out of trouble, placating the family or others, retaining his sanity, etc. The reason for a person's coming into AA is not important; any reason or even excuse will suffice. But it strikes me that the reason for staying in AA is immensely important. Getting out of trouble, placating the family or the superior — these may be good for the time being. But for the sustained, lifetime work of handling this deadly, progressive disease of alcoholism, experience has shown that such motives are inadequate, short-lived, or too fragile; they do not meet the problem head-on, and under pressure they will snap or wither. The family, the boss, the probation officer, collectively or singly, are not the problem.

The problem is me (ungrammatical and humiliating as this may be). I am truly grateful that there was a Fellowship — a group of warm, understanding people — to whom I could bring this "problem of me." Nobody lectured me; nobody gave me the moral wheeze; nor, on the other hand, did anybody stand in awe of me. The black suit and the Roman collar were merely the accidental and, therefore, unimportant attire of a sick human being. The important concern of the AAs was to reassure me that they knew what and how I was suffering and that I would "get better," as they had.

I somehow sensed immediately that the God of my understanding was present in AA by a special presence, a presence by which I could ask for and receive graces to handle my alcoholic problem, a presence that gave me these graces with and through AA people. I am grateful that within this apparently formless AA Fellowship, where only "suggestions" are made (famous last words!), there was a structured program of recovery where I would not be on my own. The Twelve Steps were there to guide me. And just over the horizon in the Twelfth Step was the promise, almost the guarantee, of something for which I had been searching over the years — a spiritual awakening!

Whatever this spiritual awakening may mean to anyone else in AA, to me it means that the God of my understanding has given me, by his special presence in AA and through AA people and the Twelve Steps, a gift that surpasses understanding — an awakening of my human spirit!

A priest

Prayer

January 1980

T HE AA PROGRAM ONLY SUGGESTS that newcomers attempt to begin to conceive of a power greater than themselves, in their own individual terms. After that, an old-timer might suggest to a skeptical newcomer — along with not picking up the first drink — faking prayer and keeping an open mind.

I came into this program a drunken atheist. Today, I pray. My being sober is a reflection of the good attributes of some higher power; it is not a reflection of any moral virtue or strength of will on my part.

This change in a drunken, hardcore, cynical atheist is a miracle beyond human comprehension. However, one aspect of the program has always been required for me to remain sober — results. Prayer works. If prayer didn't work and show results, I'd become an atheist again today.

Spirituality happens to be extremely practical. Prayer, reading the AA literature, going to meetings, using the Steps, and helping another alcohoic all combine to make my life easier and more comfortable, hour to hour, day to day.

As an atheist, I faked prayer on a trial basis in the beginning. The results have altered my view of the cosmos. An unseen realm does exist. I do not attend church, nor have I experienced a spiritual awakening; I'm still a fire-breathing cynic. Yet I pray regularly to something unseen and so vast that I, as a human being, can never understand or even name it.

I pray because of the positive results that flow from prayer. I'm a pragmatist. So, for today, I have become an agnostic, who occasionally experiences violent swings toward faith. With all the blessings that have been bestowed upon me in a year and a half, I still experience doubts and have not made the quantum leap to faith.

All this proves only one thing: that some nuts are tougher to crack than others. Today, I'm still faking prayer and getting results. Maybe God likes nuts, especially the hard ones.

R. E., Philadelphia, Pa.

A Slob's Guide to Spiritual Growth

April 1982

IT'S A SQUIRMY WORD — "spiritual." It makes me uncomfortable. It reminds me of the time I spent as a child sitting in a church and trying to look holy. "Spiritual" is confused in my mind with a kind of hymn and has connotations of mediums, levitation, and ghosts.

through the Twelve Steps. They have irresistibly drawn me outward from myself. My need for approval made me a taker. But when we are taking, there is soon little left to take from. When I have time for compassion for others — then, I hope, there will be some for me when I need human compassion. I am responsible, but I am powerless without love from Him and from you.

Once again — only love can fill the need for love. In that light, a *loving* God makes more sense than any other concept I have embraced. And I surrender to that love. I can no longer resist it. It is my need.

D. J., Alameda, Calif.

Spiritual Experience

A Slob's Guide to Spiritual Growth

IT'S A SQUIRMY word — "spiritual." It makes me uncomfortable. It reminds me of the time I spent as a child sitting in a church and trying to look holy. "Spiritual" is confused in my mind with a kind of hymn and has connotations of mediums, levitation, and ghosts.

Worse, "spiritual" implies pretensions of sainthood, a hypocritical posturing, and pretended preoccupation with wonderful thoughts — when I and everybody else know that ninety percent of my day is spent trying to keep the wolf from the door and the horse before the cart.

My spiritual inventory doesn't help much, either. This very day, as I lay in bed staring piously at the ceiling, I took the Third and Eleventh Steps

9

Worse, "spiritual" implies pretensions of sainthood, a hypo-critical posturing, a pretended preoccupation with wonderful thoughts — when I and everybody else know that ninety percent of my day is spent trying to keep the wolf from the door and the horse before the cart.

My spiritual inventory doesn't help much, either. This very day, as I lay in bed staring piously at the ceiling, I took the Third and Eleventh Steps firmly, fondly, and resolutely. I thought warm-ly of all the great tasks I would accomplish today with the aid of my trusty Third and Eleventh. Then I got out of bed.

In midwinter, with the window open and the heat turned down, getting out of a warm bed apparently is, for me, an act of will of the highest spiritual order. This monumental achievement seems to exhaust my store of spiritual strength for the day.

By ten o'clock, I have a number of creative suggestions to offer my Higher Power on how my life and will might be gainfully employed. I have a serene acceptance of God's will for me as long as it happens to conform to mine.

By 2:00 PM, I have decided to mix a little of my will for me with his, since knowledge of his will is a little slow in coming and there are problems in need of immediate attention — like meeting the payroll, hardly a matter of celestial concern.

This line of self-examination leads to certain humbling realizations that are unwanted but nevertheless gnawing little realities — potholes in the path of smooth spiritual development. For example:

1. I won't believe tomorrow what I am saying today. Many of my hard-won convictions are just expedient reactions to the situation at hand.

2. I have never seen any profound wisdom in "Everything works out eventually." Of course it does. If my car is stolen tomorrow, I can meditate on how smart I was to put off cleaning out the ashtray.

3. There are far more things I try to find the courage to change than there are things I seek the serenity to accept. Going through the day in placid acceptance of everything that happens just ain't my style.

4. I sometimes get tired of all this self-improvement and would like to just sit back and relax and enjoy life.

5. I really enjoy solitude occasionally, as opposed to constant contact with my fellow man. There are times when I prefer curling up with a good book with lots of sex and violence to putting the Big Book under my arm and sallying forth to carry the message.

Those are not proud admissions, just the truth. I lead an odd and noisy life; little happens slowly or quietly. When I read my Big Book and "Twelve and Twelve," and I assess my spiritual growth, I am filled with enormous feelings of inadequacy. Honesty, compassion, acceptance, understanding, faith, love, caring — I don't even *think* about those most of the time. My progress toward spiritual strength is a zigzag trail filled with hip-shooting reactions.

Sometimes, I have thought of creating a Slob's Guide to Spiritual Growth, for those of us who can't walk around with our hands folded and a slight, mysterious smile on our faces. It might go something like this:

1. It is better to watch the game in your undershirt with a can of cola in your hand than a can of beer.

2. When you holler at somebody, you always feel lousy afterward — like a hangover.

3. Life is a steady drizzle of small things — carry an umbrella.

4. Tomorrow is another day.

5. Never give up.

6. Concentrate on what you're doing — it beats thinking.

7. If you let the other fellow alone and don't get so upset about how he's living his life, you can watch more TV.

8. It is more fun to be happy than angry.

9. Don't take anything too seriously, including all of the above.

10. This, too, shall pass.

That's a start. All that wisdom leads me to suspect that the path of spiritual progress is perhaps not so steep and dark as I had imagined. At least, I can *try* to understand it without getting all smug and lofty.

For starters, I know that I am a walking miracle. Literally overnight, I went from years of twenty-four-hour crash drinking to total sobriety, after everything had failed except total surrender to the AA program. That is a fact I can stand on.

From that foundation, I am able to see certain glimmers of progress. For example, I can realize that I have not done anything dishonorable in at least a week. Maybe more.

Also, I have learned that using utter candor in approaching whatever progress I have made lets me feel a lot more comfortable with that progress, however slim and unspectacular it may be — it's all mine and I'm proud of getting even that far.

I have known all along, after all, that my underlying problem was not drinking but living, and only through a change of attitudes, through unquestioning acceptance of the AA program — a program of spiritual growth — could I hope to live life as forcefully, aggressively, and enthusiastically as I have. Something must have happened.

And as I peel away the layers of day-to-day expediency, I realize that my zigzag, erratic, and inconsistent course was in the general direction of progress all the time. That's good.

What right do I have to expect perfection and efficiency in my spiritual growth when the rest of my life is so full of ups and downs, ins and outs, and backs and forths? Throughout this whole adventure, the only consistency I have maintained is an absolute and total faith in AA, come what may.

Happiness happens when results exceed expectations. Maybe this is working after all. Deep down, there is also a warm, small ball of faith, always there, never dimmed, unexplainable, asking nothing, but giving much. To define it or try to bounce it would distort or destroy it. It just is, that's all.

As St. Augustine said, "God is closer to me than I am to him." I don't know exactly what that means, but it sure is true.

C. H., Fairfield, Conn.

Why God Says No

February 1958

T HE FIRST REAL AWARENESS, for most of us, of the tremendous potential continuing assistance from a Higher Power came when we realized that something beyond ourselves was removing the baffling compulsion to drink. As practical results developed, we began to respect the practical side of a spiritual life. Later we learned that God's help is not limited to our drinking problem alone, but extends into all phases of our lives.

And right there a lot of us begin to get into a certain kind of trouble.

Somehow, since we got an immediate answer for our drinking, we conclude that similar answers should come immediately — for anything else that might be disturbing us at the moment. We learn that with God all things are possible, and therefore why should we have to be disturbed or disappointed at all?

So we offer up prayers for assistance, and our requirements may be as lengthy as a child's list to Santa Claus. But God doesn't meet our demands, so we become a little miffed. And our agitation is likely to increase when we see others getting many of the advantages we'd like to have. Worse yet, we see people who aren't on a "spiritual basis" at all enjoying an outpouring of luck in all directions — a state of affairs that can lead us into blind alleys of self-pity and envy, feeling that God has cheated us.

After all, we say to ourselves (and to the Higher Power who seems to be denying us), aren't we trying to lead good lives? We're doing our best to be moral, kind, courteous, helpful, and honest. Shouldn't good things come our way, even material things? (We conveniently avoid the admission that we are trying to lead good lives only because alcohol had us trapped, backed into a corner, with no alternative except to reach out desperately for AA.) We may also have been misled by some of the current books on positive thinking, many of which contain glowing accounts of how countless perplexing problems were solved simply through spending a few minutes each day in prayer and meditation.

But first, shouldn't we consider the real meaning of Steps Three and Eleven in the AA program? In these Steps, we commit ourselves to God's will — *whatever it is and regardless of the consequences.* Our own plans may seem worthy, and our own immediate desires may be modest, but even these may somehow conflict with the plans God has for us. It may be that in his strategy, the ultimate victory hinges on *losing*, not winning, some of the battles along the way. Today's disappointment, viewed six months hence, may turn out to be one of the best breaks we ever got. And at the proper time, our own grateful hindsight will let us see the workings of God's unerring foresight.

AA's early history carries some good object lessons revealing how this principle works. At one time Bill W. and several other AA pioneers decided to solicit wealthy people for contributions to the struggling movement. When they weren't able to raise a single dime, they must have wondered if God hadn't forgotten the desperate needs of the embryo society. Yet, as it later turned out, this experience helped teach AA to be self-supporting. It certainly must

February 1982

"To whom it may concern . . . "

have been one of his mysterious ways of performing wonders.

Or take the example of Bill's business reverses in Akron, just before he met Dr. Bob. Why should God let a man sustain a defeat like that, especially a man who had known many successive defeats and was doing his level best to live a new kind of life? No considerate person in his right mind would permit a man to get in a situation like that. But God permitted it, and in groping for a way out of the mess, Bill fell back on his spiritual resources and the soul-restoring technique of helping others. Today we beneficiaries of AA's redemptive power can see that this supposed adversity was really God's heavy hand molding a magnificent movement into being.

But let's suppose, just for illustration, that God *did* give us immediate answers completely in accordance with our wishes, a blank check to do and have anything we want. How well would any of us come out on a deal like that? Since selfishness is a primary defect of alcoholics, and most of us are experts in using people and circumstances to feather our own nests, wouldn't we do the same thing to God? We would bombard him with unlimited demands, ranging from material gains to dictatorial control over the lives of others.

Since we're an impatient breed, we'd use his help to run everyone else off the road, although we'd smugly rationalize it by saying we were merely receiving what was due us. We would gloat over business successes, romantic conquests, prestige, and other "breaks" — giving little thought to the unpleasant suggestion that our gains might be defeats for somebody else. Yes, we would manipulate God as spoiled children make demands on foolish and indulgent parents.

But God is neither foolish nor indulgent, and has the wisdom to say NO. And his answers are always for our own highest good. None of this is to say that God's answers must always be "no", for all of us have known numerous times when the answer was an immediate "yes." But these requests were gratified because they were right, and were undoubtedly made in a spirit of humility and unselfishness.

Some AAs seem to achieve beautiful harmony almost immediately when they expose themselves to God's will. They develop such profound spiritual insight that they receive answers to almost all their prayers. The rest of us admire their serenity and wisdom, but continue trying to inveigle God into doing things our way.

Then we start getting the true realization, perhaps, when we, too, examine the course of our lives and discover God's unerring wisdom in times past, when he has had to listen and shake his head.

Anonymous, Jackson, Mich.

Tradition Twelve

*Anonymity is the spiritual foundation
of all our Traditions, ever reminding us
to place principles before personalities*

September 1971

E VERY SO OFTEN, I must ask ask myself, "Who do you think you are, anyway?" That question ties me to the guidepost which is our Twelfth Tradition, much as a rope tethers a grazing mule. When hooked to it, I am restrained from roaming into dangerous territories of vanity and self-pity. They always seem to be beckoning, trying to entice my hungry ego with their greener-looking fodder, and overindulgence in either could lead me back to drunkenness.

Circling this Tradition, trying to get inside its meaning by logic or some other route, time after time I have felt pulled up short by the discovery that here, in this context, "anonymity" has one simple meaning, personally applicable to me.

Newspapers, magazines, TV, movies, and radio only rarely find any particular one of us important enough for the public to care whether we are sober or not. When they do, the Eleventh Tradition amply covers that situation, in my opinion. (It never was intended to keep us from revealing our AA membership privately, however.)

But here in the Twelfth, the term "anonymity" strongly suggests to me something more than that, something at the core of nearly all AA teachings. As of today, to the best of my understanding, that something more is *humility*.

The word is one I have both fought and cherished in AA. At first, back in 1945, it made me think of the cringing, sniveling, creepy, phony "'umbleness" of Dickens' Uriah Heep. *That* was not what AA meant, I felt certain.

Then the word suggested to me the sensation of being humiliated. I found it hard to understand why and how that would help
me stay sober. Humiliation had been one of the most painful parts
of my drunkenness; did AA want me to endure more of it, sober?

It was therefore a great relief, that first year, to hear humility
discussed for hours and hours over nickel coffees in an all-night
Grand Central Station cafeteria. Humility, I was told, did not
mean being a doormat, never standing up for oneself; instead, it
meant just being openminded, no longer sure that *I* knew all the
answers.

Later, investigating religious ideas with the guidance of AA
friends, I found enormous help in Emmet Fox's explanation that
being humble did not mean being poor-spirited and spineless.
Instead, it meant being *teachable*.

After a 1946 slip, I think I took one step nearer understanding
humility when I decided to try to learn about unselfishness. For
me, that meant practicing it, going through the motions many
times, as if it were an exercise — necessary for one who had been
lost in greedy, sick self-concern. I had to find tiny things I could do
for someone else's benefit. Then I had to keep quiet about these
deeds, instead of trying to collect any credit for them.

That was not always easy, because I felt pretty sure that the
deeds should not be too easy. They should cost me at least a little,
even if it was nothing more than my time, in order to give me the
spiritual progress I sought. For my purpose, I found menial tasks
best — such as washing my group's ashtrays on the sly. The point
was, I felt, that for my own survival I had to learn to place the welfare of others before my own, and learn to do so without the reward of praise.

(Such exercises are still useful to me when I find myself wish-
ing for credit I do not get — both inside and outside AA. And I
have another bad habit to combat. Each time I go through the

lesson, I have to remind myself to be more generous about giving others credit when credit is their due. I am sometimes more prodigal with gripes than with praise, alas.)

I thought I was beginning to catch on to the meaning of humility in action. Then, late one morning, just before lunch, my boss strode into my office. "Verifax these for me," Tom said, handing me some loose pages. And he walked out.

Rage paralyzed me. I could not have felt more affronted if he had ordered me to sweep out his office. Who did he think I was? Why me, instead of a secretary? Why me, instead of a *junior* writer? I was so angry, I could not think at all — I just felt.

Finally, I went to the duplicating machine, making sure Tom saw me. I also made sure he heard me say loudly to someone, "I can't go to lunch — have to do this." Poor ole me!

Running the pages through — a two-minute operation — I tried to back off and look at myself, a trick my good psychotherapist had encouraged me to practice whenever my face felt scarlet. What I saw was a preposterously pompous forty-year-old man pouting like a four-year-old. I looked so ludicrous I began to giggle at myself, and to breathe again. Not too many years before, I had been a drunk and unemployable bum. Now I had turned into a big shot who thought he was too good for a mere mechanical task. Indeed, who did I think I was?

No longer so blinded by my own injured vanity, I remembered something else I had temporarily forgotten. Old Tom was a drunk. I mean a miserable, grouchy, guilty, scared, sweaty, nipping-all-day-but-trying-to-hide-it drunk. People laughed at the Sen Sen breath, the razor-nicked jowls, the vulgar jokes, the mug of "cold tea for my cough" stashed behind some books, the long lunch after which he always reached his daily peak of agreeableness and calm, cured of those morning shakes.

I had told him enough about my own past drunks for him to realize we were buddies beneath the skin (I was trying to maneuver him into asking how I stayed sober). So when I suddenly thought of those pitiful trembling hands, I was deeply ashamed of myself. Obviously, just before lunch he could no more put pages neatly into a copying machine than he could accurately guide a pencil. He had simply needed a favor from a friend he could trust, and he thought I was it. But I had been so conceited about myself and *my* position in the company that I had forgotten all about him and *his* problems.

I was hardly placing "principles before personalities." In my deep involvement with the most fascinating personality in the world — my own, of course — I had for a moment overlooked a prime AA principle, concern for the fellow alcoholic. I felt like such a heel that I took him to lunch in his favorite, dreary, hidden-away bar — four or five double martinis for him, pretzels and ginger ale for me.

For several weeks I wallowed in a mud puddle of guilt about that, sure I was the worst of all AA members. I practically began to proclaim with pride my preeminence in rottenness and failure. Then a dear AA friend observed one night over coffee, "Some of us will do anything for distinction, won't we?"

Shocked, I began to chuckle. Something relaxed inside. Shortly afterward, I was able to ridicule myself out of that pit of despair, as I had previously laughed myself off the peak of self-importance.

Ever since the alternate self-exaltation and humiliation of those days, almost fifteen years ago, I have been searching for a happy medium between the two extremes. I know it exists — genuine humility, with false pride absent but self-respect present — because it is demonstrated by so many of the AA personalities through whom I learn AA principles.

I think I have also caught glimpses of it in writing about our other Traditions.

Who do I think I am, anyway?

B. L., Manhattan, N.Y.

And Then an Eskimo Came Over the Hill

August 1978

FOR A LONG TIME AFTER I came to Alcoholics Anonymous, while my thinking was still cluttered up, I would listen to another telling of a familiar (though pertinent) story and would wonder, "Why do they keep telling oldies like that?"

After a while, I concluded that almost every meeting included a newcomer or two who needed to absorb that story. It wasn't intended for me, with my weeks, months, then one year of sobriety. I just tried to stay open-minded and tolerant as I heard it again and again.

But the time came when I realized, with jolting surprise, that I, too, was meant to hear these illustrative tales over and over until I knew how much each one applies to *me*.

The story that hit home hardest was the one about the Eskimo. One day, alone and thinking about AA in my life, it came to me that I had had my own little old Eskimo for more than sixty years. I had been going along smugly giving others the right to pray if they had faith in it, but knowing full well that prayer really didn't work — all because of my coincidental Eskimo who had come along when prayer failed.

The story itself concerns a man engaged in proving to a friend that there was no power in prayer. He told of having been thrown from a runaway dog sled in a lonely area of the Arctic. Lying in the snow with a broken leg, he knew he would perish if a miracle did not happen. So he prayed for one, but went on lying there. No miracle answered his prayer.

His listener said, "But you *were* saved, or you wouldn't be here to tell about it."

"Not through prayer, pal. If it hadn't been for an Eskimo who just happened to come over the ridge and see me, I'd have died."

I must have heard that story dozens of times without ever remembering one late summer twilight in 1910 when I was ten years old. A few neighborhood boys were playing hide-and-seek. Intent on really hiding, I sped silently into a house being built on a vacant lot near my home. Upstairs in that unfinished house, I found a closet. I crept inside and pulled the door shut.

My pal Bill was it, and I heard him looking for me in the house. When he came upstairs, I held the doorknob, and it did not open when he turned the handle. Long after he had gone away, I felt it time to come out of hiding. Then I found why the door had not opened: The lock had secured the door against all but a key.

Having been to Sunday school, I remembered the many times I had been told that prayers were miraculously answered. So I asked in prayer for my release. But the door did not magically open when I tried it. I got on my knees and made my wishes firmly known. No luck. In fact, nothing happened no matter how I tried prayer. So I gave up in bitter disgust at the Man Up There, and tried making noise.

A long time later, I was panicky, sweaty, and sure I would starve. It was Saturday night. Workmen would not return until Monday.

Then I heard footsteps on the stairs and Bill calling my name. I answered, and he understood my plight and ran to my house. My father came and removed the door by taking the hinges off.

Yet all my life I had disavowed the prayer-answering idea. I always spoke of an incredible coincidence when I told the story. Bill had gone home to dinner, giving up the search. His folks had a huge bowl of mashed sweet potatoes topped with marshmallows — my favorite dish. Bill had thought of me and gone to telephone me with an invitation to come share that delicacy. So I always said, "If those marshmallows had not reminded Bill of my tastes and he had not remembered an unturning doorknob when he learned I was not yet home, I'd probably have died in that closet."

I was still a comparative newcomer to AA (at the age of seventy-plus) when that Eskimo story got through my identification crust. Almost too late, I learned how prayer really works.

C. C., North Hollywood, Calif.

What Is Acceptance?

by Bill W.

March 1962

ONE WAY TO GET AT the meaning of the principle of acceptance is to meditate upon it in the context of AA's much-used prayer: "God grant me the serenity to accept the things I cannot change, courage to change the things I can, and wisdom to know the difference."

Essentially, this is to ask for the resources of grace by which we may make spiritual progress under all conditions. Greatly emphasized in this wonderful prayer is a need for the kind of wisdom that discriminates between the possible and the impossible. We shall also see that life's formidable array of pains and problems will require many different degrees of acceptance as we try to apply this valued principle.

Sometimes, we have to find the right kind of acceptance for each day. Sometimes, we need to develop acceptance for what may come to pass tomorrow and, yet again, we shall have to accept a condition that may never change. Then, too, there frequently has to be a right and realistic acceptance of grievous flaws within ourselves and serious faults within those about us — defects that may not be fully remedied for years, if ever.

All of us will encounter failures, some retrievable and some not. We shall often meet with defeat — sometimes by accident, sometimes self-inflicted, and at still other times dealt to us by the injustice and violence of other people. Most of us will meet up with some degree of worldly success, and here the problem of the right kind of acceptance will be really difficult. Then there will be illness and death. How indeed shall we be able to accept all these?

It is always worthwhile to consider how grossly that good word "acceptance" can be misused. It can be warped to justify nearly every brand of weakness, nonsense, and folly. For instance, we can "accept" failure as a chronic condition, forever without profit or remedy. We can "accept" worldly success pridefully, as something wholly of our own making. We can also "accept" illness and death as certain evidence of a hostile and godless universe. With these twistings of *acceptance*, we AAs have had vast experience. Hence, we constantly try to remind ourselves that these perversions of acceptance are just gimmicks for excuse-making: a losing game at which we are, or at least have been, the world's champions.

This is why we treasure our Serenity Prayer so much. It brings a new light to us that can dissipate our old-time and nearly fatal habit of fooling ourselves. In the radiance of this prayer, we see that defeat, rightly accepted, need be no disaster. We now know that we do not have to run away, nor ought we again try to overcome adversity by still another bulldozing power drive that can only push up obstacles before us faster than they can be taken down.

On entering AA, we become the beneficiaries of a very different experience. Our new way of staying sober is literally founded upon the proposition that "Of ourselves, we are nothing, the Father doeth the works." In Steps One and Two of our recovery program, these ideas are specifically spelled out: "We admitted we were powerless over alcohol — that our lives had become unmanageable" and "Came to believe that a Power greater than ourselves could restore us to sanity." We couldn't lick alcohol with our own remaining resources, and so we accepted the further fact that dependence upon a Higher Power (if only our AA group) could do this hitherto impossible job.

The moment we were able to fully accept these facts, our release from the alcohol compulsion had begun. For most of us, this pair of acceptances had required a lot of exertion to achieve. Our whole treasured philosophy of self-sufficiency had to be cast aside. This had not been done with old-fashioned willpower; it was instead a matter of developing the willingness to *accept* these new facts of living. We neither ran nor fought. But *accept* we did. And then we were free. There had been no irretrievable disaster.

This kind of acceptance and faith is capable of producing 100 percent sobriety. In fact, it usually does; and it must, else we could have no life at all. But the moment we carry these attitudes into our emotional problems, we find that only relative results are possible. Nobody can, for example, become completely free from fear, anger, and pride. Hence, in this life we shall attain nothing like perfect humility and love. So we shall have to settle, respecting most of our problems, for a very gradual progress, punctuated sometimes by heavy setbacks. Our old-time attitudes of "all or nothing" will have to be abandoned.

Therefore, our very first problem is to accept our present circumstances as they are, ourselves as we are, and the people about us as they are. This is to adopt a realistic humility without which no genuine advance can even begin. Again and again, we shall need to return to that unflattering point of departure. This is an exercise in acceptance that we can profitably practice every day of our lives. Provided we strenuously avoid turning these realistic surveys of the facts of life into unrealistic alibis for apathy or defeatism, they can be the sure foundation upon which increased emotional health and therefore spiritual progress can be built. At least, this seems to be my own experience.

Another exercise that I practice is to try for a full inventory of my blessings and then for a right acceptance of the many gifts that

September 1975

"Don't drink, and go to meetings."

are mine — both temporal and spiritual. Here, I try to achieve a state of joyful gratitude. When such a brand of gratitude is repeatedly affirmed and pondered, it can finally displace the natural tendency to congratulate myself on whatever progress I may have been enabled to make in some areas of living. I try hard to hold fast to the truth that a full and thankful heart cannot entertain great conceits. When we are brimming with gratitude, our heartbeats must surely result in outgoing love, the finest emotion that we can ever know.

In times of very rough going, the grateful acceptance of my blessings, oft repeated, can also bring me some of the serenity of which our AA prayer speaks. Whenever I fall under acute pressures, I lengthen my daily walks and slowly repeat our Serenity Prayer in rhythm to my steps and breathing. If I feel that my pain has in part been occasioned by others, I try to repeat, "God grant me the serenity to love their best, and never fear their worst." This benign healing process of repetition, sometimes necessary to persist with for days, has seldom failed to restore me to at least a workable emotional balance and perspective.

Another helpful step is to steadfastly affirm the understanding that pain can bring. Indeed, pain is one of our greatest teachers. Though I still find it difficult to accept today's pain and anxiety with any great degree of serenity — as those more advanced in the spiritual life seem able to do — I can, if I try hard, give thanks for present pain nevertheless. I find the willingness to do this by contemplating the lessons learned from past suffering — lessons which have led to the blessings I now enjoy. I can remember, if I insist, how the agonies of alcoholism, the pain of rebellion and thwarted pride, have often led me to God's grace, and so to a new freedom. So, as I walk along, I repeat still other phrases such as these: "Pain is the touchstone of progress." . . . "Fear no evil." . . . "This, too, will pass." . . . "This experience can be turned to benefit."

These fragments of prayer bring far more than mere comfort. They keep me on the track of right acceptance; they break up my compulsive themes of guilt, depression, rebellion, and pride; and sometimes they endow me with the courage to change the things I can, and the wisdom to know the difference.

To those who have never given these potent exercises in acceptance a real workout, I recommend them highly the next time the heat is on. Or, for that matter, at any time!

NEITHER ENDORSES NOR OPPOSES ANY CAUSES

The Shape of Things to Come

by Bill W.

February 1961

THE FIRST QUARTER-CENTURY of AA is now history. Our next twenty-five years lie in prospect before us. How, then, can we make the most of this new grant of time?

Perhaps our very first realization should be that we can't stand still. Now that our basic principles seem established, now that our functioning is fairly effective and widespread, it would be temptingly easy to settle down as merely one more useful agency on the world scene. We could conclude that "AA is fine, just the way it is."

Yet how many of us, for example, would presume to declare, "Well, I'm sober and I'm happy. What more can I want, or do? I'm fine the way I am." We know that the price of such self-satisfaction is an inevitable backslide, punctuated at some point by a very rude awakening. We have to grow or else deteriorate. For us, the "status quo" can only be for today, never for tomorrow. Change we must; we cannot stand still.

Just how, then, can AA go on changing for the better? Does this mean that we are to tinker with our basic principles? Should we try to amend our Twelve Steps and Twelve Traditions? Here the answer would seem to be "no." Those twenty-four principles have first liberated us, have then held us in unity, and have enabled us to function and to grow as AA members, and as a whole. Of course perfect truth is surely something better understood by God than by any of us. Nevertheless we have come to believe that AA's recovery Steps and Traditions do represent the approximate truths which we need for our particular purpose. The more we practice them, the more we like them. So there is little doubt that AA principles continue to be advocated in the form they stand now.

So then, if our basics are so firmly fixed as all this, what is there left to change or to improve? The answer will immediately occur to us. While we need not alter our truths, *we can surely improve their application to ourselves, to AA as a whole, and to our relation with the world around us.* We can constantly step up "the practice of these principles in all our affairs."

As we now enter upon the next great phase of AA's life, let us therefore rededicate ourselves to an ever greater responsibility for our general welfare. Let us continue to take our inventory as a fellowship, searching out our flaws and confessing them freely. Let us devote ourselves to the repair of all faulty relations that may exist, whether within or without.

And above all, let us remember that great legion who still suffer from alcoholism and who are still without hope. Let us, at any cost or sacrifice, so improve our communication with all these that they may find what we have found — a new life of freedom under God.

AA Is Getting Too Organized!

February 1961

"WE'RE GETTING ENTIRELY TOO big," he said. "And too organized. We get too much publicity. We're in danger of losing the blessings of intimacy, the person-to-person touch. We forget that this outfit is based simply on one drunk talking to another. We don't need any fancy headquarters and big conventions and TV shows."

My friend — I'll call him Al — went on: "Why, when I came in nobody talked about conferences and public relations. That sounds like Madison Avenue, not like a spiritual movement. All

this organizing for infomation and fund-raising is contrary to the spirit of AA.

"And another thing: Why are doctors and other outsiders asked to speak at our meetings? They need *us*, we don't need them."

I think you have to listen, respectfully, when the man who talks like this is a guy whose quality of sobriety commands your admiration. Loquacious, intense, burningly sincere and genuinely concerned about AA, he's almost as prodigal with words and opinions as he has been, for ten years or so, with his heart, time, money, and energy in personal Twelfth Step work.

Almost everyone would agree, I think, Al's a fine and useful AA member, doing a good job. God bless him. I can never hope to match him in energy output, time spent in AA activity, number of persons helped, or in spirituality.

I was surprised to hear him across the table echoing the very words I had once said. He was articulating my own feelings of some years ago. That this man whose AA life had inspired me so often should sound this way was disappointing. I'm sorry this sounds smug. I had discarded the views he held and thought that everyone else had changed to my new views, too — or should!

I had spent ten years nursing the feelings Al was voicing. During that time I talked much and often about the "necessity of growth"; "accepting the facts of things as they are"; "living in today, not yesterday or tomorrow." I had never applied those words to my own attitude toward AA as a whole.

Mostly I talked about how wonderful AA was *when I first*

came in. I was often heard bewailing the loss of some quality of the movement that had impressed me during my first year or so of sobriety. I face it now: I was pining day after day for the calendar to turn back, in AA's history, and leave it where I *thought* it was when I first came in — as if my feeble first glimpses of AA were the whole reality, or the ways things should be!

Memories, anyone? Is anybody here reading his own story?

While saying "it is necessary for me to grow as a person to maintain my AA sobriety," I had tacitly denied the inevitable corollary: AA grows too. Who wants to stop it? Shall we eliminate the last 100,000 or so members who came in — and close the doors, except to a screened minority, for the future?

Saying "I must continually accept the facts and truths of life as they are," I had quietly, grudgingly refused to accept the fact that AA is a worldwide movement which has caused international reverberations, and has influenced the nonalcoholic world immensely. It was worldwide when I found it (in 1945), so what I thought was just "one drunk talking to another" was already the property, not of just a few of us, but probably of the ages, for all mankind who wanted to profit by it.

Saying "I must live in today, not yesterday or tomorrow," I persisted in declaring the AA of yesterday was better, or was the *real* AA. I continually pined for AA's yesterday, feared for its tomorrow (oh, me of little faith).

While saying "Groups are getting too big — we don't get to know each other," I kept on taking new men to the biggest meetings in town and to an annual dinner in which thousands of members joined — so they could share the inspiration I found there. I didn't give a thought to the fact that each year at the dinner there were more and more faces I knew — old and new.

You know what? None of AA's new growth or procedures, I see now, has ever interfered during that delicate moment when I talk face-to-face with a scared new member. In fact, it seems to me the opportunities are now enhanced and are greater than ever. And so are the responsibilities, of course.

During my "there's too much organization" period, I was delighted to see a local central office opened so we could be surer that each prospective member who inquired got individual attention.

Oh, the human beings on its staff and guiding committee do things of which I disapprove, to be sure. So?

Because it isn't all run as I think it should be, am I to be a disgruntled "go it aloner" and refuse to help in the overall job of carrying the message? No thanks. Instead of picking up my marbles (bottles?) and going home, I prefer to stay with *my people*, and help where I can. Maybe I can improve the operation, or at least learn why it's done the way it is. The other fellows just may be right.

Sometimes I don't like a Grapevine article, or I feel that something which should be printed is censored out. I know two people who say they resent being reminded their subscriptions are running out! They deplore "promotion." But all three of us get too much good out of it to stop reading it or to stop passing copies and subscriptions along.

I think it's now my duty to do everything in my power to make our message available to everyone who has use for it. To whom can we say no — narcotic addicts, neurotics, prostitutes, ex-cons, homosexuals, people of other races, doctors, psychiatrists, or government officials who deal with alcoholics?

It's scary to realize how many people such "playing God" could condemn to death. From the ranks cited have come some of the best AA people I know. I need to do all I can to support my local service office, our world service office, and the Grapevine.

But my friend Al felt quite differently.

I gather it was ever thus in AA, and we're going to live over and over again the hard struggle that began with the writing of the book *Alcoholics Anonymous*. As I understand it, some members (conservatives?) opposed the idea. They thought it smacked of promotion, might give wrong impressions, would be "selling the program." Others (radicals?) felt deeply that such risks should be run to make the message more widely available — especially to those who could not be reached in person.

I'm selfishly glad the book got published. It and some subsequent publicity about AA saved my life. I'm glad, too, for the TV shows, movies, books, and articles about AA; also for the many doctors, clergymen, and public officials who learned all they could about AA and as a result pushed a score of my best AA friends in our direction.

I'm equally glad that the "conservatives" pointed out the dangers of promotion and firmly reminded the promoter types, like me, that we're essentially a spiritual movement. Their wise words of caution helped preserve much of what I now love best about AA.

I hope my friend Al becomes as happy and unfearful about today's Alcoholics Anonymous, all aspects of it, as I am now. There are signs. He's been elected to do a general service job. He says, " I don't like it, but here I am, so I'll do it." That's Al all right.

Anonymous, New York City

Our Primary Purpose and the Special-Purpose Group

by John L. Norris, MD

October 1977

I N RECENT YEARS, NO SUBJECT seems to have been discussed more often, in more detail, for longer hours, and with more heat than the question of special-purpose groups. Both the advocates and the adversaries of special-purpose groups hold very strong opinions on the subject, and those of us who have tried to occupy the middle ground can see the logic on both sides.

Our Third Tradition says, "The only requirement for AA membership is a desire to stop drinking." In general, we have inclined to this view: When other requirements are added that might seem to exclude some alcoholics, these should be considered AA meetings and *not* AA groups. We have never discouraged AAs from forming special-purpose meetings of any or all kinds to meet the needs of interested individuals, but we have been hesitant to consider as *groups* those that might seem to exclude any alcoholic, for whatever reason.

Many members feel that no AA group is special and, therefore, that no group should be labeled as such or even give the impression that it is "special." However, the fact is that such groups *do* exist — in the United States and Canada, at least. There are women's groups, stag groups, young people's groups, and groups for priests, doctors, lawyers, and homosexual members. These groups feel that the "labels" serve the purpose of attraction (*dou-*

ble identification) and are not intended to imply exclusion of other alcoholics.

Probably the earliest of the so-called special-purpose groups were women's groups, and it is very easy to understand how they came about. In the early days of the Fellowship, before AA was well-known and when its membership was made up largely of male alcoholics, many women felt very timid about attending such groups, and their husbands felt even more strongly about having them attend. The solution seemed to be daytime meetings made up of women, and many of these began to spring up all over our country. Beyond any doubt, they served (and probably still do serve) a very useful purpose, and many of the women who started in these groups went on to become extremely active members of regular, mixed groups of alcoholics.

The adversaries of the special-purpose group would say that this is an instance where the good became the enemy of the best, to use co-founder Bill W.'s phrase. Once AA had accepted one kind of special-purpose group, it became difficult, if not almost impossible, not to accept others.

We have no difficulty in understanding the kind of communication and understanding that can exist among groups of people who share other interests in addition to their alcoholism. It has always been hoped that doctors, priests, policemen, young people, women, etc. who meet together in special groups will also participate in

April 1959

"The problem is — how do you get them to take the first drink?"

the activities of regular, mixed AA groups. We live in a world made up of all kinds of people, who function in a variety of professions, and it is in this world that we have to function as individuals. If AA is a preparation and support for normal living, then it would seem that the most meaningful AA activity would occur in groups made up of all kinds of people who follow all kinds of professions.

The proliferation of so many kinds of special groups has been a matter of concern, and we sometimes wonder where this will end. Will we soon be having Catholic groups. Protestant groups, Jewish groups, atheist groups, agnostic groups, groups made up of members of one political party or another? Certainly, we hope not, and we don't anticipate any such thing. However, we do feel that we should be aware of a possible trend and perhaps bend every effort to encourage our similarities and not our particularities.

I mentioned earlier that we have never discouraged special-purpose *meetings* but have been hesitant to list as *groups* those that might seem to preclude other alcoholics' attending. Perhaps we might talk a little bit about the differences between an AA meeting and an AA group. Our directories state: "Traditionally, two or more alcoholics meeting together for purposes of sobriety may consider themselves an AA group, provided that, as a group, they are self-supporting and have no outside affiliation." And in the beginning of our Fellowship in countries outside the United States and Canada, we agreed on six points that describe what an AA group is. They are:

"(1) All members of a group are alcoholics, and all alcoholics are eligible for membership. (2) As a group, they are fully self-supporting. (3) A group's primary purpose is to help alcoholics recover through the Twelve Steps. (4) As a group, they have no outside affiliation. (5) As a group, they have no opinion on outside issues. (6) As a group, their public relations policy is based on attraction rather than promotion, and they maintain personal anonymity at the level of press, radio-TV, and film."

Without a doubt, meetings are the primary activity of each AA group and the most common way of carrying the message to newcomers and to other members who want to maintain recovery. When we make a distinction between AA groups and AA meetings, we are emphasizing a *concept* rather than the *format* of what actually happens when AAs get together. We think of an AA group as something that continues to exist even when there is no meeting taking place, because a group does many other things besides hold meetings. On the other hand, special-purpose *meetings*, which take care of the needs of interested individuals, are usually informal gatherings with no particular structure.

At the 1973 General Service Conference, workshops on "The AA Group" were held and went into overtime because of lengthy discussion on the subject of special-purpose groups. By request of this Conference, the subject was scheduled for full-scale discussion at the 1974 Conference. The time allotted for it again proved to be insufficient and a special session — lasting four hours — was called. The final action was that the AA General Service Office should list *all* groups in accordance with the definition of an AA group listed in the front of all our directories.

In the final analysis, perhaps, what we are really dealing with in special-purpose groups is communication among AA members and how to improve it so that we can do a better job of carrying the AA message to alcoholics of all kinds.

The Washingtonians

July 1976

A LCOHOLICS ANONYMOUS WAS ONLY ten years old when Bill W., AA's co-founder, wrote: "Those who read the July [1945] Grapevine were startled, then sobered, by the account which it carried of the Washingtonian movement. It was hard for us to believe that 100 years ago the newspapers of this country were carrying enthusiastic accounts about 100,000 alcoholics who were helping each other stay sober; that today the influence of this good work has so completely disappeared that few of us had ever heard of it. . . .

"May we always be willing to learn from experience!" Bill cautioned.

Founded by six drunks in 1840, the Washingtonians had grown in membership to hundreds of thousands in a short twelve years, and then destroyed themselves as an organization and dropped out of sight. By 1852, all that remained of their spectacular power as a method of treatment was the Home for the Fallen in Boston.

In a talk on the Traditions shortly before his death, Bill said that

the Washingtonians had done things "which were very natural to do, but which had turned out to be utterly destructive. And it was this spectacle of the past, brought before us as our Traditions were evolving, that confirmed that we were probably very much on the right track in this matter of no public controversy; in this question of paying our own bills; in this question of not becoming involved with other enterprises, and so on down the line. And above all, it confirmed the great protective guide of our anonymity Tradition."

Later, in the book *Alcoholics Anonymous Comes of Age,* Bill wrote: "In many respects the Washingtonians were akin to AA. . . . Had they stuck to their one goal, they might have found the full answer. Instead, the Washingtonians permitted politicians and reformers, both alcoholic and nonalcoholic, to use the society for their own purposes. . . . Within a very few years they had completely lost their effectiveness in helping alcoholics, and the society collapsed.

"The lesson to be learned from the Washingtonians was not overlooked by Alcoholics Anonymous. As we surveyed the wreck of that movement, early AA members resolved to keep our Society out of public controversy."

And to a friend Bill wrote, "I wish every AA could indelibly burn the history of the Washingtonians into his memory. It is an outstanding example of how, and how not, we ought to conduct ourselves. In a sense, Alcoholics Anonymous has never had a problem seriously threatening our overall unity. Yet I notice that some AAs are complacent enough to suppose we never shall."

Bill also recalled the fate of the Washingtonians before 1,500 AAs gathered at the annual banquet in New York City on November 7, 1945. "In short, the Washingtonians went out to settle the world's affairs before they had learned to manage themselves. They had no capacity for minding their own business. . . . The negatives within them overthrew the positives.

"That won't happen here," Bill urged in closing, "if we remember, publicly and privately, our own simple principles of honesty, tolerance, and humility, and that we live only by the grace of God."

Traditions! Words to remember! Thanks, Bill. Thank you, Washingtonians.

D. P., Ogden, Utah

Are We Letting Others Do Our Work?

December 1978

W ITHIN AA, CONCERN IS OFTEN expressed over the steadily increasing number of agencies in the alcoholism field. Are such agencies taking over our work? This topic might be compared to the weather. We keep talking about it, and we are wasting time on such a debate, because there is nothing we can do about it. The "others" are here to stay. Let's cooperate with the treatment facilities, the detox centers — the "others." We need them.

The more important question is: Are we *letting* others do our work? There is no way that the "others" can do for the sick and suffering alcoholic what we, the recovering alcoholics, can do. Our threefold malady must be treated in all three areas to effect full recovery from our "seemingly hopeless state of mind and body."

We can assist "others" to do *their* work by placing sick alcoholics in a treatment facility so that they will not die, so that they can recover physically; so that they can then do *our* work by trying to carry the message of recovery to healthier, more receptive individuals.

The fact that our co-founder Bill was led to none other than a medical doctor was part of the great miracle of our Fellowship. As an MD, Dr. Bob treated many early AAs, without charge, for the physical part of our threefold malady — *but* he always remembered that he must return again and again to help the newcomer with the other two areas of our disease. These are the emotions or mental quirks that only another alcoholic can identify with, and the spiritual disintegration that only another alcoholic can comprehend. Let's not shirk our sponsorship responsibility in these areas.

Let the "others" do their work. Let the "others" dry out our prospects. Let the "others" clean and feed our prospects physically. But let us be there to talk with them, and walk with them from the recovery room to an AA contact, to an AA meeting, and to a new way of life.

After many years of complaining that we have no place to take drunks, we now do have a place — and we do take them there. Then, often, we feel we have done our job. Let others handle it. But we know that when they are released from any institution, they need a guiding hand and heart or they will head for the bottle, where they instinctively know they will find comfort. Let's be there to offer that guiding hand and heart.

Too often, the hand and heart of AA are no longer there, and some of us old-timers are letting this happen, because we don't stress to the younger member that sobriety depends largely upon carrying the *message — not the body*. The newer member is detox-oriented and is ready, at the ring of the phone, to taxi the drunk to the nearest facility. We, as older members, feel we have done our part. We have "baby-sat" for hours on end, administered the honey and the TLC, carried the body, and then tried to carry the message; now we feel it's time for newer members to have their turn. But let's urge them to use Chapter 7 of the Big Book, "Working with Others," where we are told, "You can help when no one else can. You can secure their confidence when others fail . . . Helping others is the foundation stone of your recovery."

We older members should remind the newer member of the responsibilities of a sponsor; that as a sponsor, he or she is "a leader. The stakes are about as big as they could be. A human life and usually the happiness of a whole family hang in the balance. What the sponsor does and says,. . . how well he handles criticisms, and how well he or she leads the prospect on by personal spiritual example — these qualities of leadership can make all the difference, often the difference between life and death." Bill wrote that for us in discussing the Ninth Concept.

Let us not be a taxi service to and from treatment centers, or a clerk handling an alcoholic's admission to the hospital of his choice; let us not enable the drinking prospect to continue on the path of destruction, or enable the continued search for the "easier, softer way." The "others," too, have found that the easier, softer way is enabling the drunk to stay drunk, and they are reluctant to readmit the repeaters, the perennial "slippers."

Many alcoholism counselors are very good at their profession and do try in their professional capacity to help the alcoholic. They seem to do it best when they are able to convince the prospect that the spiritual principles of the Twelve Steps of AA offer the total sobriety that will enable him "to become happily and usefully whole."

H. R., Miami, Fla.

Those 'Goof Balls'

by Bill W.

November 1945

MORPHINE, CODEINE, CHLORAL HYDRATE, Luminal, Seconal, Nembutal, Amytal — these and kindred drugs have killed many alcoholics. And I once nearly killed myself with chloral hydrate. Nor is my own observation and experience unique, for many an old-time AA can speak with force and fervor on the subject of "goof balls."

Excepting an infrequent suicide, nobody uses these drugs in the expectation of death. To many alcoholics still in the drinking state, they represent blessed relief from the agonies of a hangover.

Some of us, perfectly sober for months or years, contract the habit of using sedatives to cure insomnia or slight nervous irritability. I have the impression that some of us get away with it, too, year after year, just as we did when we first began to drink alcohol. Yet experience shows, all too often, that even the "controlled" pill-taker may get out of control. The same crazy rationalizations that once characterized his drinking begin to blight his existence. He thinks that if pills can cure insomnia, so may they cure his worry.

Now a word about the use of morphine by physicians. Sometimes, a general practitioner, not knowing his patient is already loaded with barbiturates, will give a morphine injection. A friend of mine died like that. Sober about three years, he got into an emotional jam. Pills led to alcohol, and this combination to still more pills. His doctor found an excited heart. Out came the needle, and a few hours later out went a very good friend. Another close friend, sober three years, also fell on evil days — pills and liquor. At the end of about three weeks of this diet, he was placed one evening in a sanitarium. Nobody told the doctor there about the pills with which his system was already loaded. The patient was "eased" with a shot of codeine. Before daylight he was dead.

Near the end of my own drinking career, I had an alarming experience. Chloral hydrate was prescribed for one of my terrible hangovers. The doctor warned me to stick rigidly to his dosage. But I kept possession of the bottle. While my wife slept quietly beside me, I reached under the mattress, took out the flask, and guzzled the whole business. I had a narrow shave. Moral: When a doctor gives a legitimate sedative prescription, don't let the alcoholic have the bottle.

As a matter of fact, our friends the doctors are seldom directly to blame for the dire results we so often experience. It is much too easy for alcoholics to buy these dangerous drugs, and once possessed of them, the drinker is likely to use them without any judgment whatever. Sometimes, his well-meaning friends, unable to see him suffer, hand him pills themselves. It's a very dangerous business.

It's even dangerous to give a suffering alcoholic a drink if he is already loaded with pills. Years ago, I had an experience of this

VICTOR E.

sort. We had a prospect in tow whom I shall call Slim. He had finally consented to go to a hospital. On the way, he had a few — but only a small quantity compared to his customary capacity. Just before we reached the hospital, Slim's speech suddenly got very thick, and he passed out. I had to get a porter to help him to a cab. As he could usually manage a couple of bottles a day when active, I couldn't understand this performance at all. Arrived at the hospital, Slim was still slumped in his seat, and I couldn't move him. Our good friend Dr. Silkworth came out and peered in the cab door. One look was apparently enough. Said he to me, "How is this man's heart?"

Confidently, I replied, "He's got a heart like an elephant. Told me so himself. But I don't see how he got drunk so fast. I gave him very little liquor."

Out came the doctor's stethoscope. Turning then to me, he said, "Not much use bringing this man in here. He can't last long. What else has he been taking besides liquor?"

Stunned, I replied, "Nothing that I know of."

Very gingerly, an attendant carried Slim inside. Out came the stethoscope again. The doctor shook his head, saying, "This poor chap has been loaded with barbiturates for days. When you gave him alcohol, even a little, it fired off the accumulated charge of sedative he had in him. See how blue he is? His heart isn't really working much. It's just jittering. I can't even count it."

The doctor rushed to the phone and called Slim's wife. To my horror, she confirmed the fact that he had been taking heavy doses of Amytal for about ten days. The doctor gently told her she had better hurry, else she might be too late. Then he called a famous heart specialist for consultation and told him to hurry, too. They

September 1974

laid Slim on a bed upstairs. The great specialist came and drew out his stethoscope. At once, he looked very serious, and motioning us out into the hall, he said that he would leave a prescription but that he did not think my friend could possibly live through the night. Dr. Silkworth agreed.

During these proceedings, I had been praying as I never had prayed before. After the two doctors had pronounced the death sentence on Slim, I told them of my prayers and explained, cheerfully as I could, that I had been reading Dr. Alexis Carrel's book *Man the Unknown*, in which prayer was described as effecting miraculous cures. The great specialist took his leave. Dr. Silkworth and I went downstairs to wait for the prescription to come in. A boy finally brought two capsules from the drugstore. The doctor looked at them, saying he hated to give them, they were so powerful. We went upstairs and as we stepped off the elevator we saw someone coming down the hall jauntily smoking a cigarette. "Hello, boys," roared Slim. "What am I supposed to be doing in here?"

Never, so long as I live, shall I forget the relief and astonishment that spread over the doctor's countenance as he quickly tested Slim's heart. Looking at me, he said, "This man's heart is now normal. Fifteen minutes ago I couldn't count it. I thought I knew these alcoholic hearts pretty well. But I've never seen anything like this — never. I can't understand it." What miracle saved Slim, no one can say. He left the hospital in a few days, without ill effects from his experience.

As for me — well, I guess I learned my lesson then and there. No more "goof balls" unless the doctor says so — not for me. No thank you!

As Different as We Choose to Be

May 1984

CONSIDERING THE PANIC that the question of AA and drug addicts is causing in California, it could be more appropriately described as "alcoholics versus drug addicts" or "us against them."

There are several different opinions being expressed in California on how we should deal with this "problem." Some feel we should just not let "them" in; better to lose a few dope fiends (who may or may not be alcoholic) than to jeopardize the program that saved our lives. They either decide to be at least partly alcoholic, or they don't stay. They should also be willing to make this decision within their first two or three meetings.

Others I have spoken to feel that AA has come of age, so to speak, and should open its doors to all chemically dependent people whether they drink or not.

Personally, I don't fit into either category. There seems to be a middle group that feels the job of deciding who is a member belongs to the individual and God. There seems to be a great deal of anger in my area when discussing drug addicts and AA, and where I come from, that kind of anger is usually generated by fear.

I would like to share one dually addicted AA member's experience and — because I can't help it — opinion. Dual addicts are different from "pure" addicts. I say this because it is my opinion that a dual addict is just an alcoholic who had chemical problems other than alcohol. It happens to be so in my case.

I grew up in the 1960s. Hippies, peace marches, the Beatles, drugs in general, gurus, and finding yourself were in. I was *not*. Being completely inadequate in all areas had become almost a natural state for me. Then, I found alcohol — peppermint schnapps, to be exact — and life became a real possibility. I became an intellectual, glamorous, and witty fourteen-year-old alcoholic. From the first drink (which I never forgot), I knew that I had found the answer to all of life's problems. I just had to figure out how to drink enough to maintain superiority without getting arrested or killed.

When I was fifteen, someone turned me on to pot. I was having trouble staying awake, so someone gave me whites — I could drink all night and still be standing! Someone else asked if I was ready for a spiritual experience, and I tried my first hit of acid (LSD). Heroin was suggested — I was available. I continued to drink and indulge myself in whatever chemical came my way. In my mind, drinking and drugs were inseparable. It was a way of life. The point I am trying to make is that from the time I was fifteen years old, I exhibited all of the classic signs of an alcoholic: blackouts, inability to predict my behavior, inability to have just one drink, etc. But I didn't know that.

It was not cool to be a lush, and God knows we had to be *cool*. Some of my friends died being cool. And unfortunately for you, that's how I came into AA — *too cool!* There is a statement of policy making the rounds in AA groups today that, considering my attitude and inability to accept my alcoholism, might have made it impossible for me to stay in Alcoholics Anonymous had it been used when I was new. It reads in part: "These newcomers are truly welcome here as members of our Fellowship, provided their primary addiction is to alcohol — something they alone can decide. We ask only that when discussing their problems, they confine themselves to those related to their alcoholism."

There is more to the statement, but it is that portion I would like to address myself to. I have already told you how difficult it was for me to admit my alcohol problem. I also had a serious attitude problem. If I was told to do something, I just couldn't do it; if I was told *not* to do something, it was absolutely essential that I do it. If I had been told when I was new that I couldn't talk about drugs in meetings, I would have had to talk about them all the time. If AA members then would have reacted as hostilely as some do today, I would have said, "Later."

I was *incapable* of telling you my problems in the beginning — primary or otherwise. I didn't trust anyone, and I felt alone and isolated. I will continue to thank God I came into an AA group that was spiritually fit enough that they did not find it necessary to

censor my conversation or my actions in order to protect themselves. When I was new, I did talk about drugs, and I used a lot of
four-letter words to do it! Somehow, my group managed to allow
me the dignity to choose to change these things and the freedom to
do it when I *could*, and not when *they* thought I *should*.

I had finally found a place where — weird as I was — I was accepted and encouraged to stay. I was given love and understanding
beyond my comprehension, and when I got really wild, one of the
old-timers would take me aside after the meetings and explain to
me the damage I was doing, or could do, and suggest alternatives.
In turn, I came to feel very protective of AA and of my group. I developed a real desire to be a contributing member of AA.

I found that feeling different or having an edge on the other
AA members by being an alcoholic-addict was not appealing to
me. I do not refer to myself as an alcoholic-addict, for the very reasons I mentioned in the beginning. I truly feel that I am an alcoholic who had problems with other chemicals, and if I participate in
our program of recovery by practicing these spiritual principles in
my life, it just doesn't occur to me to stick needles in my arm or
smoke those funny cigareetes. I have found a great freedom in
being one among many.

I do, however, understand the need to identify — that's why I
believe AA talks should never be censored. When I am asked to

December 1973

speak at an AA meeting, I share my experience with drugs as part of my story — because it *is* part of my story, just as children, five marriages, prison, and sleeping in parks are part of someone else's story. I wouldn't think of telling you not to share all of you with me.

There seems to be a real tolerance of people in my home group. "The only requirement for membership is a desire to stop drinking," and we seem to have no trouble sticking to our single purpose, which is to carry the message to still-suffering alcoholics, however damaged and confused they are in the beginning. If we believe what we hear in AA everywhere, miracles happen here. But they take time.

It is very hard for me to believe that a few hundred misplaced druggies could destroy AA. It is very easy for me to believe that the kind of blind anger that fear brings could. I'm talking about the kind of fear that leads us to take sides against each other and require sick minds to make rational decisions, like "Is your primary addiction to alcohol?" — the kind of fear that caused the early members of AA to make lists of membership requirements to protect their groups from "them." There is a fine line between upholding our singleness-of-purpose Tradition and limiting or restricting our membership. The day AA appears to be rejecting people who may be alcoholic, we will begin to die. The bottom line is: We are all we have. What good will it do us if, while defending our "rights," we destroy AA? It has always been said that if AA is ever destroyed, the danger will come from within. Can any of us survive without the Fellowship of AA?

I have a few ideas to share that might help. Since treatment facilities seem to be sending us so many people who admittedly have no alcohol problem, can we send letters to the administrators explaining what AA is, what we do and do not do, just as we send anonymity letters to newspapers and TV and radio stations?
Could we, the members with a little time, remember that this might be such newcomers' only contact with AA, and treat them with tolerance and patience? Can we refer drug addicts to Narcotics Anonymous, quietly, after the meeting? Can some of us with dual addiction start NA meetings, with some healthy recovery going on? Can we alcoholics who have chemical problems other than alcohol relinquish our uniqueness for the unity that puts our common welfare first? Can we remember that *all* people who suffer from alcoholism are welcomed in AA — even if they can't admit

their problem? Can we remember that the changes did not occur overnight in any of us, and give the new ones a chance to *want* to change?

May the power that presides over us all continue to do so.

D. G., Huntington Beach, Calif.

Back to Basics

September 1977

PERHAPS IT'S THE NATURE OF THE BEAST, but it's a well-known fact that drunks tend to complicate the hell out of things. Recently, through a series of miracles and incredible strokes of good luck, and with a pile of help from some beautiful people and my Higher Power, I broke all the odds and celebrated my fourth AA birthday.

My wife made a cake, and at our small meeting that night, I was asked to chair. I did, and I'd no sooner started talking than I realized what I was saying had nothing to do with AA.

Period.

Recently, I'd gotten into one of those self-help awareness books, all about curing your tush or something, and the meeting I was chairing was straight out of the awareness book. Maybe that would have been all right, because perhaps we need to go a step beyond sometimes (although I've since changed my mind and live straight out of the Big Book) — except for one vital fact.

Sitting down at the other end of the table was a guy named Dick. And Dick, bless him, had a plain, old-fashioned, gut-level, puke-in-the-mornings-and-see-spiders-and-snakes, bust-up-your-marriage-and-lose-your-job, convulsion-and-screaming-fit *drinking* problem.

Really. Dick was an alcoholic brand-new to the program, and he obviously couldn't care less whether or not I'd found peace and tranquility through this new method that involved harnessing the cosmic forces inside my central being.

As a matter of fact, Dick was trying to get a cup of coffee to his mouth, and most of it went down his front. But he got some in the right place, and then he looked up and saw me staring at him.

He smiled.

And I remembered just who the hell I was in the whole lash-up. I wasn't a guru, or some philosopher looking for the answer to Great Questions.

I was and am a drunk.

Four years ago, I looked just like Dick. Worse, because I had puke on my sleeve when I came to the first meeting and I didn't get *any* coffee in the right place.

I'm a drunk. And all the cosmic forces, all the awareness books or self-help gimmicks, all the super-duper-go-gettum-in-the-bushes new and whippy ideas brought out in shiny new packages and books each month can't change it.

I'm a drunk, and I'd like to thank Dick for bringing me back to basics. I'd like to thank him for jerking me away from the insanity of thinking I'll ever be anything but a drunk; thank him for pulling me back to a program that works for me and keeps me alive and functioning. And sober.

But most of all, I'd like to thank Dick for that smile. That's where it's at.

G. P., Elbert, Colo.

Tradition Ten

*Alcoholics Anonymous has no opinion
on outside issues; hence the AA name
ought never be drawn into public controversy*

May 1971

I COULD HEAR THEM down the street, before seeing them. Outside our AA meeting room, John and Jane were having at each other again, as they often did, in a political argument — good-natured, but earnest and loud. It was the year of a national election, long past, before I had ever heard of our Traditions. When I got to the door, I saw that one combatant wore a donkey pin, the other an elephant. Both also wore exasperated looks on their red faces, and neither would listen to a word the other said.

Seeing me, they quit yelling and went into the meeting room with me, apparently leaving their strong differences outside. Just inside the door, they removed their political buttons.

"Why do that?" I asked. "Isn't it just as important to express your convictions in AA as anywhere else?"

John said, "National politics has no place in AA."

"What if I spoke to a new member I wanted to help, and she saw my political affiliation was different from hers?" Jane explained. "It might stand in the way of her listening to the AA message. What matters in AA is that we all have one thing in common — our drinking problem. Our various disagreements outside AA don't count here."

Being fresher from the barrooms than they were, I remembered a sign I had seen in one: "Politics, religion, and ladies are not appropriate topics of conversation in a saloon." The peace-ensuring wisdom of that had impressed me even when drunk. These AAs were smart, too, I thought; their practice of leaving arguments outside not only prevented their accidentally keeping some alcoholics out, it also helped hold together those already in the Fellowship by cutting down reasons for quarrels.

In retrospect, nearly a quarter-century later, that incident is now recognizable as my first brush with our Tenth Tradition, although it happened some time before the Traditions were written. In 1948, such experience-rooted, wise behavior was just called "the AA way."

Somehow, by instinct or the grace of God, the earliest AAs apparently arrived at this intelligent custom by coping with actual dilemmas. For instance, though surrounded by arguments following the repeal of prohibition, they knew enough to avoid the appearance of lining AA up with either the wets or the drys of the 1930s, long before such wisdom was codified as Tradition Ten. Not only would such alignment have split the then-tiny, struggling band of nameless drunks into bitterly fractious factions, but taking sides in such a struggle would also have brought the Fellowship the enmity of everyone outside AA who differed with whatever the AA party line might have been.

Wet alcoholics like me (believing liquor should be legal) would have stayed away in droves from our movement if it had been dry (demanding national or local prohibition), and vice versa. So I suggest that, in a very real sense, "the AA way" later described in this Tradition saved my life. It made possible my belonging to AA, even though I was soon to learn that I disagreed with many AA members on various other topics as well.

If AA had tied itself up with one particular Christian denomination, with humanism, with Islam, or with one particular school of psychology-psychiatry in the big wars beginning to brew in the 1930s, look how many of us would have had additional strong reasons for refusing to go to AA!

Among the most controversial matters of the 1970s are: a war, race, some young people's behavior, poverty, and drugs. It is notable that AA has not divided itself into camps on these issues. I would not dream of dragging any one of them into an AA relationship, nor of trying to find out who in AA agrees with me on those topics and who does not. It is much more important to me to keep uppermost in my mind that our common endeavor — recovery from alcoholism — is the most important part of my relationship with other AAs.

But outside AA, as a private citizen not identified as an AA member, I am, of course, free to act as I choose on those subjects, just as any other concerned person is. Instead of limiting my freedom, this Tradition gives me complete liberty outside the Fellowship, and frees me to concentrate on recovery alone while I am in AA circles.

Only when I began preparing this series of articles did I discover how beautifully many other Traditions support this one. Number One (common welfare) reminds me that our common bond is more important than our various differences outside AA. Two (group conscience) tells me that leaders are only servants in AA, not governors with the power to take us into public controversies. Three (membership requirement) reminds me that alcoholics who want our help need not agree with us on *any* issues. Four (group autonomy) declares that each group can run its own affairs

VICTOR E.

— as long as it does not drag the rest of us into a public battle.

Number Five (primary purpose) emphasizes to me the fact that my chief AA business is carrying the message to alcoholics, not trying to make the rest of the Fellowship see how right I am in my various convictions (prejudices?). Six (neither endorsing nor opposing) specifically warns me of the dangers of any AA involvement in the world's quarrels. The words "neither endorsing nor opposing," you have probably noticed, are from the Grapevine-originated AA Preamble, of course, not from the Tradition itself. But have you ever noticed how well the Preamble summarizes many of the Traditions — and how closely it parallels the wording of the fifth paragraph in the Big Book's original foreword. Obviously, the sense of the Traditions was being expressed in AA actions back in 1938-39, years before they were formally drawn up and adopted.

Tradition Seven (self-support) suggests that the acceptance of any outside contributions could subtly link my AA group to non-AA causes. The caution in Number Eight against turning AA membership into a profession helps keep us out of competition, and therefore out of controversy, with the medical, legal, religious, and other professions.

Number Nine's advice about avoiding a monolithic AA organization also makes it simpler for us to observe Ten — we would have to be much more organized than we are in order to move the entire Fellowship into any partisan posture. The anonymity suggested by Eleven and Twelve helps safeguard us against being carried into publicized debates by some nationally known AA figure.

As of now, I'm convinced I have hardly skimmed the top off the deep riches of our Traditions. Writing articles on them is grad-

July 1976

ually teaching me how very far I have to go to incorporate them into my own AA thinking, let alone my personal life outside AA.

If our Traditions were simply organizational policies, or public relations procedures applicable only to groups or to the Fellowship as a whole, it seems to me they would be highly changeable from culture to culture, and from time to time. But I suspect they will outlast many other aspects of AA, because they increasingly seem in my view to suggest immutable spiritual principles for this one individual's life.

The Tenth is an excellent illustration. Its sense would enormously benefit my relationships with people in or out of AA — if I used it. How great it would be if I could always keep irrelevant, controversial matters out of some of my personal friendships, work relationships, even family ties, and concentrate instead on our areas of agreement, the important bonds between us.

In childhood, I felt that people with any affiliations different from mine were somehow against me. No matter how much I might like you, if you were anything other than an individual of one certain color, of one particular denomination (especially one regional branch), of one specific political persuasion, and of one limited socioeconomic class, I was sure you were an enemy even if you did not act like one.

A lot of that garbage is now cast aside, thanks to our Steps, but I have not yet learned to live comfortably with some people whose opinions are different from mine, even when those opinions are not an integral or necessary element of our relationship. I still let such differences stand between me and some beloved members of my own family, instead of concentrating on the things we have in common, the ways in which we do agree and are alike, the things most truly important in maintaining a loving relationship, as I think a good AA should.

Oh, if only the whole world valued its common good as loudly as it pursues its individual controversies! That is the essence of Tradition Ten, as I understand it — and we all know whose inventory we take in AA, right?

B. L., Manhattan, N.Y.

Over 40 Billion Problems Served

October 1983

S AYS THE AA PREAMBLE: "Our primary purpose is to stay sober and help other alcoholics to achieve sobriety." Remember? You should. We usually read it aloud at the beginning of every AA meeting.

But lately at discussion meetings, after the chairperson finishes some qualifying remarks, he or she pauses, then asks, "Who has a problem to be discussed?" This despite the fact that we are all there to try to solve our "common problem" — alcoholism! — "and help other alcoholics to achieve sobriety." And we have just stated it in so many words.

May I inspire you with a few of the earthshaking "problems" I've heard introduced at recent discussions? No? Well, that's too bad. Please extinguish all smoking materials and fasten your seat belts, because I'm about to do just that. Here goes.

Lola wants to talk about her overwhelming fear of heights. Caligula hates Ma Bell with a passion; when he gets a wrong number, he is fond of beating up telephone booths. And Mad Morris — well, the judge awarded his wife a divorce and his pickup truck at the same time, and what's a guy gonna do? And there's poor Portney, who complains that his brother hasn't spoken to their mother for a year. Timid Tessie wants some "input" on the subject of sex; she feels her aunt may have a problem, she says. And then there's Irving, who wants a constitutional amendment to do away with all holidays. They make lonely people lonelier, says he. And more.

This phenomenon is not merely local; it is widespread. My travels around the U.S. bear this out. I'm told the current thing is to awaken people to their "personhood"; try to get them "in touch with their feelings"; encourage them to "ventilate" their emotions, because they have a perfect right to their "space." Well, this li'l old country boy has no quarrel with that. Nope. Hop to it — do your thing. (Just don't bug *me* with it, please.)

In some sections of the U.S. I've visited, I've observed some members, disgusted at this departure from the AA program, get up and walk out. Some don't return. Shame on *them*! The pioneers of our program experienced many attempts to expand (read "dilute") the purpose of Alcoholics Anonymous, but *they* didn't quit — they hung in there. Where would we all be today if they had left in a righteous huff? So don't swim away from your life preserver. Besides — we need you.

My overriding concern, however, is with the fact that the hours spent solving the problems of Ma Bell and her attacker, Lola's acrophobia, Mad Morris's pickup truck, Tessie's inhibited aunt, Portney's complaint, etc. usually end up with no one telling us *how to go one day without one drink!* And it seems to me that's what Alcoholics Anonymous meetings are all about — or should be. How come we're suddenly the McDonald's of psychiatry? (40 BILLION PROBLEMS SERVED!)

Yes, I realize that the emotional problems we have are undoubtedly related to our alcoholism, but I also know that although my grandmaw is related to me, I don't drag her to AA meetings, the poor old soul. I go for my alcoholism. Don't you?

Years ago, they told us that AA wouldn't get our wives back, wouldn't restore lost jobs (wouldn't get back pickup trucks or Ma Bell's love); but if we treated our alcoholism *not as a symptom of something else* but as a *terribly destructive entity in itself* — well, by golly, we just might make it, one day at a time. And they were right, and still are.

Speaking of symptoms: It is generally accepted that inflated egos are symptomatic of having punished the strong waters. But when we turn our discussion meetings into seminars wherein we explore — *and prescribe for* — everyone's emotional, marital, legal, psychiatric, and sexual problems, well, sir, it kinda looks like that ole ego is ballooning up again. Yessir, we've just saddled up old Silver — Superman rides again! Whoopee!

I know. Some readers are going to be a bit outraged by this love letter. I'll perhaps be branded as "quaint" and "old-fashioned" and "hard-core AA" (what's "soft-core AA"?) and maybe a bit senile, standing in the way of "progress." Perhaps I'll be told it's time I went to the locker room and turned in my uniform. Alas, that's gratitude for you. But let me say this:

Don't you know I love you? Honest I do. I just want you to be with us next year.

F. L., Bangor, Me.

Is Public Controversy Ever Justified?

January 1977

I T HAS NOW BEEN SEVERAL months since a prestigious research organization released a lengthy report on its study of alcoholism. From that necessarily technical report, the press and other media seized upon the one element sensational enough to make news: the statement that some alcoholics can and do return to normal drinking. Several of my friends bitterly denounced the report. Many other AA members, identifying themselves as such, wrote angry letters to newspapers and magazines.

Perhaps by this time tempers have cooled enough to let us examine the issue involved in the light of AA principles — assuming that, just before press time for this magazine, we have not been prodded into renewed rage by another supposedly authoritative assurance that alcoholics need not remain abstinent.

An AA member who criticizes such reports usually expresses one concern: that they may harm alcoholics still drinking and encourage some recovered alcoholics to resume drinking. Therefore, it could be argued that AA members, drawing upon considerable experience in this area, have a duty to expose the fallacies in the report.

In my opinion, we have no such duty *as AA members*. On the contrary, we have a long-standing Tradition about public controversy. At almost every AA meeting, we hear that our Fellowship does not engage in such controversy. Tradition Ten explicitly states that "Alcoholics Anonymous has no opinion on outside issues; hence the AA name ought never be drawn into public controversy."

The Tradition does not disapprove of individuals' becoming involved, provided they don't use the AA name or announce that they are members. In fairness to AA, however, it's plain that no person should leap into a public controversy as an AA member, thus giving the impression that the Fellowship itself is taking a position. There are good reasons why we have always avoided such controversies in the past, and it's not likely that there will be justification for becoming involved in the future.

Still, it could be argued, AA has always insisted that controlled drinking is an impossibility for the alcoholic. "We are like men who have lost their legs; they never grow new ones," the Big Book says. "Neither does there appear to be any kind of treatment which will make alcoholics of our kind like other men. We have tried every imaginable remedy. In some instances there has been brief recovery, followed always by a still worse relapse. Physicians who are familiar with alcoholism agree that there is no such thing as making a normal drinker out of an alcoholic. Science may one day accomplish this, but it hasn't done so yet."

We should remember that this is offered as an opinion, not as a dogma to be defended at all costs. In 1939, when the Big Book was published, a large number of doctors and social workers probably thought that alcoholics should be able to become controlled drinkers at some point. AA members did not set out to do battle with any of these people and, for that matter, didn't even argue with alcoholics who thought they could still drink in a controlled manner. Far from warning them of dire consequences, the Big Book authors merely said, in effect, that the proof of the pudding was in the eating. "We do not like to pronounce any individual as alcoholic," they wrote, "but you can quickly diagnose yourself. Step over to the nearest barroom and try some controlled drinking. Try to drink and stop abruptly. Try it more than once. It will not take long for you to decide, if you are honest with yourself about it. It may be worth a bad case of jitters if you get a full knowledge of your condition.''

In other words, the AA founders were not zealously committed to the task of convincing any person that he might be an alcoholic, or of citing scientific proof that he could never be a controlled drinker. This was something the individual would have to decide for himself, even at the cost of getting drunk again. Is it irresponsible to tell an alcoholic to try drinking again if he thinks he can get away with it? Not really, because any person who believes that he can drink will probably do it no matter what is said to him. Our experience has certainly shown us that alcoholics do not usually respond to logic or intellectual arguments.

When I was drinking, I would have listened to any person, no matter how sleazy his credentials, who told me I could keep on drinking. This questionable reassurance would have counted for more than the advice of 100 experts taking the opposite view. I believed what I wanted to believe, and other members have told me the same thing about themselves. That being so, I do not think many alcoholics are endangered by a scientific report. True, it's much better to have a prominent think tank suggest that you can drink, but any friendly bartender or drinking companion will serve just as well.

Another argument in favor of entering the controversy could be that *controlled* drinking is not an outside issue, since rejection of this goal is vital to AA's program and methods. We should remember, however, that the professional field *is* external to AA, and it is made up of people with all shades of opinions and beliefs. AA members who work in the field of alcoholism do not really have the right or the duty to speak for AA as a whole, and there will be a great deal of resentment and opposition from professional workers if we try to shape general opinion.

AA's role in the broad field of alcoholism, as I understand it, is simply to offer our program to those who want it and to cooperate with other alcoholism workers and agencies to help alcoholics, without marrying AA to any specific cause or opinion. Many outside workers and agencies share AA's views on alcoholism and the recovery process. Others do not and are even critical of AA. In any case, these are outside opinions, even when relating directly to AA's interests.

We discovered long ago that our success in following the AA program and helping alcoholics depends largely on our own practices and beliefs, and that it isn't necessary to have the agreement of outsiders. Some professionals in alcoholism, for example, think that AA's spiritual program is unnecessary and irrelevant, and others believe that AA should relax its Tradition of anonymity. They have a right to hold such opinions, just as we have a right to hold opposite views.

It might also be argued that certain issues are more important than others, that the controversy over controlled drinking warrants parting from tradition so that individual members and the Fellowship can put AA's name on the line in defense of total abstinence as the only way to recovery. Would this ever be justified? Well, co-founder Bill W. apparently had such issues in mind when he wrote in *Twelve Concepts for World Service:*

"...we cannot and should not enter into public controversy, *even in self-defense* [emphasis added]. Our experience has shown that, providentially, it would seem, AA has been made exempt from the need to quarrel with anyone, no matter what the provocation. Nothing could be more damaging to our unity and to the worldwide goodwill which AA enjoys, than public contention, no

December 1968

"My father has a better quality of sobriety than your father!"

matter how promising the immediate dividends might appear.

"Therefore, it is evident that the harmony, security, and future effectiveness of AA will depend largely upon our maintenance of a thoroughly nonaggressive and pacific attitude in all our public relations. This is an exacting assignment, because in our drinking days we were prone to anger, hostility, rebellion, and aggression. And even though we are now sober, the old patterns of behavior are to a degree still with us, always threatening to explode on any good excuse. But we *know* this, and therefore I feel confident that in the conduct of our public affairs we shall always find the grace to exert an effective restraint."

As I reread this, I was reminded of my own feelings some years ago when the question of an alcoholic's return to controlled drinking was raised. A nonalcoholic friend whom I greatly respected told me that he didn't think the AA program brought *real* recoveries from alcoholism. He insisted that real recovery would enable the alcoholic to become a moderate drinker, neither addicted to alcohol nor dependent on AA meetings. Around the same time, some doctors in Cincinnati and other researchers in England were saying that alcoholics ought to be able to drink again with safety and that some were doing so. In one report, there was also a veiled criticism of AA and a hint that the insistence on total abstinence as a condition for recovery might prevent some people from receiving help.

What effect did these pronouncements have on me? Well, it's right there in the quotation on the Twelfth Concept: My friend's statement and the doctors' reports made me angry, hostile, rebellious, and aggressive. I was so mad at my friend that I didn't even attempt to answer his (I thought) appallingly stupid declaration. As for the experts in Cincinnati and England, I decided sorrowfully that they would have the destruction of thousands of alcoholics to answer for when they arrived at the pearly gate!

Upon examining my feelings, however, I came to see that I was concerned more about my own ego than about the welfare of still-practicing alcoholics. I closely identified myself with AA, and I sometimes obtained approval and respect by informing others that I was an AA member. I wanted people to praise AA as the most effective force in the field of alcoholism. I felt cheated and hurt by any criticism of AA, because it was also a criticism of a way of life in which I had a major investment.

But this, I had to admit, was simply an echo of my drinking

behavior: seeking the approval of others or bolstering my own self-esteem by association with a cause or group. It was unrealistic then to expect universal approval, and it is the same in sobriety. No matter how well we AAs do our job or how conscientiously we follow our program, certain people will criticize us. Nor can we expect universal agreement on anybody's theory, even the question of an alcoholic's ability to return to controlled drinking. It seems self-evident to us that we are right — all our experience shouts it — but we have to let the facts speak for themselves. Even if our belief proved right in the long run, we would be wrong as individuals and as a society if we became involved in angry accusations and bitter denunciations.

For that matter, it is not surprising that controversy has developed about patterns of recovery for the alcoholic, and I am no longer upset by it. I now see this as a healthy sign that research and study on alcoholism are continuing to grow. In every professional field, there are controversies and conflicting opinions. It is hard to believe, but a recent *Wall Street Journal* story pointed out, only partly tongue-in-cheek, that aeronautical engineers still argue about what causes an airplane to fly. And the professional and technical journals in every field are full of lively and heated disputes about matters most of us would have thought settled long ago. It is only logical, therefore, that the increasing professionalization of the alcoholism field should be marked by criticism of older theories and discussion of new ones.

Meanwhile, of course, there's plenty of opportunity for AA members and friends of AA to enter any controversy, *if they can do so without involving the AA name or the Fellowship as a whole.* I've noticed, for example, that several professionals in the alcoholism field have attacked the think tank's report, so it is being properly challenged by knowledgeable and experienced people. This is the way new ideas and theories are tested and publicized among professionals, and I'm all for it when it moves along in a spirit of friendly debate. That friendly spirit comes hard for us, as recovered alcoholics, and I suppose that's why Bill W. urged AAs to avoid public controversy.

There will always be controversies and rumors of controversies. After all, if engineers can't even agree about why an airplane flies, why shouldn't there be disputes about the nature and treatment of alcoholism?

M. B., Toledo, Ohio

ALCOHOLICS ANONYMOUS IS A FELLOWSHIP

Twelve Suggested Points for AA Tradition

by Bill W.

April 1946

NOBODY INVENTED ALCOHOLICS ANONYMOUS. It grew. Trial and error has produced a rich experience. Little by little we have been adopting the lessons of that experience, first as policy and then as tradition. That process still goes on and we hope it never stops. Should we ever harden too much, the letter might crush the spirit. We could victimize ourselves by petty rules and prohibitions; we could imagine that we had said the last word. We might even be asking alcoholics to accept our rigid ideas or stay away. May we never stifle progress like that!

Yet the lessons of our experience count for a great deal — a very great deal, we are each convinced. The first written record of AA experience was the book *Alcoholics Anonymous*. It was addressed to the heart of our foremost problem — release from the alcohol obsession. It contained personal experiences of drinking and recovery and a statement of those divine but ancient principles which have brought us a miraculous regeneration. Since publication of *Alcoholics Anonymous* in 1939 we have grown from 100 to 24,000 members. Seven years have passed; seven years of vast experience with our next greatest undertaking — the problem of living and working together. This is today our main concern. If we

235

can succeed in this adventure — and keep succeding — then, and only then, will our future be secure.

Since personal calamity holds us in bondage no more, our most challenging concern has become the future of Alcoholics Anonymous; how to preserve among us AAs such a powerful unity that neither weakness of persons nor the strain and strife of these troubled times can harm our common cause. We know that *Alcoholics Anonymous* must continue to live. Else, save few exceptions, we and alcoholics throughout the world will surely resume the hopeless journey to oblivion.

Almost any AA can tell you what our group problems are. Fundamentally they have to do with our relations, one with the other, and with the world outside. They involve relations of the

AA to his group, the relation of his group to Alcoholics Anonymous as a whole, and the place of Alcoholics Anonymous in that troubled sea called modern society, where all humankind must presently shipwreck or find haven. Terribly relevant is the problem of our basic structure and our attitude toward those ever-pressing questions of leadership, money, and authority. The future may well depend on how we feel and act about things that are controversial, and how we regard our public relations. Our final destiny will surely hang upon what we presently decide to do with these danger-fraught issues!

Now comes the crux of our discussion. It is this: Have we yet acquired sufficient experience to state clear-cut policies on these, our chief concerns? Can we now declare general principles which could grow into vital traditions — traditions sustained in the heart of each AA by his own deep conviction and by the common consent of his fellows? That is the question. Though full answer to all our perplexities may never be found, I'm sure we have come at last to a vantage point whence we can discern the main outlines of a body of tradition; which, God willing, can stand as an effective guard against all the ravages of time and circumstance.

Acting upon the persistent urge of old AA friends, and upon the conviction that general agreement and consent between our members is now possible, I shall venture to place in words these suggestions for *an Alcoholics Anonymous tradition of relations — twelve points to assure our future:*

Our AA experience has taught us that:

1. Each member of Alcoholics Anonymous is but a small part of a great whole. AA must continue to live or most of us will surely die. Hence our common welfare comes first. But individual welfare follows close afterward.

2. For our group purpose there is but one ultimate authority — a loving God as He may express Himself in our group conscience.

3. Our membership ought to include all who suffer alcoholism. Hence we may refuse none who wish to recover. Nor ought AA membership ever depend upon money or conformity. Any two or three alcoholics gathered together for sobriety may call themselves an AA group.

4. With respect to its own affairs, each AA group should be responsible to no other authority than its own conscience. But when its plans concern the welfare of neighboring groups also, those groups ought to be consulted. And no group, regional committee, or individual should ever take any action that might greatly affect AA as a whole without conferring with the trustees of the Alcoholic Foundation [now the AA General Service Board]. On such issues our common welfare is paramount.

5. Each Alcoholics Anonymous group ought to be a spiritual entity *having but one primary purpose* — that of carrying its message to the alcoholic who still suffers.

6. Problems of money, property, and authority may easily divert us from our primary spiritual aim. We think, therefore, that any considerable property of genuine use to AA should be separately incorporated and managed, thus dividing the material from the spiritual. An AA group, as such, should never go into business.

Secondary aids to AA, such as clubs or hospitals which require much property or administration, ought to be so set apart that, if necessary, they can be freely discarded by the groups. The management of these special facilities should be the sole responsibility of those people, whether AAs or not, who financially support them. For our clubs, we prefer AA managers. But hospitals, as well as other places of recuperation, ought to be well outside AA — and medically supervised. An AA group may cooperate with anyone, but should bind itself to no one.

7. The AA groups themselves ought to be fully supported by the voluntary contributions of their own members. We think that each group should soon achieve this ideal; that any public solicitation of funds using the name of Alcoholics Anonymous is highly dangerous; that acceptance of large gifts from any source, or of contributions carrying any obligation whatever, is usually unwise. Then, too, we view with much concern those AA treasuries which continue, beyond prudent reserves, to accumulate funds for no stated purpose. Experience has often warned us that nothing can so surely destroy our spiritual heritage as futile disputes over property, money, and authority.

8. Alcoholics Anonymous should remain forever non-professional. We define professionalism as the occupation of counseling alcoholics for fees or hire. But we may employ alcoholics where they are going to perform those full-time services for which we might otherwise have to engage nonalcoholics. Such special services may be well recompensed. But personal "Twelfth Step" work is never to be paid for.

9. Each AA group needs the least possible organization. Rotating leadership is usually the best. The small group may elect its secretary, the large group its rotating committee, and the groups of a large metropolitan area their central committee, which often employs a full-time secretary. The trustees of the Alcoholic Foundation are, in effect, our general service committee. They are the custodians of our AA tradition and the receivers of voluntary contributions by which they maintain AA General Headquarters and our general secretary at New York. They are authorized by the groups to handle our overall public relations and they guarantee the integrity of our principal publication, The AA Grapevine. All such representatives are to be guided in the spirit of service, for true leaders in AA are but trusted and experienced servants of the whole. They derive no real authority from their titles. Universal re-

spect is the key to their usefulness.

10. No AA group or member should ever, *in such a way as to implicate AA,* express any opinion on outside controversial issues — particularly those of politics, alcohol reform, or sectarian religion. The Alcoholics Anonymous groups oppose no one. Concerning such matters they can express no views whatever.

11. Our relations with the outside world should be characterized by modesty and anonymity. We think AA ought to avoid sensational advertising. Our public relations should be guided by the principle of attraction rather than promotion. There is never need to praise ourselves. We feel it better to let our friends recommend us.

12. And finally, we of Alcoholics Anonymous believe that the principle of anonymity has an immense spiritual significance. It reminds us that we are to place principles before personalities; that we are actually to practice a truly humble modesty. This to the end that our great blessings may never spoil us; that we shall forever live in thankful contemplation of Him who presides over us all.

May it be urged that, while these principles have been stated in rather positive language they are still only suggestions for our future. We of Alcoholics Anonymous have never enthusiastically responded to any assumption of personal authority. Perhaps it is well for AA that this is true. So I offer these suggestions neither as one man's dictum nor as a creed of any kind, but rather as a first attempt to portray that group ideal toward which we have assuredly been led by a Higher Power these ten years past.

Dr. Bob:
The Man and the Physician

September 1978

IT IS VERY DIFFICULT TO SPEAK OF Dr. Bob without going into eulogistic superlatives. While he lived, he laughed them off. And now, though he is dead, I feel that he still laughs them off. I sat beside him many times at the speakers' table and watched him squirm as some florid introduction was being given him. Many a chairman of the meeting strove to rise to the responsibility of introducing him by referring to him as co-founder of the "greatest, most wonderful, most magnificent, most momentous movement of all time.'' Dr. Bob whispered to me on one of these occasions, ''The speaker certainly takes in a lot of territory and plenty of time.''

While Dr. Bob thoroughly appreciated the spirit of personal gratitude that usually prompted such superlatives, he never took them seriously as applicable to himself. He rose up to tell with all humility the simple story of an alcoholic's return to sobriety. He seldom called upon his vast experience with others. He simply repeated in different ways the story of one man's great return. And that was his own.

He could have gone scientific and statistical, for he heard more confessions of sprees and lost weekends than anyone else alive. But he never did it that way. He always remained plain. Dr. Bob had once been lost in an alcoholic fog himself. He recalled that he, too, had been proud, resentful, full of rancor, cocky, self-sufficient, and selfish. But whether he spoke at the banquet table or ministered to an alcoholic in the ward, he was kind but firm, serious and sympathetic, always unmindful of race, color, creed, or previous state of alcoholic servitude.

Dr. Bob was a humble man. His humility was born, no doubt,

March 1975

''And now I'd like to introduce my co-founders — Mother and Dad.''

of his humiliations before his good wife, Anne, and his colleagues in the medical profession. This led to the great step of becoming humble before his God. Here was the crisis in his life: At last, he found the God who he knew would help him if he would only place a humble confidence in him. This is the story of Dr. Bob. It is the story, too, of the Twelve Steps that logically follow, once the situation is faced with honest realism.

Looking back over his life, one might say Dr. Bob was two people, two personalities, even in his drinking days. After his return to sobriety, he still remained two personalities. As he made his rounds through St. Thomas Hospital, he did so as Dr. R. H. S., medical practitioner. But as he came to Room 390, the alcoholic ward, he put off the cloak of science and professionalism and became just plain Dr. Bob, a man eager, willing, and able to help his fellowman. As he left the hospital each day, two men went out through the door — one a great MD, the other a great man.

It was quite natural that Dr. S. sought hospitalization for alcoholics. He had been sending the sick to St. Thomas Hospital for years, and alcoholism to him was a sickness as real as pneumonia, but not so easy to treat. The new treatment was to be physical, psychological, social, and spiritual. The whole patient was to be treated, because the whole man was sick.

Many of his colleagues in the medical profession disagreed with Dr. S., some bitterly. It was fortunate that he had been associated with the nursing sisters at St. Thomas Hospital. It was very fortunate, even providential, that he met the Sisters of Charity of St. Augustine. For in the long, long history of their order, they had taken care of all manner of disease, dereliction, and misfortune, and they were now willing to try the newer method of treating alcoholism. Thus, for the first time, a ward in a general hospital was opened to Alcoholics Anonymous.

Dr. S. and the sisters soon learned to diagnose more accurately and prescribe more effectively. Here was a new type of patient needing a new type of treatment. The disorder seemed more on the psychological and spiritual than on the physical side. Here was a patient whose thinking was all beclouded; whose attitudes were wrong; whose philosophy of life was all mixed up; whose sense of values was distorted; whose spiritual life was nonexistent. The patient was indeed a definite challenge to the skill, patience, and prayer of all who worked at the hospital with Dr. S. in the noble art of healing a terribly wounded personality.

What success attended his efforts, as well as the efforts of the sisters and all who worked with the many patients who passed through that ward, is now a matter of history. It will ever remain a monument to the memory of R. H. S., MD — and Dr. Bob, the man.

J. G., Ohio

Bill's Wife Remembers When

by Lois W.

December 1944

AS THE WIFE OF AN EARLY AA, I think that some of our experiences and my reactions to my husband's changed life may be interesting to other wives. Bill was an alcoholic, I believe, from the first drink he ever took, just a few months before our marriage. From then on, for seventeen years, I did everything I could think of to keep him away from liquor.

I will tell a little of our life before AA to help explain some of my later emotions. Bill and I had no children, so I soon felt that my job in life was to help Bill straighten himself out. As time went on, he earnestly tried to stop drinking. He was always very remorseful and perplexed the mornings after. We would then resolve to lick this liquor situation together, launching off on some new tack.

As his drinking got worse, all decision and responsibility had to be taken by me. It was lucky that we were companionable, for gradually, as our social contacts were broken, we were thrust back on each other for company. In order to get away from alcohol over the weekends, I used to engineer some sort of outing, as we both loved the outdoors. If our pocketbook was flat, we might take the subway to the Dyckman Street ferry and hike along the Palisades to some scenic spot, where we would nibble our sandwiches and gaze at the view. Or we might ferry to Staten Island and walk there, perhaps broiling a steak over a campfire. We hired a rowboat at Yonkers and, using a bath towel as a sail, floated up the Hudson to a spit of land near Nyack, where we camped and tried to sleep. We once went so far to get away from alcohol that we both gave up

our jobs and took a whole year off. This we spent motorcycling and camping over half the United States.

These trips, although good for Bill's health, did nothing toward his permanent sobriety. In fact, his alcoholism grew steadily more serious. He lost job after job, until I became entirely hopeless about him.

And then, suddenly and finally, Bill straightened out through the help of an old friend. At once, I was convinced of his complete change and was, of course, extremely happy. Bill began to go to religious meetings and to work feverishly with alcoholics. I would go to meetings, too, and would try to share his newfound enthusiasms. He always had some drunk in tow and would work all night or get up in the middle of the night to go to the suburbs if one called him. We had drunks all over the house; sometimes, as many as five lived there at one time.

One drunk committed suicide in the house after having sold about $700 worth of our clothes and luggage. Another slid down the coal chute from the street to the cellar when we refused him the front door. Two others took to fighting, and one chased the other all around the house with a carving knife. The intended victim was saved by a third drunk, who delivered the knife-minded one a knockout blow. An alcoholic who was living in the basement was invited up for a pancake breakfast. After eating his share, he suddenly put on his hat and started out the door, remarking that he was going to Childs for *plenty* of pancakes.

Bill had found himself a job about this time. It used to take him away from home a great deal, and I was left with one or more alcoholics to look after. Once, one of these boys lay in the vestibule all night and screamed invective at me because I would not let him in. He was so loud, the passersby all stopped, looked, and listened.

Another time, it was 4:00 AM before I succeeded in towing a drunk home. He was anxious to be at his job the next morning, and we had gone out around midnight to look for a doctor, having been unable to get one to come to the house at that hour. I helped his shaky steps up and down stoops, lit his cigarettes for him, and finally, when he could not rouse a doctor, held a drink to his lips in a bar. When I asked him how he then felt, he said, "Well, a bird can't fly on one wing." After a few more drinks, I managed to get him home, but he did not get to his job the next morning.

I was once suddenly taken sick, and when my sister arrived to nurse me, she found five men milling around in the living room, one of them muttering, "One woman can look after five drunks, but five drunks cannot look after one woman."

Now to describe my reactions to it all. When Bill first sobered up, I was terribly happy, but soon, without realizing it, I began to resent the fact that Bill and I never spent any time together anymore. I stayed at home, while he went off somewhere scouting up new drunks or working with old ones. My life's job of sobering up Bill, with all its former responsibilities, was suddenly taken away from me. I had not yet found anything to fill the void. And then there was the feeling of being on the outside of a very tight little clique of alcoholics into which no mere wife could possibly enter. I did not understand what was going on within myself until, one Sunday, Bill asked me to go with him to a meeting. To my own surprise as well as his, I burst forth with "Damn all your meetings!" and threw my shoe at him as hard as I could.

This display of bad temper woke me up. I realized that I had been wallowing in self-pity; that Bill's change was simply miraculous; that his feverish activity with alcoholics was absolutely necessary to his sobriety; and that if I did not want to be left way behind, I had better jump on the bandwagon, too!

'Let's Keep It Simple . . .' but How?

by Bill W.

July 1960

THIS GRAPEVINE WILL BE READ as we celebrate AA's Twenty-Fifth Anniversary in July at Long Beach, California. We shall be stepping over a new threshold into our future. We shall rejoice as we think of the gifts and the wonders of yesterday. And as we rededicate ourselves to fulfilling the immense promise of AA's tomorrow, we shall certainly survey how we stand today. Have we really kept AA simple? Or, unwittingly, have we blundered?

Thinking on this, I began to wonder about our fundamental structure: those principles, relationships, and attitudes that are the substance of our Three Legacies of Recovery, Unity, and Service. In our Twelve Steps and Twelve Traditions, we find twenty-four definitely stated principles. Our Third Legacy includes a charter for world service that provides thousands of general service representatives, hundreds of local committee members, eighty [now ninety-one] General Service Conference delegates, fifteen [now twenty-one] General Service Board trustees, together with our headquarters' legal, financial, public relations, and editorial experts and their staffs. Our group and area services add still more to this seeming complexity.

Twenty-two years ago last spring, we were just setting about the formation of a trusteeship for AA as a whole. Up to that moment, we had neither stated principles nor special services. Our Twelve Steps weren't even a gleam in the eye. As for the Twelve Traditions — well, AA had only forty members and but three years' experience. So there wasn't anything to be "traditional" about. AA was two small groups: one at Akron and another in New York. We

were a most intimate family. Dr. Bob and I were its "papas." And what we said in those days went. Home parlors were meeting places. Social life ranged around coffeepots on kitchen tables. Alcoholism was, of course, described as a deadly malady. Honesty, confession, restitution, working with others, and prayer were the sole formula for our survival and growth. These were the uncomplicated years of halcyon simplicity. There was no need for the maxim "Let's keep it simple." We couldn't have been less complicated.

The contrast between then and now is rather breathtaking. To some of us, it is frightening. Therefore we ask, "Has AA really kept faith with Dr. Bob's warning, 'Let's keep it simple'? How can we possibly square today's Twelve Steps, Twelve Traditions, General Service Conferences, and International Conventions with our original coffee-and-cake AA?"

For myself, I do not find this difficult to do. Genuine simplicity for today is to be found, I think, in whatever principles, practices, and services can permanently ensure our widespread harmony and effectiveness. Therefore, it has been better to state our principles than to leave them vague; better to clarify their applications than to leave these unclear; better to organize our services than to leave them to hit-or-miss methods, or to none at all.

Most certainly, a return to the kitchen-table era would bring no hoped-for simplicity. It could mean only wholesale irresponsibility, disharmony, and ineffectiveness. Let's picture this: There would be no definite guiding principles, no literature, no meeting halls, no group funds, no planned sponsorship, no stable leadership, no clear relations with hospitals, no sound public relations, no local services, no world services. Returning to that early-time brand of simplicity would be as absurd as selling the steering wheel, the gas tank, and the tires off our family car. The car would be simplified, all right — no more gas and repair bills, either! But our car wouldn't go any place. Family life would hardly be simplified; it would instantly become confused and complicated.

A formless AA anarchy, animated only by the "Let's get together" spirit, just isn't enough for AAs here and now. What worked fine for two score members in 1938 won't work at all for more than 200,000 of them in 1960. Our added size and therefore greater responsibility simply spell the difference between AA's childhood and its coming of age. We have seen the folly of attempting to recapture the childhood variety of simplicity in order to sidestep the kind of responsibility that must always be faced to "keep it simple" for today. We cannot possibly turn back the clock, and shouldn't try.

The history of our changing ideas about "simplicity for today" is fascinating. For example, the time came when we actually had to codify — or organize, if you please — the basic principles that had emerged out of our experience. There was a lot of resistance to this. It was stoutly claimed by many that our then-simple (but rather garbled), word-of-mouth recovery program was being made too complicated by the publication of AA's Twelve Steps. We were "throwing simplicity out the window," it was said. But that was not so. One has only to ask, "Where would AA be today without its Twelve Steps?" That these principles were carefully defined and published in 1939 has done only the Lord knows how much good. Codification has vastly simplified our task. Who could contest that now?

In 1945, a similar outcry arose when sound principles of living and working together were clearly outlined in AA's Twelve Traditions. It was then anything but simple to get agreement about them. Yet who can now say that our AA lives have been complicated by the Traditions? On the contrary, these sharply defined principles have immensely *simplified* the task of maintaining unity. And unity for us AAs is a matter of life or death.

The identical thing has everywhere happened in our active services, particularly in world services. When our first trusteeship for AA was created, there were grave misgivings. The alarm was great because this operation involved a certain amount of legality, authority, and money, and the transaction of some business. We had been running happily about saying that AA had "completely separated the spiritual from the material." It was therefore a shocker when Dr. Bob and I proposed world services; when we urged that these had to head up in some kind of permanent board, and further stated that the time had come — at least in this realm — when we would have to learn how to make "material things" serve spiritual ends. Somebody with experience had to be at the steering wheel, and there had to be gas in the AA tank.

As our trustees and their co-workers began to carry our message worldwide, our fears slowly evaporated. AA had not been confused — it had been simplified. You could ask any of the tens of thousands of alcoholics and their families who were coming into AA because of our world services. Certainly, their lives had been simplified. And in reality, so had ours.

When our first General Service Conference met in 1951, we again drew a long breath. For some, this event spelled sheer disaster. Wholesale brawling and politicking would now be the rule. Our worst traits would get out in front. The serenity of the trustees and everybody else would be disturbed (as indeed it sometimes was!). Our beautiful spirituality and the AA therapy would be interfered with. People would get drunk over this (and indeed a few did!). As never before, the shout went up, "For God's sake, let's keep this thing simple!" Cried some members, "Why can't Dr. Bob and Bill and the trustees go right on running those services for us? That's the only way to keep it simple."

But few knew that Dr. Bob was mortally sick. Nobody stopped to think that there would soon be less than a handful of old-timers left; that soon they would be gone, too. The trustees would be quite isolated and unconnected with the Fellowship they served. The first big gale could well bowl them over. AA would suffer heart failure at its vital center. Irretrievable collapse would be the almost certain result.

Therefore, we AAs had to make a choice: What would really be the simpler? Would we get that General Service Conference together, despite its special expense and perils? Or would we sit on our hands at home, awaiting the fateful consequences of our fear and folly? What, in the long run, we wondered, would really be the better — and therefore the simpler? As our history shows, we took action. The General Service Conference of Alcoholics Anonymous has just held its tenth [in 1985, its thirty-fifth] annual meeting. Beyond doubt, we know that this indispensable instrument has cemented our unity and has ensured the recovery of the increasing hosts of sufferers still to come.

Therefore, I think that we *have* kept the faith. As I see it, this is how we have made AA truly simple!

Some may still ask, "Are we nevertheless moving away from our early Tradition that 'AA, *as such,* ought never be organized'?" Not a bit of it. We shall never be "organized" until we create a government; until we say who shall be members and who shall not; until we authorize our boards and service committees to mete out penalties for nonconformity, for nonpayment of money, and for misbehavior. I know every AA heart shares in the conviction that none of these things can ever happen. We organize our principles merely so that they can be better understood, and we continue so to organize our services that AA's life-blood can be transfused into those who must otherwise die. That is the all-in-all of AA's "organization." There can never be any more than this.

A concluding query: "Has the era of coffee and cake and fast friendships vanished from the AA scene because we are going modern?" Well, scarcely. In my hometown, I know an AA who has been sober several years. He goes to a small meeting. The talks he hears are just like those Dr. Bob and I used to hear — and also make — in our respective front parlors. As neighbors, my friend has a dozen AA cronies. He sees them constantly over kitchen tables and coffee cups. He takes a frequent whack at Twelfth Step cases. For him, nothing has changed; it's just like AA always was.

At meetings, my friend may see some books, pamphlets, and Grapevines on a table. He hears the secretary make her announcement that these are for sale. He thinks the New York intergroup is a good thing, because some of his fellow members were sponsored through it. On world services, he is not so clear. He hears some pros and cons about them. But he concludes they are probably needed. He knows his group sends in some money for these undertakings, and this is okay. Besides, his group's hall rent has to be paid. So when the hat comes by, he cheerfully drops a buck into it.

As far as my friend is concerned, these "modernizations" of AA are not a bit shattering to his serenity or to his pocketbook. They merely represent his responsibility to his group, to his area, and to AA as a whole. It has never occurred to him that these are any but the most obvious obligations.

If you tried to tell my friend that AA is being spoiled by money, politics and overorganization, he would just laugh. He'd probably say, "Why don't you come over to my house after the meeting, and we'll have another cup of coffee."

Tradition Six

*An AA group ought never endorse, finance or
lend the AA name to any related facility
or outside enterprise, lest problems of
money, property, and prestige
divert us from our primary purpose*

August 1970

BEFORE I UNDERSTOOD even dimly what AA was, I was sure I could improve it. Looking back, I realize now that my pure gall was appalling, since it was rooted so firmly in ignorance. I knew almost nothing about the externals of the Fellowship and much less about its spiritual principles. Since I was too proud to admit that there was anything I did not know, I almost never asked questions.

Practically nothing in the very skimpy AA literature we had then (in 1945) explained how AA or its component units functioned, so my knowledge was based on what I heard and saw in one group. Then as now, we AA members (like other human beings ev-

VICTOR E.

erywhere, I suppose) talked a bewildering melange of facts, guess-work, inspired wisdom, gossip, and nonsense. Yet I assumed that what I heard was the whole AA truth, and armed only with my small collection of quick impressions and misinformation about AA, I wanted to change it.

Surely, for example, AA should be informing the medical profession about the facts of our disease as *we* understood them. (The Yale — now Rutgers — School of Alcohol Studies and the National Council on Alcoholism had barely got started, and this was nine years before the American Medical Association estab-lished its alcoholism committee.)

The government, I was sure, should change laws relating to alcoholics. (The North American Association of Alcoholism Pro-grams and the National Center for Control and Prevention of Alcoholism were then impossible dreams.)

Detoxification centers, vocational rehabilitation, and other services improved understanding by social workers, school kids, psychologists, and cops — all these and more were badly needed. Why, I carped, was AA not getting busy?

Just suppose for a minute that our Fellowship had indeed been misguided right smack into all those activities. What a tan-gled web we could have woven! How many drunks would have been ignored, left to die, as we mounted our political and fund-raising campaigns! How many enemies AA would have made for itself if it had tried to dictate to the medical, clerical, and legal professions!

If my AA group had had prestige, money, and power at stake, I fear my own sobriety would have found little support at our meet-

October 1964

ings. There would have been no room for it on the agenda. Many of us would have left, I fear — *sic transit* glorious sobriety, and maybe AA itself.

I am certain now that if any AA-run governmental programs on alcoholism had been set up and had gone bust, my resentments would have burst through my tender, new sobriety. Suppose we had started an official AA club and it had been raided because of gambling, or AA-run retreats for alcoholics had become subjects of gossip. What then? I would have gotten either emotionally embattled or, more probably, alcoholically embottled.

As always, AA as a whole proved much wiser than I as an individual, and my group just plugged along, trying to do its own thing. Even without such complications, we had trouble enough just trying to figure out *what* our own thing really was. The Traditions had not been written yet.

At first, we felt we had to do at least three things: (1) provide a place where members could play cards, eat, and have coffee at any time, (2) maintain an office with telephones as a central clearing-house for Twelfth Step work and information about meetings, (3) keep our own AA meetings and Twelfth Step work going.

The first two involved us in legal corporations, finances, real-estate management, building maintenance, cafeteria operation, a paid secretary, and, naturally, rules and officers. As a result, new-comers who just needed the message often got shortchanged because we were too busy with serious problems like a drunken chef, typewriter repairs, club dues, revising bylaws, a temperamental janitor, and deciding who could and could not use the phone or which brand of coffee to buy.

We made it almost impossible for newcomers to tell the difference between joining a club and simply becoming a sober AA. I know. I was one of those newcomers.

People who did not get elected to boards or did get demoted from jobs proceeded to get drunk. Criticism of the cafeteria cashier's report became resentment of "AA's financial structure," yet! Two fellows I liked were displeased by the cafeteria food, blamed AA, and left. (No wonder! They had heard little else except the food discussed at their first meetings. They were dead within a year, of alcoholism.)

The solution my group finally found, nearly a quarter-century ago, was quite simple. We decided that, no matter how exciting and how needed such business enterprises were, an AA group ought to stay out of them, because discussions of money, property, and prestige kept us wildly distracted from the Twelve Steps.

As an AA group, we decided to carry the message, period. So we dropped the food business and real-estate management. Some individuals formed separate nonprofit corporations, outside AA, to run clubs or day centers for AAs who wanted such amenities. As for the local central office (or intergroup), it was eventually operated and supported by *all* the groups nearby.

This arrangement has worked beautifully ever since, both in New York and elsewhere. And now, of course, other services seriously needed by alcoholics are at last beginning to get under way — but *not* under the auspices of AA. Food, clothing, shelter, and medical assistance are often necessary for the alcoholic's recovery. But other organizations, efficiently operated and professionally experienced in these matters, can handle them better than an AA group.

Nevertheless, let's not overlook a fact seldom recognized, in conversation or in print: Many of the great improvements in the treatment of alcoholics during the last thirty-five years have been brought about quietly, behind the scenes, by anonymous AA members, acting as private citizens interested in a public-health

problem. The Sixth Tradition leaves every AA member the freedom to do that, if he cares to, so long as his actions do not constitute AA endorsement (or criticism) of any enterprises, nor "lend
the AA name" to them.

(There's another side to this coin, too. Once upon a time, a
non-AA alcoholism program tried to create the impression, false-
ly, that it was endorsed by AA. But the attempt backfired. The
professionals at whom the program was aimed thought it was just
an extension of AA and would not come near it! I know. I was the
guilty one.)

Adherence to our primary purpose makes AA unique — and
also gives us a special responsibility, it seems to me. We are the
only people who have our own personal experience to share. And
we are the only people who try to do nothing except help the individual alcoholic because we have to, to stay sober ourselves. We
help him, not for the sake of society or of science, but for the sake
of our own sobriety.

As a result, other programs in the alcoholism field have come
to depend heavily on AA's continuing integrity. At every single
professional meeting, it is a conspicuous fact that nonalcoholics
count absolutely on the aid of sober, conscientious AAs who
remember: *When anyone, anywhere, reaches out for help, I want
the hand of AA always to be there. And for that: I am responsible.*

B. L., Manhattan, N.Y.

Services Make AA Tick

by Bill W.

November 1951

A COFFEEPOT SIMMERS on the kitchen stove, a hospital sobers
the stricken sufferer, general headquarters broadcasts the
AA message; our service lifelines span the seven seas. All these
symbolize AA in action. For action is the magic word of Alcoholics Anonymous. So it is that every AA service daily proves that so-
called "material activities" can lead to magnificent spiritual
results.

Once upon a time, all AA meetings were held in homes. There

weren't any committees, and nobody put up a cent. We hadn't even a name, and "founders" were unheard of. It was that simple.

Yet we did enjoy one "service" — a valuable one, too. Wives baked cakes and brewed strong coffee for us alkies huddling together in the front parlors, still terrified that our new program might not work after all. Those wifely dispensations of good cheer smoothed the way and so lightened our burden of doubt. Thus, from the very beginning, did such gracious service make AA tick.

By and by, meetings got big. Our front parlors couldn't hold them. We had to move into halls. Gathering places seldom came free, so we must needs pay rent. Landlords weren't a particle interested in the spiritual advantages of group poverty. So someone passed the hat, and we dropped money into it voluntarily. We knew we couldn't meet or function as a group unless we did. We grudgingly learned that rent was necessary to ensure sobriety — our spiritual dividend, life itself.

This rent-paying process also produced the first AA "official." The gent we picked to pass the hat soon became our treasurer. Then phone calls had to be answered, letters written, literature or-

February 1961

"Take me to your humble, trusted servant."

dered and distributed. The now familiar group secretary put in his
— or her — appearance. Presently newspaper interviews had to be
given, preachers and doctors canvassed, hospital arrangements
made, banquets set up. Not by anybody, either. Somebody special
had to be picked to do these chores. That "somebody" became the
group service chairman.

Of course this was all quite troublesome, for it marred our
sometimes fallible serenity. Squabbling began, dark forecasts of our
future were made, and everybody yearned to go back into the parlors. But we didn't because we couldn't. We saw we'd have to have
service committees or fail to function, perhaps fall apart entirely.
We'd actually *have to organize services in order to keep AA
simple.*

Hospitals, we early found, disliked drunks. We had been noisy
nuisances who ducked paying bills and seldom got well. Yet we
quickly saw that many an alcoholic might never get a real chance
with AA unless hospitalized. What could we do?

At first, we went in for home "tapering." But instead of
"tapering off," our new clients usually "tapered on" — and right
back into the bars again. Some groups tried to organize "AA hospitals" with MDs on call. This carried matters too far; it put our
groups straight into serious business. All these early attempts were
busts. We finally learned that each AA group ought to be *primarily
a spiritual entity, not a business corporation.* Then individual AAs
and their friends began to set up rest homes and drunk farms as
private enterprises. This worked a lot better, but still it wasn't
enough.

At length the medics began to come to our aid. Agreeing with
our hard-earned conclusion that doctoring ought to be the affair of
doctors, they commenced to help us make hospital connections.
Our first attempts to cooperate with hospitals in city areas often
led to damaging confusion. Anybody sponsored anybody, and
those hospital bills still didn't get paid. Cocksure AAs told doctors
how to run wards. This easygoing lack of head or tail in our hospital relations didn't keep AA simple at all. Confusion was general
until some hospitals bluntly told metropolitan AA groups that responsible members with whom they could consistently deal would
have to be named — or else. Nobody, said the hospitals, could possibly cooperate with an anarchy.

It began to dawn upon AA that *group responsibility would
have to reach much further than the meeting hall doorstep* on

Tuesday and Thursday nights only. Otherwise, the new man approaching our door might miss his chance, might lose his life.

Slowly, most reluctantly, groups in densely populated areas saw they would have to form associations, open small offices, pay a few full-time secretaries. Terrific outcries went up. To many, this really meant destructive organization, politics, professionalism, big expense, a ruling officialdom, and government. "Believe us," they argued, "a local central office could cost metropolitan AA members 50 cents a month apiece. That could turn into a damned head tax — what about our AA Tradition of no 'fees or dues'?"

Of course these exaggerated fears never materialized. We have lots of good intergroup associations now, voluntarily supported. The newcomer is getting a better break; the hospitals are pleased. The office of one large association has sponsored and hospitalized 7,000 alcoholics. Prompt interview and phone service is planting the seeds of recovery in other thousands. Local meeting directories are issued, public relations and dinners set up. We found these last couldn't be carelessly left to anybody who happened to feel like giving interviews or printing up a bundle of tickets and handbills. In short, intergroups do those area chores that no single individual or group could. They unify regions; they make AA tick.

By 1937, some of us realized that AA needed a standard literature. There would have to be a book. Our word-of-mouth program could be garbled, we might be destroyed by dissension over basic principles, and then our public relations would surely go to pot. We'd fall flat on our obligation to the alcoholic who hadn't yet heard unless we put our knowledge on paper.

But not everybody agreed. Many were badly scared by this proposal. Money in some quantity would be needed, there would be huge disputes over authorship, royalties, profits, prices, and the contents of the book itself. Some truly believed that this seemingly reckless project would blow our little Society to bits. "Let's avoid trouble, let's keep things simple," they said.

Well, we did quarrel violently over the preparation and distribution of that AA book. In fact, it took five years for the clamor to die down. Should any AAs dream that the old-timers who put the book together went about at the time in serene meditation and white robes, then they had best forget it. The inspiration readers now say they find in the volume must have got there by the grace of God only!

Yet see what has happened. Two-hundred-thousand AA

books circulated in this year 1951, silently scattering our message worldwide, lighting the path of progress for nearly every incoming member. Without doubt, that book is the backbone of our unity; it has unbelievably *simplified* our task. Although its preparation was in part a very "material" proceeding indeed, those early labor pains of its creation did help form our Society and cause it to function. The spiritual result in sobriety, happiness, and faith is altogether beyond any reckoning.

This group of headquarters services enables AA to function as a whole. They guard our Traditions; they issue our principal literature. They watch over our general public relations and so relate us rightly to the world outside. They mediate our difficulties; they guide our policy. Therefore, these indispensable services are AA's principal lifelines to the millions who do not know.

It is this world center of service which constitutes the principal bequest in our recently announced Third Legacy. And it is by the terms of this Legacy of Service that the General Service Conference of Alcoholics Anonymous, a representative body of state and provincial [now Conference area] delegates, assumed control and guidance of these principal affairs of AA last April.

That event marked the passing of responsibility for our world services from Dr. Bob, our friends, and myself, to you — the members of Alcoholics Anonymous. Support and guard these assets well; the lives and fortunes of millions, the very survival of AA itself may depend much upon how well you discharge this, your newfound obligation.

Let us make our services respectable; let us rank them in importance with the Twelve Steps of recovery and the Twelve Principles of AA Tradition. Let us forget our fear of overorganization; let us remember that AA as a whole cannot be organized, but that we must so organize and support our special services that AA can function. Let us forget our early fears of professionalism, of the accumulation of wealth, of government. Experience, now fortified by our Traditions, has already assured us none of these evils are likely to descend upon us.

Above all, let's change our old attitude about money. Collectively, AA members earn an enormous income because of their sobriety, it's a one-half a billion-dollar bonanza each year. Can we not wisely, gratefully, and humbly reinvest a tiny fraction of this vast sum in those vital services that make AA tick? I think we can, and I think we shall. For in our own lives we have seen sobriety produce money, and in our AA services we have seen a little money produce incalculable spiritual dividends. Let's think this all through again.

By our Twelve Steps we have recovered, by our Twelve Traditions we have unified, and through our Third Legacy — Service — we shall carry the AA message down through all the corridors of time to come. Of this, I am happily confident.

Tradition Eight

Alcoholics Anonymous should remain
forever nonprofessional, but our service centers
may employ special workers

December 1970

ONE OF MY FINGERS, all by itself, has only scant strength and skill; but when it is used with all the others, it feels pretty powerful and seems to know what it is doing.

I've also noticed that if I cut a finger and bandage it, then try not to use it for a few days, the whole hand suddenly gets clumsy and inefficient. If one finger is out of whack, they all are.

Just so, it seems to me, with AA's Traditions. They work best as a complete system, with each one supporting all the others. Besides, I understand them better as a hooked-together whole. In fact, I cannot always tell where one leaves off and the next begins.

The Eighth is a good example. When I start ruminating about it, about nonprofessionalism, I find my thoughts wandering off into the Second (our leaders), the Sixth (non-AA enterprises), the Seventh (financial independence), and the Ninth (style of organization).

It helps me to think of the Traditions as different facets of the same crystal. They are, perhaps, even better understood as varied aspects of an integrated, unified style of life which we call "the AA way." Or as twelve different perspectives on the spiritual (i.e., "of the spirit — not material") experience which is at the core of survival for each of us as individuals, as well as survival of the Fellowship itself.

It is largely our Traditions that make AA unique, in my opinion. They are guidelines possessed by no other body of people I know of. They could not have been planned in advance, because

August 1958

"I make three meetings a week — London, Rome, and Cairo."

when AA got started no one could then foresee in just what shapes it would develop, or which problems would come up. So the Traditions, like the Steps, got written down and adopted *after* the problems had come up and had been solved. The Traditions are an agreed-upon distillation of much past experience, twelve descriptions of ideal AA behavior.

Fortunately for me, I was in AA while some of that experience was being experienced. I suffered through some of the mistakes that the Traditions can now help any member avoid. I often received the nourishing fruit of a Tradition, under some other name, when my sobriety was languishing and spindly.

To illustrate: The last winter of my pre-AA alcoholism (December 1944) was miserably bleak, dark, and cold. Walking into that old Manhattan AA office on West 41st Street was like suddenly finding, around the corner from bitter winds, an unexpected, warm spring day. Like first crocuses, illogical hopes unbelievably popped up to be wondered at. The woman behind the desk was the first AA to twelfth-step me, and she said, among many other cherished words, that she was *not* paid to help me and that I need not cringe in shame and ignorance before any imagined, awesome expertise of older members (nor need I phony up my case history to hold their interest). AAs were not professionals, not experts, but just former drunkards who helped each other stay sober, she pointed out.

That meant I could fit in, as they did, if I wanted to! And suddenly a long-frozen longing to belong thawed inside me — a sharp, lovely, barely remembered yearning from childhood. I could acknowledge it now because, for once, I dared hope for relief.

Real recovery, the summertime fullness of my own sobriety, was still some years away, but even from the fringes of AA, where I was to huddle fearfully most of my first two years, I could feel in my bones that what my first twelfth-stepper and the other "real" members said made good sense.

Nonalcoholics had often reached *down* to try to help me. AA members, being just drunks like me, simply reached *out* to help.

My alcoholic experiences with professional experts, such as clergymen, physicians, policemen, and others paid to help, had not filled me with love or trust. But the folks in this AA thing were not fingerwaggers, reminding me that they were morally superior. These AAs were my own kind, barroom kin, and I believe that is one of the big reasons I lingered on in the AA neighborhood.

In retrospect, I am now certain that the characteristic of AA described in this Eighth Tradition is responsible in large measure for my being alive and sober today. I was, when I first came to AA, so childishly resentful of authority, so jealous of anyone who might know more than I, that I fear I would not have loitered around AA if it had consisted of "experts" paid to help me.

Eavesdropping avidly on the "grown-ups" (then my private name for sober members), I began to grasp some of the things they were talking about. For example, it finally became apparent even to me, back in 1945, that New York AA had to have someone who would be responsible full-time for making sure that our telephones got answered; that calls for help were referred quickly to some dependable, sober member near the caller; that new prospects who wandered in were twelfth-stepped; that information on times and locations of all the Greater New York meetings was kept up to date; that mail asking for help was answered; that the rent and telephone bills were paid; and that the place was cleaned up occasionally.

Unless we made one person responsible full-time for all these chores, all of us would suffer — especially newcomers. We wanted prospects to get instant and careful help, not to be forgotten about. We needed a central storehouse of accurate information, easily available, about where a Tuesday-night meeting might be found near the Flatbush section of Brooklyn, or somewhere in Queens or Staten Island.

So we agreed that we had to have a full-time secretary who would provide these services for all members of all groups in the vicinity. And we decided it had to be someone who could be fired if she did not do the job properly. That would make her responsible to those she served. (Oops! Slipping over into the Ninth and Second Traditions, see?)

It never occurred to anyone, I believe, that we ought to hire a nonmember in order to keep AA nonprofessional. It seemed perfectly obvious that the only sort of person equipped for this job would be a member of some experience both in sobriety and in local AA. No nonmember could possibly understand all that had to be done, and how to do it in the traditional AA ways. Of course, our secretary would also have to be someone with office skills — able to write letters, handle typing and filing, keep records, write checks, etc.

Our hunt for such a person brought us smack up against the pay question. Practically everybody around who was qualified, in both AA knowledge and office skills, had to have a job-with-pay in order to eat. We certainly could not ask or expect any alcoholic trying to stay sober in AA to give up a good-paying office job and starve to death in order to work for AA for nothing. We wanted to pay our own way, to depend on no one's charity (Seventh Tradition, right?); we wanted to pay for the best, and get it, whether it was coffee or secretarial skill we bought.

In later years, I have spoken often, and with embarrassing loudness, to the effect that AA salaries, whether at GSO, the Grapevine, or local central offices, ought always to be at least as good as, if not better than, those in profit-making commercial enterprises if we expect to hire and keep the best-qualified workers.

In 1945, the dilemma was solved when we decided to hire a certain AA woman and pay her for her office skills used in the service of AA, just as she would have been paid for her office skills if used in the service of some other agency or employer.

Perhaps that is why, when I was asked, many years later, whether I would do a writing job for pay for our AA General Service Board, I could say "Yes" with a clear conscience. Since I earned my living by writing, I was simply selling that skill to AA exactly as I often sold it to various other clients. The board paid me for my professional service. But notice: AA has never paid me (nor has it ever paid anyone) to admit I was powerless over alcohol, to go to meetings, to take my personal inventory and discuss it with someone, to make amends to those I have harmed, to admit it when I am wrong, to use prayer and meditation, and to show responsible concern for newcomers. In short, I have never known any of the workers hired in our offices and service centers to get paid for staying sober!

Sometimes, the term "professional AA" is used in another way by Traditions lawyers I have known — to put down any AA member who happens to earn a living using occupational skills (as a doctor, typist, psychologist, educator, public relations person, fund raiser, or whatever) in some non-AA agency concerned with alcoholism.

The term, as an opprobrious or belittling epithet, is undeserved, I think, unless the person is being paid for staying sober the AA way.

As far as I can see, in the Fellowship today no sober AAs are professional AAs, no matter what jobs they do. In AA concerns, we are all just amateurs together. And an amateur, of course, can be defined as "one who does something for love, not for pay." That's how each of us works the AA program, isn't it?

To reinforce and further clarify this concept, we have the AA style of organization (or *dis*organization!). But here I am beginning to slip over into the next Tradition.

B. L., Manhattan, N.Y.

Tradition Nine

AA, as such, ought never be organized;
but we may create service boards or committees
directly responsible to those they serve

February 1971

T WO FLAKED-OUT FELLOWS were shown in a popular William Steig cartoon a few years ago. The caption was something like "One of these days we've got to get organized around here."

I remember expressing the same sentiment while drinking. I not only said it, I did it. To me, getting organized meant getting things arranged in a highly systematic manner, in preparation for getting them done. (You don't necessarily pay your bills, but you do make a neat list of creditors.) During self-enforced droughts, I would zealously overorganize everything in sight in round-the-clock spurts — only to blow it all, later, in a flood of ethanol.

And so I welcomed the idea of an "organization" — which I supposed AA was — for getting something done about the trouble I was having with my drinking.

I approached AA twenty-six years ago in total darkness as to how it did things. (How often is it approached any other way?) I guess I expected to find a written constitution, bylaws, dues, and paid sergeants of some kind trained to discipline the backsliders. After all, there was a telephone listing, and I had been invited to come to an office. That sounded pretty organized to me.

But the first members I met unwittingly sowed confusion by using familiar terms in an unfamiliar context. Such words as "member, join, meeting, officer, committee," etc. do not mean the same in AA as outside it, but how was I to know that?

My confusion grew as I heard and saw AA people behaving differently from each other, saying wildly disparate things, sometimes contradicting each other. Some even drank!

I asked about the president of AA, and they said there wasn't any; yet they had a chairman, a secretary, and elections. There was no ritual for joining, they said; yet the secretary usually announced, "If you want to join this group, see me after the meeting."

They said there were no musts, but that to do certain jobs one must have been sober at least three months. They insisted they were alcoholics, not ex-alcoholics; yet most never touched a drop.

Obviously, I was seeing only the lowest-grade members of this outfit, I became pretty sure. I kept nosing around to find the generals, so I could get the real score. I never found any top brass.

But, despite the vast ignorance of the noncom troops, AA *got things done.* The telephone got answered; meetings were held, with prearranged programs; coffee got served; a book and pamphlets were distributed. So AA must be systematized in *some* way, I had to conclude. But how? Was there a secret hierarchy of authorities who enforced the statutes by *making* members do things?

Such were the expectations — shaped, of course, by the experiences of my non-AA lifetime — with which I arrived at the door of the Fellowship. With growing delight, and often chagrin, I have learned how mistaken I was.

Now I am convinced that one sure way to destroy AA would be for us to set up a rigid organization patterned after the non-AA societies we all know. Yet we cannot be a laissez-faire body, willing always to "Let George do it." Instead, each of us is expected, it seems to me, to assume enough personal responsibility on his own for the Fellowship to get its major function (Tradition Five) accomplished.

What giant problems our first members faced! They had to find ways to get things done without slipping into either the bedlam of autonomy unlimited or the trap of overorganizing and underaccomplishing. The dilemma could easily have overwhelmed them, in my opinion. Organizing can itself be addictive, my personal experience indicates. It's easy to get so fascinated with the process of organizing that I can lose all sight of what I am organizing for. I marvel that any of the first ten years' members stayed sober at all.

Tradition Nine describes the masterful solution worked out during the first ten years of AA experience. Since so many alcoholics rebel against authority in human form, we just dispense with it altogether. The first seven words of Tradition Nine say that we have no bosses — echoing Tradition Two.

But the last fourteen words describe the system and orderliness necessary for our outfit to get *things done*.

My personal AA life illustrates both the problem and its solution. Like a tantrum-throwing four-year-old, I figuratively stamped my foot and refused to pay attention to the Twelve Steps. I mistakenly believed them to be rules for staying sober, instead of a simple description of how our first members actually did recover. After enough slips, however, I saw that in AA I had the freedom to try out, on my own, the Steps suggested as a program of recovery. But I had to make myself do them, because no one in AA could force me to.

I tried to be bossy in AA, and I got drunk. I learned to empty ashtrays for the group, and I began staying sober.

A few years back, we floundering fathers of a certain Greenwich Village group found ourselves about to be replaced. To make life easier for our successors than it had been for us, we wrote out what each steering committee member (trusted servant) had done, exactly how, when, and where. (This was before the General Ser-

vice Office published its excellent pamphlet "The AA Group.")
We bound these information sheets in a notebook for our new
secretary-treasurer.

About three months later, we learned that the group was
behind in "gifts" to our landlord (a church) and had not paid its
intergroup pledges or several GSO bills for literature.

Swift to find a scapegoat, we turned on Ernie, the new secretary-treasurer, and demanded, "Why didn't you pay those
things?"

Indignantly, he told us, "Because I didn't know I was supposed to, and I don't know where to pay them, anyhow."

In my most tolerant bleeding-deacon voice, I chirped, "But
Ernie, exactly what is to be paid, and when, and to whom, is all
spelled out for you in that book."

"What book?" he asked.

"That black notebook we gave you."

"Oh, that!" Ernie replied with disgust. "I've never opened
it," he announced proudly. "Nobody in AA is going to tell *me*
what to do!"

Several chronic beginners tipsily applauded.

That nutty contretemps put the AA organization problem
into a beautiful nutshell, it seems to me. How do we avoid offend-
ing each other with government — which inevitably means giving
some members authority over others — and still escape chaos? As
the late Bernard Smith so eloquently put it at our 1970 International Convention in Miami Beach, the answer is in the way our Ninth
Tradition insures AA against anarchy while at the same time insul-
ating us against any form of AA government. Ernie, working with
the other new officers of the group, later came upon that answer
himself.

My fellow founders and I had had our feelings hurt when
somebody first suggested there might be a better arrangement than
our paternalistic one, and the new officers took over. We finally
realized, though, that the AA custom of rotation in office can be a
healing experience for those who can take it and understand the
spirit behind it. Rotation is not spelled out in any Step or Tradition. (Neither are many other good AA ideas, such as the 24-hour
plan, going to meetings, significance of the first drink.) But it
mercifully helps solve the seniority problem we older members can
inflict on newer ones, and I think it is within the spirit of Traditions
Two and Nine, if not in their wording.

The genius embodied in the Tradition Nine phrase "responsible to those they serve" escaped my detection for a long time, because it sounded too noble and elegant to be more than a truism. When I worked on some AA committees, however, it came to life for me, and I now consider it an astonishing and challenging notion.

What if those of us who professionally serve others outside AA — whether we are doctors, taxi drivers, professors, or Playboy bunnies — had to report not to some boss or professional association with punishment powers, but instead to our *clients*? In effect, that *is* the case with AA officers and committees, isn't it?

Once, an AA committee I belonged to heard of a member who was representing himself as an AA official and collecting money thereby. We instantly launched into a discussion of what to do to him. Think about that. . . .

It took us an hour or so to realize that we had only the right to pray for him, not the authority to punish him. It was an exciting realization, and I continue to stand in awe of this principle: No matter how much you or I may misbehave, no matter how bad a member one of us may be, there is no one in AA with formal authority to fine us, censure us, or kick us out of the Fellowship. That seems to me a clear implication of both Traditions Nine and Three (requirement for membership).

I've learned, too, that I can misuse this Tradition as I have several others, to excuse my own failings. When I foul up, I can shrug my shoulders and say, "After all, we're not supposed to be well organized." But that's just a cop-out, I fear; Number Nine does *not* say we ought to be inefficient, lazy, dishonest, or irresponsible.

Of course, the lack of authority in AA can exasperate high-pressure types. I think of one of our most popular AA pamphlets, "What Happened to Joe." The actual writing and production of it took less than four months. But before that, discussions of it had lasted *fourteen years!* Interminably, committees worried about whether to do it at all, then about how to do it, what it should say and not say, and on and on.

The process would have been much more efficient if some boss had made the decisions and given the orders. But that is not the AA way. In order to be responsible to those they serve, AA servants work carefully, coolly, prayerfully. An AA pamphlet *should* be based on such preparation, it seems to me, if it is to represent responsibly the entire Fellowship, as all those published by AA World Services, Inc., do.

If AA were organized the way other outfits are, we could move faster, but would the result be more beneficial to *all* of us, both present members and those yet to come? For our simple stated purpose, our exasperatingly patient committees and boards are ideal, in my opinion. If we took on additional functions — such as managing buildings, providing shelter or medical services, running cafés — an entirely different kind of organizational system would of course, be needed. Many AA operators of clubhouses and rest farms have unhappily found that out.

If we tried to organize in the conventional, orthodox ways, we could well become totally *dis*organized. If we had to thrash out complete agreement on such issues as rules and authority and power and money, we'd split apart. Instead, we let each man hold his own ideas, discipline himself, and march to his own drumbeat. And in our joint determination to do this, we stay truly united after all.

It has been said that, if we want personal recovery, we owe this to AA's future: "to place our *common* welfare first; to keep our Fellowship united. For on AA unity depend our lives and the lives of those to come."

B. L., Manhattan, N.Y.

Why Alcoholics Anonymous Is Anonymous

by Bill W.

January 1955

AS NEVER BEFORE, the struggle for power, importance, and wealth is tearing civilization apart. Man against man, family against family, group against group, nation against nation.

Nearly all those engaged in this fierce competition declare that their aim is peace and justice for themselves, their neighbors, and their nations: Give us power and we shall have justice; give us fame and we shall set a great example; give us money and we shall be comfortable and happy. People throughout the world deeply believe that, and act accordingly. On this appalling dry bender, society seems to be staggering down a dead-end road. The stop sign is clearly marked. It says "Disaster."

What has this got to do with anonymity, and Alcoholics Anonymous?

We of AA ought to know. Nearly every one of us has traversed this identical dead-end path. Powered by alcohol and self-justification, many of us have pursued the phantoms of self-importance and money right up to the disaster stop sign. Then came AA. We faced about and found ourselves on a new high road where the direction signs said never a word about power, fame, or wealth. The new signs read, "This way to sanity and serenity — the price of self-sacrifice.

The Twelve Steps and Twelve Traditions states that "Anonymity is the greatest protection our Society can ever have." It says

July 1979

"You stick with me, Hester, and they'll think we belong to some kind of club, or something."

also that "The spiritual substance of anonymity is sacrifice."

Let's turn to AA's twenty years of experience and see how we arrived at that belief, now expressed in our Traditions Eleven and Twelve.

At the beginning we sacrificed alcohol. We had to, or it would have killed us. But we couldn't get rid of alcohol unless we made other sacrifices. Big shot-ism and phony thinking had to go. We had to toss self-justification, self-pity, and anger right out the window. We had to quit the crazy contest for personal prestige and big bank balances. We had to take personal responsibility for our sorry state and quit blaming others for it.

Were these sacrifices? Yes, they were. To gain enough humility and self-respect, to stay alive at all we had to give up what had really been our dearest possession — our ambitions and our illegitimate pride.

But even this was not enough. Sacrifice had to go much further. Other people had to benefit too. So we took on some Twelfth Step work; we began to carry the AA message. We sacrificed time, energy, and our own money to do this. We couldn't keep what we had unless we gave it away.

Did we demand that our new prospects give us anything? Were we asking them for power over their lives, for fame for our good work, or for a cent of their money? No, we were not. We found that if we demanded any of these things our Twelfth Step work went flat. So these natural desires had to be sacrificed; otherwise our prospects received little or no sobriety. Nor, indeed, did we.

Thus we learned that sacrifice had to bring a double benefit, or else little at all. We began to know about the kind of giving of ourselves that had no price tag on it.

When the first AA group took form, we soon learned a lot more of this. We found that each of us had to make willing sacrifices for the group itself, sacrifices for the common welfare. The group, in turn, found that it had to give up many of its own rights for the protection and welfare of each member, and for AA as a whole. These sacrifices had to be made or AA couldn't continue to exist.

Out of these experiences and realizations, the Twelve Traditions of Alcoholics Anonymous began to take shape and substance.

Gradually we saw that the unity, the effectiveness — yes, even the survival — of AA would always depend upon our continued willingness to sacrifice our personal ambitions and desires for the common safety and welfare. Just as sacrifice meant survival for the individual, so did sacrifice mean unity and survival for the group and for AA's entire Fellowship.

Viewed in this light, AA's Twelve Traditions are little else than a list of sacrifices which the experience of twenty years has taught us that we must make, individually and collectively, if AA itself is to stay alive and healthy.

In our Twelve Traditions we have set our faces against nearly every trend in the outside world.

We have denied ourselves personal government, professionalism, and the right to say who our members shall be. We have abandoned do-goodism, reform, and paternalism. We refuse charitable money and prefer to pay our own way. We will cooperate with practically everybody, yet we decline to marry our Society to anyone. We abstain from public controversy and will not quarrel among ourselves about those things that so rip society asunder — religion, politics, and reform. We have but one purpose: to carry the AA message to the sick alcoholic who wants it.

We take these attitudes not at all because we claim special virtue or wisdom; we do these things because hard experience has told us that we must — if AA is to survive in the distraught world of today. We also give up rights and make sacrifices because we ought to — and, better yet, because we want to. AA is a power greater than any of us; it must go on living or else uncounted thousands of our kind will surely die. This we know.

Now where does anonymity fit into this picture? What is anonymity anyhow? Why do we think it is the greatest single protection that AA can ever have? Why is it our greatest symbol of personal sacrifice, the spiritual key to all our Traditions and to our whole way of life?

The following fragment of AA history will reveal, I deeply hope, the answer we all seek.

Years ago a noted ball player sobered up through AA. Because his comeback was so spectacular, he got a tremendous personal ovation in the press and Alcoholics Anonymous got much of the credit. His full name and picture, as a member of AA, were seen by millions of fans. It did us plenty of good; alcoholics flocked in. We loved this. I was specially excited because it gave me ideas.

Soon I was on the road, happily handing out personal interviews and pictures. To my delight, I found I could hit the front pages, just as he could. Besides, he couldn't hold his publicity pace, but I could hold mine. I only needed to keep traveling and talking. The local AA groups and newspapers did the rest. I was astonished when recently I looked at those old newspaper stories. For two or three years I guess I was AA's number one anonymity breaker.

So I can't really blame any AA who has grabbed the spotlight since. I set the main example myself, years ago.

At the time, this looked like the thing to do. Thus justified, I ate it up. What a bang it gave me when I read those two-column spreads about "Bill the Broker," full name and picture, the guy who was saving drunks by the thousands!

Then this fair sky began to be a little overcast. Murmurs were heard from AA skeptics who said, "This guy Bill is hogging the big time. Dr. Bob isn't getting his share." Or, again, "Suppose all this publicity goes to Bill's head and he gets drunk on us?"

This stung. How could they persecute me when I was doing so much good? I told my critics that this was America and didn't they know I had the right of free speech? And wasn't this country and every other run by big-name leaders? Anonymity was maybe okay for the average AA. But co-founders ought to be exceptions. The public certainly had a right to know who we were.

Real AA power-drivers (prestige-hungry people, folks just like me) weren't long in catching on. They were going to be exceptions too. They said that anonymity before the general public was just for timid people; all the braver and bolder souls, like themselves, should stand right up before the flash bulbs and be counted. This kind of courage would soon do away with the stigma on alcoholics. The public would right away see what fine citizens recovered drunks could make. So more and more members broke their anonymity, all for the good of AA. What if a drunk was photographed with the governor? Both he and the governor deserved the honor, didn't they? Thus we zoomed along, down the dead-end road!

The next anonymity-breaking development looked ever rosier. A close AA friend of mine wanted to go in for alcohol education. A department of a great university interested in alcoholism wanted her to go out and tell the general public that alcoholics were sick people, and that plenty could be done about it. My friend was

a crack public speaker and writer. Could she tell the general public
that she was an AA member? Well, why not? By using the name
Alcoholics Anonymous she'd get fine publicity for a good brand
of alcohol education and for AA too. I thought it an excellent idea
and therefore gave my blessing.

AA was already getting to be a famous and valuable name.
Backed by our name and her own great ability, the results were immediate. In nothing flat her own full name and picture, plus excellent accounts of her educational project and of AA, landed in
nearly every large paper in North America. The public understanding of alcoholism increased, the stigma on drunks lessened, and
AA got new members. Surely there could be nothing wrong with
that.

But there was. For the sake of this short-term benefit, we were
taking on a future liability of huge and menacing proportions.

Presently an AA member began to publish a crusading magazine devoted to the cause of Prohibition. He thought Alcoholics

Alcoholics Anonymous is a fellowship of men and women who share their experience, strength and hope with each other that they may solve their common problem and help others to recover from alcoholism. The only requirement for membership is an honest desire to stop drinking... AA has no dues or fees. It is not allied with any sect, denomination, politics, organization or institution... Does not wish to engage in any controversy. Neither endorses nor opposes any causes. Our primary purpose is to stay sober and help other alcoholics to achieve sobriety.

HERE IS THE ORIGINAL WORDING of the Preamble, as it was
first introduced in the June 1947 Grapevine. Written by the
then editor to describe AA to the Grapevine's non-AA readers, it
has become a part of AA literature. It came to be called the Preamble because it is so often read at the opening of AA meetings.

Much of the phrasing was borrowed from the Foreword to the

Anonymous ought to help make the world bone dry. He disclosed himself as an AA member and freely used the AA name to attack the evils of whiskey and those who made it and drank it. He pointed out that he too was an "educator," and that his brand of education was the "right kind." As for putting AA into public controversy, he thought that was exactly where we should be. So he busily used AA's name to do just that. Of course, he broke his anonymity to help his cherished cause along.

This was followed by a proposal from a liquor trade association that an AA member take on a job of "education." People were to be told that too much alcohol was bad for anyone and that certain people — the alcoholics — shouldn't drink at all. What could be the matter with this?

The catch was that our AA friend had to break his anonymity; every piece of publicity and literature was to carry his full name as a member of Alcoholics Anonymous. This, of course, would be bound to create the definite public impression that AA favored

---

original edition of *Alcoholics Anonymous*, where "an *honest* desire to stop drinking" is described as "the only requirement for membership." The Preamble soon began to appear in Conference-approved literature and in many other AA publications.

At the 1958 General Service Conference, a delegate asked about the words "honest desire to stop drinking," suggesting that since "honest" does not appear in the Third Tradition, it might be deleted from the Preamble. In discussion, most Conference members felt that as AA had matured, it had become almost impossible to determine what constitutes an honest desire to stop drinking, and also that some who might be interested in the program could be confused by the phrase. Thus, as part of the evolution of AA, the phrase had been dropped from common usage. The mid-summer 1958 meeting of the General Service Board ratified the deletion, and since then the Preamble has read simply "a desire to stop drinking."

At the same time, the phrase "AA has no dues or fees" was clarified to read as it presently does: "There are no dues or fees for AA membership; we are self-supporting through our own contributions." The current version of the Preamble appears on page one of every issue of the Grapevine, and on the copyright page of this book.

"education," liquor-trade style.

Though these two developments never happened to get far, their implications were nevertheless terrific. They spelled it right out for us. By hiring out to another cause, and then declaring his AA membership to the whole public, it was in the power of an AA to marry Alcoholics Anonymous to practically any enterprise or controversy at all, good or bad. The more valuable the AA name became, the greater the temptation would be.

Further proof of this was not long in showing up. Another member started to put us into the advertising business. He had been commissioned by a life insurance company to deliver a series of twelve "lectures" on Alcoholics Anonymous — *and naturally our friend himself* — all in one good-looking package.

At AA Headquarters, we read the proposed lectures. They were about 50 percent AA and 50 percent our friend's personal religious convictions. This could create a false public view of us. Religious prejudice against AA would be aroused. So we objected.

Our friend shot back a hot letter saying that he felt "inspired" to give these lectures, and that we had no business to interfere with his right of free speech. Even though he was going to get a fee for his work, he had nothing in mind except the welfare of AA. And if we didn't know what was good for us, that was too bad! We and AA's Board of Trustees could go plumb to the devil. The lectures were going on the air.

This was a poser. Just by breaking anonymity and so using the AA name for his own purposes, our friend could take over our public relations, get us into religious trouble, put us into the advertising business and, for all these good works, the insurance company would pay him a handsome fee.

Did this mean that any misguided member could thus endanger our Society any time or any place simply by breaking anonymity and telling himself how much good he was going to do for us? We envisioned every AA advertising man looking up a commercial sponsor, using the AA name to sell everything from pretzels to prune juice.

Something had to be done. We wrote our friend that AA had a right of free speech too. We wouldn't oppose him publicly, but we could and would guarantee that his sponsor would receive several thousand letters of objection from AA members if the program went on the radio. Our friend abandoned the project.

But our anonymity dike continued to leak. AA members

began to take us into politics. They began to tell state legislative committees — publicly, of course — just what AA wanted in the way of rehabilitation, money, and enlightened legislation.

Thus, by full name and often by pictures, some of us became lobbyists. Other members sat on benches with police court judges, advising which drunks in the line-up should go to AA and which to jail.

Then came money complications involving broken anonymity. By this time, most members felt we ought to stop soliciting funds publicly for AA purposes. But the educational enterprise of my university-sponsored friend had meanwhile mushroomed. She had a perfectly proper and legitimate need for money and plenty of it. Therefore, she asked the public for it, putting on drives to this end. Since she was an AA member and continued to say so, many contributors were confused. They thought AA was in the educational field or else they thought AA itself was raising money when indeed it was not and didn't want to.

So AA's name was used to solicit funds at the very moment we were trying to tell people that AA wanted no outside money.

Seeing what happened, my friend, wonderful member that she is, tried to resume her anonymity. Because she had been so thoroughly publicized, this has been a hard job. It has taken her years. But she has made the sacrifice, and I here want to record my deep thanks on behalf of us all.

This precedent set in motion all sorts of public solicitations by AAs for money — money for drying-out farms, Twelfth Step enterprises, AA boardinghouses, clubs, and the like — powered largely by anonymity breaking.

We were next startled to learn that we had been drawn into partisan politics, this time for the benefit of a single individual. Running for public office, a member splashed his political advertising with the fact that he was an AA and, by inference, sober as a judge! AA being popular in his state, he thought it would help him win on election day.

Probably the best story in this class tells how the AA name was used to back up a libel lawsuit. A member, whose name and professional attainments are known on three continents, got hold of a letter which she thought damaged her professional reputation. She felt something should be done about this and so did her lawyer, also an AA. They assumed that both the public and AA would be rightfully angry if the facts were known. Forthwith, sev-

eral newspapers headlined how Alcoholics Anonymous was rooting for one of its lady members — named in full, of course — to
win her suit for libel. Shortly after this, a noted radio commentator
told a listening audience, estimated at twelve million people, the
same thing. This again proved that the AA name could be used for
purely personal purposes — this time on a nationwide scale.

The old files at AA Headquarters reveal many scores of such
experiences with broken anonymity. Most of them point up the
same lessons.

They tell us that we alcoholics are the biggest rationalizers in
the world; that fortified with the excuse we are doing great things
for AA we can, through broken anonymity, resume our old and
disastrous pursuit of personal power and prestige, public honors,
and money — the same implacable urges that when frustrated once
caused us to drink; the same forces that are today ripping the globe
apart at its seams. Moreover, they make clear that enough spectacular anonymity breakers could someday carry our whole society
down into that ruinous dead end with them.

So we are certain that if such forces ever rule our Fellowship,
we will perish too, just as other societies have perished throughout

---

VICTOR E.

*This is the first Victor E. cartoon strip, which appeared in the
July 1962 Grapevine. Each month since then, Victor has stood
nervously in front of that saloon door with an urge to go in and
have that first drink. Each time, his Higher Power — or something
— has intervened, and Victor has walked, run, or been pushed off
the scene without having that drink.*

Victor is not a very good AA; evidently, he has never really human history. Let us not suppose for a moment that we recovered alcoholics are so much better or stronger than other folks; or that because in twenty years nothing has ever happened to AA, nothing ever can.

Our really great hope lies in the fact that our total experience, as alcoholics and as AA members, has at last taught us the immense power of these forces for self-destruction. These hard-won lessons have made us entirely willing to undertake every personal sacrifice necessary for the preservation of our treasured Fellowship.

This is why we see anonymity *at the general public level* as our chief protection against ourselves, the guardian of all our Traditions, and the greatest symbol of self-sacrifice that we know.

Of course no AA need be anonymous to family, friends, or neighbors. Disclosure there is usually right and good. Nor is there any special danger when we speak at group or semipublic AA meetings, provided press reports *reveal first names only.*

But before the general public — press, radio, films, television, and the like — the revelation of full names and pictures is the point of peril. This is the main escape hatch for the fearful destructive

July 1962

gotten the program. If he had, he would not still be hanging around the saloon door. But whatever his reservations, whatever his shortcomings, he has not taken a drink.

In July 1985, he celebrates his twenty-third anniversary without a drink — twenty-three years of some kind of frantic sobriety! Quite a victory. Just shows you what prolonged association with AA and the Grapevine can do.

forces that still lie latent in us all. Here the lid can and must stay down.

We now fully realize that 100 percent personal anonymity before the public is just as vital to the life of AA as 100 percent sobriety is to the life of each and every member. This is not the counsel of fear; it is the prudent voice of long experience. I am sure that we are going to listen; that we shall make every needed sacrifice. Indeed we have been listening. Today only a handful of anonymity breakers remain.

I say all this with what earnestness I can; I say this because I know what the temptation of fame and money really is. I can say this because I was once a breaker of anonymity myself. I thank God that years ago the voice of experience and the urging of wise friends took me out of that perilous path into which I might have led our entire Society. Thus I learned that the temporary or seeming good can often be the deadly enemy of the permanent best. When it comes to survival for AA, nothing short of our very best will be good enough.

We want to maintain 100 percent anonymity for still another potent reason, one often overlooked. Instead of securing us more publicity, repeated self-serving anonymity breaks could severely damage the wonderful relations we now enjoy with press and public alike. We could wind up with a poor press and little public confidence at all.

For many years, news channels all over the world have showered AA with enthusiastic publicity, a never-ending stream of it, far out of proportion to the news value involved. Editors tell us why this is. They give us extra space and time because their confidence in AA is complete. The very foundation of that high confidence is, they say, our continual insistence on personal anonymity at the press level.

Never before had news outlets and public relations experts heard of a society that absolutely refused personally to advertise its leaders or members. To them, this strange and refreshing novelty has always been proof positive that AA is on the square, that nobody has an angle.

This, they tell us, is the prime reason for their great goodwill. This is why, in season and out, they continue to carry the AA message of recovery to the whole world.

If through enough anonymity lapses we finally caused the press, the public, and our alcoholic prospects themselves to wonder about our motives, we'd surely lose this priceless asset and, along with it, countless prospective members. Alcoholics Anonymous would not then be getting more good publicity; it would be getting less, and worse. Therefore the handwriting on the wall is clear. Because most of us can already see it, and because the rest of us soon will, I'm fully confident that no such dark day will every fall upon our Society.

For a long time now, both Dr. Bob and I have done everything possible to maintain the Tradition of anonymity. Just before he died, some of Dr. Bob's friends suggested that there should be a suitable monument or mausoleum erected in honor of him and his wife, Anne, something befitting a founder. Dr. Bob declined, with thanks. Telling me about this a little later, he grinned and said, "For heaven's sake, Bill, why don't you and I get buried like other folks?"

Last summer I visited the Akron cemetery where Bob and Anne lie. Their simple stone says never a word about Alcoholics Anonymous. This made me so glad I cried. Did this wonderful couple carry personal anonymity too far when they so firmly refused to use the word "Alcoholics Anonymous," even on their own burial stone?

For one, I don't think so. I think that this great and final example of self-effacement will prove of more permanent worth to AA than could any spectacular public notoriety or fine mausoleum.

We don't have to go to Akron, Ohio, to see Dr. Bob's memorial. Dr. Bob's real monument is visible throughout the length and breadth of AA. Let us look again at its true inscription — one word only, which we AAs have written. That word is sacrifice.

INDEX

committees, 72-73
Publicity
  negative, 272-278
  positive, 280-281

Rationalizing, 43-46
Reaching out, 85
Reality, acceptance of, 58-61,
  172-174
  See also Truth
Recovery through the Steps,
  125-129
Rejection, 15-17, 157
Resentments, 43-46
Responsibility Declaration, 254
Responsibility, personal, 53-56
Rotation, 109-113, 266-267
Rowland H., 163, 164, 165, 166,
  167, 168
Rule-makers, 41-43
Rutgers School of Alcohol
  Studies, 251

St. Augustine, 188
St. Matthew, Gospel According
  to, 132
St. Thomas Hospital (Akron,
  Ohio), 241
Second Step, 19, 77, 198
  on finances, 77
Second Tradition, 95-100, 101,
  224, 237
  and humility, 101
  See also Group conscience
Seixas, Dr. Frank, 75
Self-centeredness, 32
Self-esteem, 150
Self-honesty, 79-80
Self-pity, 25-30, 58-61
Self-support, 91-92, 267, 277
  See also Seventh Tradition
Selfish program, 153-155
Sense of humor, 82
Sensitivity, 82
Serenity Prayer, 79, 80, 152-153,
  159, 197, 198, 200

Service, 138-141
Service committees, 256-259
Service, Legacy of
  Bill W. on, 254-259
Seventh Step
  on finances, 78
Seventh Tradition, 102, 114-119,
  225, 238
  and humility, 102
Sex, 50-53
Sharing experience, 93-95
Shoemaker, Dr. Samuel, 164, 166
Shyness, 84
Silkworth, Dr. William Duncan,
  11-14, 75, 165, 167, 215, 216
  on slips, 11-14
Sisters of Charity of St.
  Augustine, 241
Sixth Step, 78
  on finances, 78
Sixth Tradition, 102, 225,
  237-238, 250-254
  and humility, 102
Slips, 9-11, 11-14, 168-171
Slogans, 85
Smith, Bernard, 267
Sober living, 64-67, 148-153
Speaking at meetings, 93-95
Special-purpose groups, 206-209
Special-purpose meetings,
  206-208
"Spiritual awakening," 179-183
Spiritual growth, 184-188
Spiritual side of program,
  176-183
Spirituality, 188-191
Sponsoring your doctor, 75-76
Sponsorship, 83-87, 92-93
Sponsor-sponsee relationship,
  83-87
Steig, William, 160, 264
Still-suffering alcoholic, 14-15
Surrender, 157-159, 180

Tenth Step, 19-20, 28, 45, 78, 160
  on finances, 78